6.00

D0758750

Hoover Institution Studies: 27

AKEL:

The Communist Party of Cyprus

COMPARATIVE COMMUNIST PARTY POLITICS

Jan F. Triska, Editor

AKEL:

THE COMMUNIST PARTY OF CYPRUS

T. W. ADAMS

Hoover Institution Press

Stanford University   Stanford, California

The Hoover Institution on War, Revolution and Peace, founded at Stanford University in 1919 by the late President Herbert Hoover, is a center for advanced study and research on public and international affairs in the twentieth century. The views expressed in its publications are entirely those of the authors and do not necessarily reflect the views of the Hoover Institution.

Standard Book Number 8179-3271-2
Library of Congress Catalog Card Number 70-126963
©1971 by the Board of Trustees of the Leland Stanford Junior
   University
All rights reserved
Printed in the United States of America

To my son Anthony

In memory of his namesake, my father

WITHDRAWN
UTSA LIBRARIES

Contents

Preface

As the final version of this manuscript was being prepared, many important events were unfolding on the Cypriot stage. On March 8, there was an unsuccessful assassination attempt on the life of the President of the Republic, Archbishop Makarios, in all probability perpetrated by some die-hard supporters of *enosis* (union of Cyprus with Greece). The activities of these terrorist groups were followed throughout 1969 and are considered in some detail in Chapter 4. One of the individuals initially suspected in the assassination attempt, former Minister of Interior Polykarpos Georghadjis, was found in his car with six bullets in his body on March 16. In both instances, individuals were arrested and some were held without trial on the basis of a detention law passed in February after the wave of terrorism reached the crisis stage for the government. In Cyprus violence usually breeds more violence; the island of Aphrodite once again was stained with blood.

The tragic events of this period will surely prove to have relevance to the subject of this book, but at this time it is difficult to trace the connection. The communists did not appear to be a target of the terrorists, nor did they seem to have taken any active part in the violence. Between March 5 and 8 the Communist Party of Cyprus (AKEL) was holding its Twelfth Party Congress in the capital city of Nicosia. Other than a few resolutions on some new subjects, the Congress was no different from previous ones. It reelected Ezekias Papaioannou as General Secretary and stressed the well-worn slogan against the "Western imperialists," who were accused of transforming Cyprus into a "center of war, intrigue, and spying against the people." (See Appendix F for some examples of the Twelfth Congress resolutions.)

One rather unusual development at the Congress came in General Secretary Papaioannou's opening speech, when he named my other two books and referred to this present, though then unpublished, study: "According to authoritative information," he said, this book "will attempt to serve as a wedge in relations between Makarios and AKEL" (*Haravghi,* March 6, 1970). This was a rather empty claim, since the "wedge" already exists; the Archbishop is merely tolerating the communists because they are mainly Greeks and he has no desire to split the Greek Cypriot community while the problems with the Turkish Cypriot community remain unsolved. If the break between Makarios and the communists ultimately does come about, and this book contributes, so be it.

Furthermore, Papaioannou stated that "the aim of these books [the *U.S. Army Handbook for Cyprus, Cyprus Between East and West,* and this book] is to prepare the American people psychologically for American imperialist intervention in Cyprus under the excuse that the island is in danger of becoming the 'Cuba of the Mediterranean.' " This is erroneous. I have tried to make this study as balanced as a Western scholar could make it; if the Cypriot communists do not agree with my facts (or conclusions), I would suggest that they open up their archives to anyone who is interested.

Nonetheless, this is the first attempt at a thorough study published in English of the history and activities of AKEL on the politically sensitive island of Cyprus. The specific project has been in gestation since 1965, when the Relm Foundation through a generous grant sponsored the first of four annual visits I was to make to the Republic of Cyprus for field research. My interest in Cyprus, however, goes back fifteen years, when I was captivated by the island on my first visit in 1955—an exciting time to be there. Since then, I have returned to the island nine different times, the highlight being the two-month stay in April and May of 1969 which gave me a chance to witness and even participate in some historic happenings. More than that, though, I had the opportunity on each visit to see and interview most of the persons still living who played roles in the introduction, spread, or containment of the communist movement there. In addition to the numerous interviews in Cyprus, valuable and novel data were also obtained from personal interviews and conversations with informed persons in Greece, Turkey, England, and the United States.

One important English-language source of published primary information I used was the Joint Publications Research Service of the U.S. Department of Commerce. From their files since 1957 I was able to glean the translated versions of the AKEL Constitution, the various party programs, numerous speeches and articles, and news accounts of AKEL activities in such publications as *Haravghi, Neos Democratis, Neolaia,* and *Ergatiko Vima.* From the Foreign Broadcast Information Service, I have been able to follow in translation the daily news reports of the party since 1964. Certain other key documents or newspaper accounts were translated by authoritative individuals specifically for this study.

Also, I have read with profit a number of unclassified reports which have originated with the Greek, Turkish, Cypriot, British, and American governments. These have been obtained on a privileged basis and therefore cannot be referenced. Certain memoranda and papers from Ploutis Servas were helpful, and the short paper by Andros Nicolaides, "The Appeals of Communism in Cyprus," prepared for a graduate course at George Washington University in 1965, was also useful.

A number of colleagues helped verify and supplement my own collection of information, and for this I am very grateful. While I am responsible for the conclusions and interpretation of the data, I am indebted to Professor Jan Triska of Stanford University for the thorough outline he worked out for the purposes of studying non-ruling communist parties; this outline asked the questions and forced the answers which have helped to make this study as complete as it is.

Finally, I wish to express thanks to my family for their indulgence, to Jean Dupont Miller for her excellent job of editing, to Gretchen P. Kohlweiler and Mary Lippolis for typing the various drafts, and to Beverley C. Dowdy for her devoted assistance in preparing the final manuscript.

T.W.A.

Federal Executive Institute
Charlottesville, Virginia
March 1970

Editor's Introduction

This study of the AKEL, the communist party of Cyprus, is one of a series of monographs which together comprise comparative politics of non-ruling communist parties (NRCPs). The series is concerned with the state of the non-ruling communist parties in the world, with the causes of their emergence, and in particular with the question: *Why are NRCPs strong in some national states and not in others?* The theoretical focus of the series is on (a) the *varieties* of the NRCPs and their individual mutations and variations from the prescriptive Bolshevik organizational model; (b) the *causes* of these varieties, and identification of those environments within which NRCPs operate which have been most variety-productive; and (c) the *consequences* of these varieties, i.e., the particular conditions these varieties have produced which make for similarities or differences among the NRCPs.

The series examines three major assumptions:

1) Traditionally, whatever its immediate objectives and preoccupations, every NRCP has professed the principal long-range aspiration of becoming a ruling party, i.e., each has hoped to follow the path of those parties which—like the Czechoslovak, the Yugoslav, the Polish, or the Chinese party— became ruling communist parties (RCPs). However, the less an NRCP is willing to sponsor solely the interests of the RCPs, the more it tends to deviate from this aspiration. Moreover, the peaceful coexistence strategy of the U.S.S.R. since the Twentieth Congress of the CPSU has not supported the aspiration of the NRCPs to all-out struggle for power in their national states.

2) The NRCPs tend to be progressively more nationally than internationally oriented, and their national orientation tends to increase in direct proportion to the growing disunity among the RCPs (a result, in turn, of the proliferation of RCPs in the world). The NRCPs, in other words, are—like the RCPs— subject to growing positive interaction with their immediate operational environment and hence become progressively

less heterogeneous with their national environment. (If an NRCP is small, weak, and operating in an indifferent or hostile national environment, it is probable that its cadres are almost completely alienated from its national environment, and that its perceived operational environment is an extension of that perceived by the ruling communist parties.)

3) The greater the coincidence between means and/or goals of an NRCP and its operational environment, the more influential the NRCP. NRCPs have declined or been unsuccessful in those countries—such as Ireland, Canada, and the United States—where their operational environment has been unalterably hostile; they have gained or been successful in those parts of the world where they have adjusted to their operational environment—as in Italy and France—or where the operational environment has favored NRCP means and/or goals, as in Asia. (NRCPs operating in an unfriendly environment in developing nations and which side with the Chinese Communist Party in advocating uprisings and violence in underdeveloped countries create a danger of general war which the peaceful coexistence policy of the U.S.S.R. was designed to avoid.)

Among other assumptions examined empirically in the series—some of them current in the various writings on the subject—are the following: "Communism breeds on poverty and underdevelopment"; "The achievements of communism are the achievements of organization"; "Communist ideology is an imperfect theory of modernization"; and "The behavior of an NRCP is determined by its functions within its operational environment."

In the sense that "freedom of formation of associations to seek to control the state prevails only in the Western democracies and in states modeled after them,"[1] the NRCPs are *political parties* in those states where such freedom, however minimal, exists; but even in non-democratic states they have competitors for rule. The NRCPs differ from the RCPs not only in that the ruling parties are not parties at all in the above sense, but they are by definition without competitors for rule. This difference has important consequences: The extant political and social system usually has a far greater impact on an

---

[1] V. O. Key, Jr., *Politics, Parties, and Pressure Groups,* 2d ed. (New York: Crowell, 1953), p. 223.

NRCP than on an RCP, while the relative impact of the NRCP on its operational (national) environment is normally incomparably smaller. This difference is observable and measurable in the social composition of the NRCPs; in their structures, operational codes, and strategies; and in their relations with other CPs, both ruling and non-ruling.

What constitutes a communist party? Some communist parties call themselves communist, whereas others, such as the Irish Workers' League, are truly communist in all save name. Still others, such as the Mexican Workers' and Farmers' Party, have strong communist leanings but exist independently of, and sometimes in competition with, the local communist party. Some countries have both a communist party-states oriented party and a "national" communist party; some countries have these plus a Trotskyite party. Where communism is illegal, numerous left-wing parties may preach Marxist slogans but maintain few connections with the Communist party-states.

We are concerned here only with those parties which perceive themselves to be a part of the world communist movement and are so perceived by the party-states, thus automatically excluding all Trotskyite and "national" communist parties, as well as left-wing parties which do not acknowledge the party-states' leadership. Furthermore, we count only one party per country, selecting that party most closely identified with the communist system.

The common outline divides this study into six principal parts: Chapter 1 concerns the historical setting, concentrating on the emergence, evolution, and organizational strength of the NRCP. Here we search for causal relations—why and how an NRCP came into being, which phenomena influenced its evolution; which developments contributed to its strength. Chapter 2 deals with the NRCP in terms of its role and organization, i.e., its status, membership, and structure. Chapter 3 has to do with the NRCP national environment (its geographic and demographic locale, and the prevailing social, political, economic, military, belief, and other relevant systems). The intercourse between the NRCP and its national environment, and hence the past and present national operational code of the NRCP, are treated in Chapter 4. Chapter 5 deals with the NRCP's international operational code. And Chapter 6 stipulates the principal determinants of the NRCP's behavior. In addition, the Introduction to the case study concentrates on what the author believes to be the unique features of his particular NRCP, what distinguishes it from other national parties. The Summary briefly reviews the high spots of the case study, emphasizing causal explanations of the NRCP's emergence, its strength, and its present orientation.

A few additional words concerning some of the components of the outline are in order.

First, there has been no attempt made as yet to span the gaps between models constructed by three authors who have made important theoretical contributions to the study of NRCPs, namely Gabriel Almond,[2] Hadley Cantrill,[3] and Lucian Pye.[4] Chapter 2 should remedy this deficiency, at least in part, by emphasizing *role* and *status* of the party. The chapter describes functions of the NRCP which are assumed to signify the (roughly) three states of party development:

1) In developing nations—in non-politicized, non-community societies—revolutionary NRCPs are a dynamic force. Here they perform, in addition to their own unique objectives, the role of socializers toward modernity.[5] Here they feed the aspirations and ambitions of persons frustrated by an economy that cannot accommodate their skills. The high want/get ratio resulting from such economic conditions, we hypothesize, both alienates and brings into the CP those wishing to transform their societies rapidly and make them part of the modern world.

2) In societies where only some segments of the population have not been integrated and incorporated into the social and political system, the NRCPs attempt to integrate alienated (political and social) individuals for articulation of their dissatisfaction and protest. These *sub-cultural* NRCPs, habituated to defending the negative interests of isolated sections of the society, function more as *social* parties than as political parties. Seton-Watson has described what happened when a sub-cultural

[2] *The Appeals of Communism* (Princeton: Princeton University Press, 1954).

[3] *The Politics of Despair* (New York: Collier Books, 1962).

[4] *Guerrilla Communism in Malaya* (Princeton: Princeton University Press, 1956).

[5] Pye, *op. cit.*, p. 344; Hugh Seton-Watson, *From Lenin to Khrushchev* (New York: Praeger, 1961), p. 320.

NRCP left the protest field to enter responsible government in postwar France: The Communists had traditionally viewed the parliament as a useful forum for propaganda, and "it was not easy to discard this mentality. Denunciation and demagogy were easier and more enjoyable than responsibility."[6]

3) Finally, when NRCPs have gone beyond social protest and assumed political responsibility, their deviant and revolutionary character tends to be replaced by legitimacy and social plausibility, and their difference from other political parties tends to be reduced, sometimes to zero. From an ideological protest movement, the *electoral* NRCP tends to become a pragmatic and non-heretic political force. Italian and French CPs are probably the outstanding examples of NRCPs in this stage of operation.

Chapter 2 also focuses on status: Is the NRCP *influential?* (What is its political weight?) Is it *militant?* (Has a militant politics normally farther-reaching consequences within the immediate political process?) Is it *tolerated?* (Might the same NRCP be perceived as radical in one system and conservative in another? Is it *changing* its status? (What are the NRCP elite's present aspirations as compared to those of yesterday? How flexible is the elite's perception of its own role? Could an NRCP typology rank-order NRCPs according to their willingness to experiment and change their organizational forms?) And what are its *prospects?* (Does the NRCP "have a future"?) Inasmuch as all these variables have negative counterparts, twenty different combinations are possible, from one extreme (influential, militant, tolerated, changing NRCPs with positive prospects) to the other (non-influential [impotent], bargain-oriented, not tolerated, unchanging NRCPs with negative prospects).

With appropriate indicators, the several NRCP types may be of research value in further refining the NRCP types in the world and then matching the differences with (a) the kind of membership-leadership, rank and file, and supporters they attract; (b) socialization processes within the NRCPs; (c) environmental conditions as correlated with party transition from one type to another; etc.

As to the structure of the NRCP: Scholars (Duverger)[7]

[6] Seton-Watson, *op. cit.,* p. 294.
[7] Maurice Duverger, *Political Parties* (London: Methuen and Co. Ltd., 1954).

often assume that CPs are rigid hierarchial orders, that the party occupies the whole time of its elites, and that the party organization does not allow its members to participate fully in ordinary ways in the wider social community. Party demands create a rigid personality type, and the party recruits personalities predisposed to fit easily into the party order.

But is this true of the new parties whose leaders were recruited at the end of the Stalin era and have no personal experience of the Comintern organization in its last years? The major figures in the Cuban party, for instance, all began their party careers in the last years of the Stalin era or later, as did many, perhaps most, of the leaders of sub-Saharan parties, the Burmese party, and many of the newer Latin American parties. It is not possible that these new leaders will diverge from the old stereotype? If they are not rigid authoritarian personalities and if their party organizations are more flexible, leaders now may be more readily responsive to environmental influences than were those of the Stalinist period. New parties with youthful leadership also should be more eclectic in their regard for the history of the CPSU, the Comintern, etc., and more willing to experiment with new strategies and new relationships with other political groups. The Sino-Soviet split should foster such eclecticism.

Chapter 3 describes attributes in the environment that may make the objective of the NRCP, namely its transformation into an RCP, possible or easy. For instance, is the political system similar in some respects to that in a communist party-state: dictatorial, one-party, controlled press, etc.? Is the economy largely government controlled? Does the environment present problems similar to those solved more or less successfully by the CP in China, in the Soviet Union, or in Yugoslavia? Are the relations between the state and the Soviet Union and/or China, and/or Yugoslavia friendly and conducive to the growth of a local CP organization, or favorable to the growth of non-communist parties and groups that partially imitate Soviet or Chinese organizations and methods?

The social fabric, and in particular the social structure, of a given country is an important factor affecting the success of an NRCP. If there is little divergence in primordial loyalties within a country, the effectiveness of communist appeal to primordial sentiments is likely to be slight. The more recent difficulties of CPs in the Middle East, for example, might be due in part to shifts in communist appeals from intellectuals to class loyalties in nations relatively lacking in ethnic diversity.

As to the political system, both Max Weber[8] and Duverger have stressed the "natural emergence" of parties, given certain conditions in the political environment of a given state. Weber's formulation of party evolution encompasses as causative factors both the development of a national legislature and the growth in size of the electorate. Duverger, whose work is perhaps more relevant for the study of NRCPs, deals in part with externally created parties which emerge outside the legislature and invariably pose some sort of challenge to the ruling group, particularly in terms of representation. Duverger also stresses that externally created parties may be associated with (1) expanded suffrage, (2) strongly articulated secular or religious ideologies, or (3) nationalistic or anti-colonial movements. This broader handling of causality is more applicable to a study of NRCPs because their development may well deviate from any general pattern in response to partisan strategies devised by one or more communist party-states.

The concern with party organization (see Chapter 4) is widespread in the literature. Sigmund Neuman,[9] for example, postulates that one of the functions of the modern society is to transform parties of individual representation into parties of integration. Duverger's overly complex scheme of party organizations may be contrasted with overly simplified concepts, such as the dichotomous schemes of Thomas Hodgkin ("elite parties" vs. "parties of personalities");[10] Ruth Schachter ("patron parties" vs. "mass parties");[11] Martin Kilson ("caucus-type parties" vs. "mass-type parties");[12] or even John Kautsky ("traditionalist nationalists" vs. "modernist

[8] *The Theory of Social and Economic Organization* (Glencoe: The Free Press, 1947).

[9] *Modern Political Parties* (Chicago: University of Chicago Press, 1956).

[10] *African Political Parties* (Baltimore: Pelican, 1960).

[11] "Single Party Systems in West Africa," *American Political Science Review*, LV (1961), pp. 294–307.

[12] "Authoritarian and Single Party Tendencies in African Politics," *World Politics*, XV, No. 2 (January 1963).

nationalists").[13] However, such typologies, while useful in ranking parties along a single continuum, are not necessarily useful for our purpose of explaining the relations between environmental influences and the changing organizational structures and behavior patterns of NRCPs. Here the linkage between NRCP characteristics and environmental influences is especially important.

A number of creative people have contributed to this series. In addition to the authors of the series, in this case Professor T. W. Adams, I would like to thank Wallace Berry, Jack Kangas, Carole Norton, Naralou Roos, John Rue, and Maurice Simon for their imaginative contributions and valuable assistance.

Jan F. Triska

Stanford University
September 1970

[13]*Political Change in Underdeveloped Countries* (New York: Wiley, 1962); see also Colin Leys, "Models, Theories, and the Theory of Political Parties," *Political Studies,* VII (1959), pp. 127–46; Neil A. McDonald, *The Study of Political Parties* (New York: Doubleday, 1956); and Charles E. Merriam and Harold F. Grosnell, *The American Party System,* 4th ed. (New York: Macmillan, 1949).

Abbreviations of Cypriot Organizations

AKEL   Progressive Party of the Working People, the Communist Party of Cyprus

DEK   Democratic National Party, the most right-wing of all the parties in Cyprus; led by 1968 presidential candidate Dr. Takis Evdokas; believes in "instant *enosis*" and is considered the only open political faction that is anti-Makarios

DEOK   Democratic Labor Federation of Cyprus, a splinter group of the SEK

EDEK   Democratic Union of the Center Party; democratic socialist party founded by Dr. Vassos Lyssarides; in favor of "self-determination" for Cyprus

EDMA   United Democratic Regeneration Front; right-wing, founded by former EOKA district leaders but largely inactive now

EDON   United Democratic Youth Organization, communist

EK   Unified Party, the party initially led by the Clerides-Georghadjis coalition which has business interests behind it, as well as the Church and the rest of the SEK labor movement; often called the party in favor of continued independence for Cyprus

EKA   Union of Cypriot Farmers, communist

EM   *Ethnikon Metapon* (National Front), the leading clandestine pro-*enosis* terrorist group which harassed the Makarios government in 1969–70.

EME   Hellenic Mines Corporation

EOKA   National Organization of Cypriot Fighters, pro-*enosis*

KME   Cyprus Mines Corporation, U.S. corporation

KTIBF	Cyprus Turkish Trade Union Federation; anti-communist, founded in 1954
OEKA	Organization for Control of the Communist Menace
OHEN	Orthodox Christian Union of Youth
PEK	Pan-Agrarian Union of Cyprus; right-wing; advocates rural development program, crop insurance, entry into EEC, and expanded medical and educational program for farmers
PEKA	EOKA veterans' organization, right-wing
PEO	Pan-Cyprian Federation of Labor; formal organization of the "Old Trade Unions" group; communist; affiliated with the World Federation of Trade Unions
PEOM	Pan-Cyprian Organization of Secondary School Students, communist.
PEON	Pan-Cyprian National Youth Organization, independent
PK	Progressive Party, a small pro-*enosis* movement led by newspaper editor Nicos Samson
POAS	Pan-Cyprian Federation of Independent Trade Unions, anti-communist moderates
POGO	Pan-Cypriot Federation of Women's Organizations, communist
PP	Progressive Movement, a pro-*enosis* conservative party led by Mayor Ioannides of Nicosia; has some backing from the Church part of the SEK labor movement, and the farmers' group PEK
SEK	Confederation of Cypriot Workers; formal organization of the "New Trade Unions"; anti-communist; founded in 1943; affiliated with the International Confederation of Free Trade Unions

Introduction

"We used to say in jest that anyone who understood the situation in Cyprus had been misinformed!" Thus reminisced the last British Governor of Cyprus, Sir Hugh Foot (Lord Caradon), after his years of service in the Crown Colony. The observation, in jest or not, has relevance for anyone who has looked at the intricate human problem of Greek versus Turk, but it has a special meaning for anyone who attempts a study of the communist movement in the island.

There exists today a considerable difference of opinion in the West regarding the strength and effectiveness of AKEL, the Communist Party of Cyprus. This is so because much of what is written about the party comes from polemicists and journalists who are strongly biased, or simply sensationalistic, and very little of this reportage is in English. AKEL, the acronym for Anorthotikon Komma Ergazomenou Laou (Progressive Party of the Working People), is numerically the strongest organized political force on the island, and is one of the two legal communist parties in the Middle East.* (MAQI in Israel is the other.)

Skillfully managed by a devout and long-time Marxist, Ezekias Papaioannou, AKEL's membership comes almost entirely from the Greek Cypriot community, which constitutes four-fifths of the island's people. At its Eleventh Party Congress in 1966 the party claimed 14,000 members, possibly amounting to 50 per cent of all the admitted communists in the Middle East. Adding their considerable support in the labor movement and other front groups, the communists in Cyprus have a following, including overlappings, of possibly 70,000 out of the 1967 estimated population of 614,000.

Anorthotikon has a number of similar meanings in Greek, such as: elevated, restored, built-up, reformed, erected, and progressive. AKEL uses the word in the sense of wanting to raise the standards of the masses by new measures; hence "progressive" is the commonly used English equivalent.

Through its front groups and an elaborate network of local cadres, AKEL has usually been credited with control of some 30 per cent of the electorate. That estimate is an old and inconclusive guess, based on the first elections of 1959 and 1960, in which AKEL acted in coalitions. Only one presidential election has been held since then and reliable data could not be drawn from that. Typically, most of the published statistics concerning AKEL or its fronts come from communist sources and therefore have a political coloration. The next AKEL Party Congress has been announced for March 1970 and the membership claims could again be revised.

Nevertheless, one thing is clear: on a percentage basis the Communist Party of Cyprus is probably the largest non-ruling communist party in the world today; its claimed membership is approximately 4 per cent of the adult population and is fairly stable.[*] In the Republic's Parliament, AKEL holds 10 per cent of the total seats and 14.3 per cent of the 35 Greek Cypriot representatives. Why so large a communist party in so small a place is indeed a good question. (See postscript for the 1970 election results, p. 205.)

Communism in Cyprus originated in the early 1920's around the southern port city of Limassol. There some idealists had read Marx and aspired to use his theories to rid the island of its social ills. In 1923 the advent to power of the Labour Party in England helped raise hopes of success, but the first Communist Party of Cyprus, Kommonistikon Komma Kyprou (KKK), initially did not have enough appeal to develop a strong following among the superstitious peasants or the other working classes. After island-wide riots toward which the KKK was sympathetic, the movement was officially banned by the British colonial government in 1933 along with a number of other Greek organizations. The AKEL was formally founded in 1941 by the remaining hard-core communists and a group of leftist intellectuals.

During World War II, AKEL conducted political education courses in the volunteer Cyprus Regiment and converted

---

[*]The official 1967 estimate of the adult population over 20 years of age is 345,500. The 14,000 claimed members of AKEL in 1966 works out to be 4.1 per cent of the adult population, which is on a percentage basis larger than that of the Italian Communist Party.

many young soldiers to communism.* Toward the end of World War II, AKEL gained considerable ground through the diligent efforts of its own organized labor leaders, who were aided by the liberal policies of the new Labour government in England. Sensing the possibility that the communists might seize power in the mainland during the 1947–49 Greek Civil War, AKEL waged an intensive campaign for *enosis* (union) with Greece. Its main issue was anticolonialism and it was popular.

Owing to indifference on the part of the "nationalists" (the usual denotation of the island's anti-communist forces), AKEL became a strong political organization and showed its strength by winning a number of municipal elections in the mid-1940's. In 1945 AKEL felt secure enough to declare itself an official communist party. Realization of the party's growing power regenerated nationalistic and moral front groups under the leadership of the Greek Orthodox Church (the ethnarchy) to oppose AKEL. After certain miscalculations in both the labor and the political area, AKEL had a purge in 1949 which brought the present leadership to power. Unable to capture the banner of *enosis* from the Church, the party gradually slipped from its postwar position of strength. By 1954, the charismatic Archbishop Makarios III (the current President of the Republic) was able to cut in half the control that AKEL had been exercising over nearly 40 per cent of the population.

A serious communist blunder was made during the declared Emergency Period (1955–59), when AKEL lost much of its following in the Greek Cypriot populace by not joining Col. George Grivas (Digenis) and his pro-*enosis* EOKA (National Organization of Cypriot Fighters) in harassing the British. Although AKEL, under proscription by the British for its subversive activities, did conduct an undercover campaign for unconditional self-determination for Cyprus, this was never meant as support for *enosis,* and tended to split the rebel forces. Thus AKEL unwittingly played into British hands.

After the party was legalized again in 1959, AKEL became bold and defiant but certainly not militant. In this period

*One of these early converts stated that had it not been for the training in Marxism which he received during his time as a soldier he would never have passed his entrance examinations to Oxford after the war.

there is adequate evidence that AKEL was tightly controlled by Moscow. Russian propaganda in Greek was sent to Cyprus daily from Radio Budapest and a clandestine communist radio, "The Voice of Truth," steadily poured out the communist line.

The final Zurich and London Agreements of 1959, which gave Cyprus independence, were soon challenged by AKEL. The communists claimed the treaties were a complete renunciation of the principles of self-determination for which the Greek Cypriots—but ironically not themselves—had shed so much blood during the previous four years. Moreover, the communists saw the resulting establishment of the British Sovereign Base Areas as neo-colonialism, and likened them to the American base in Okinawa. Not long after, U. S. communication facilities on Cyprus also became a communist propaganda target.

In the 1959 presidential elections, after forming a front with certain nationalists who were also opposed to the Zurich-London Agreements, AKEL helped garner a 35 per cent electoral return for the anti-Makarios forces. Despite this activity, AKEL was awarded five seats in the Parliament the following year via an electoral arrangement with Archbishop-President Makarios, who saw no advantage in isolating the communists. The communists were given no portfolios in the Cabinet, but still managed consistently to support the government on major issues—to support it, in fact, to a greater extent than even some ministers did.

Among other things, AKEL has encouraged a non-aligned foreign policy and a close affinity between Makarios, Tito, and Nasser. The President of the Republic often reaffirms his intention not to join any military alliances and to continue as far as possible to vote in the U. N. General Assembly with the Afro-Asian bloc. In the foreign policy area AKEL has no trouble lining up with Makarios, and by following him in all other areas the party hopes to give itself a "patriotic" image in order to cover its failure to participate in the self-determination struggle of the late 1950's.

The chief determinant of AKEL's behavior is the avoidance of open conflict with the nationalist forces, for it undoubtedly fears more than anything else another period of proscription. AKEL thus functions legally and peacefully, and takes great pains to avoid making extreme statements which might be construed as undermining the Republic. While this may be AKEL's great political weakness, it is paradoxically its strength as well: if AKEL were ever outlawed again, it would probably not be capable of operating effectively underground, and that could mean the end of active communism in Cyprus. Only time, however, could prove that for sure.

As part of its tactical support for Makarios, AKEL espouses in public the cause of "self-determination," but it is not clear how AKEL really stands on *enosis*. Throughout history the *enosis* issue has been the bête noire for Cypriot communists. In private conversations party members would probably show little interest in union with a "monarcho-fascist" Greece, where communism is banned. Yet the communists' failure to plead the case of *enosis* is an "academic" question for the nationalists, since *enosis* and self-determination—which the communists do preach with ostensible enthusiasm—are synonymous to most Greek Cypriots. This widely held interpretation has been most advantageous for AKEL. Of late, the communists are also being aided by a growing realization in the island that the probability of *enosis* is becoming more and more unlikely.

Another AKEL issue has been the demand that there be new election laws which would introduce the principle of proportional representation. The communists assert that although the AKEL coalition polled an estimated 35 per cent of the vote in the 1959 presidential election, it got only 10 per cent of the parliamentary seats which were agreed upon before the single-list balloting took place. When the next parliamentary elections are held in the summer of 1970 AKEL might seek another election pact for a larger though still minority share of seats. Or it might suit the communists' long-range plans to continue to stress the unity of all Greek Cypriots, since AKEL may not be ready for an electoral battle soon; by so doing AKEL could probably buy time and build up its sympathizer strength with the aim of making a parliamentary bid for power—or at least to make a major contest—in some future election. Meanwhile, Makarios appears content to avoid parliamentary elections as long as he can because of the existing intercommunal problems with the Cypriot Turks. Fortunately for AKEL, the 1960's were not the appropriate time frame in which to argue over Greek Cypriot domestic politics.

The government thus far has allowed AKEL to operate openly. While the Archbishop occasionally comes out against AKEL in his public pronouncements, until 1969 he has not allowed his own amorphous Patriotic Front to split into political parties. This move may help counter AKEL's influence among the farmers and workers, but as long as elections are postponed interest in party politics is not intense. Makarios evidently assumes that he can keep the communists within his flock and can control their rank and file through the Church. Moreover, it is thought that the Archbishop uses AKEL to dissipate dissension within his own political following, including even the pro-*enosis* terrorist groups which flourished in 1969. Also, AKEL could be a political asset in the Greek Cypriot efforts to derive maximum support for its non-aligned foreign policy—a legal communist party helps avoid criticism from Eastern countries. In any event, as long as the intercommunal tensions which began in 1963 remain unsolved, the communists are still part of the Greek community. In Makarios' eyes, the number one danger is the Turk! In short, Cypriot communism is tolerated by the Greek-community dominated government because there are presently more important problems with which to cope.

AKEL's tactical line has been essentially one of labeling the Soviet Union the defender of the Greek Cypriot struggle for self-determination; it has explicitly aligned itself with Moscow in the Sino-Soviet dispute, realizing that the Chinese brand of revolution is not for Cyprus. The U.S.S.R.'s current interest in the island is to prevent it from being a viable NATO base and to inhibit any pro-Western orientation in the government's foreign policy, possibly even to move that policy toward a pro-Soviet posture. AKEL has suggested with success that Cyprus accept Soviet barter trade agreements, economic aid, and technical assistance from Soviet bloc nations. In terms of Soviet theory, in which "national democracy" is a necessary precursor to a "socialist peoples democracy," the communists in Cyprus appear to be in the first phase of the traditional campaign, which requires them to be "anti-imperialist" and "pro-national liberation," and to put forth slogans such as "Liquidate the Aftermath of Colonialism" and "Attain Full National Independence."

AKEL had swung into accord with most of the nationalist aims before a Russian "about-face" in January 1965, when the Soviets openly supported the Turkish objective of an independent federated Republic of Cyprus. It has become clear why the Russians have made overtures to Ankara: friendly Turkey is a much larger gain than a restive little Cyprus. The Turks probably accept Russian support as a demonstration of their independence from the U.S., as well as a prop for their own bargaining position in any bilateral talks with Greece on the future of the island.

The Soviet Union's rapprochement with Turkey, however, put AKEL in a most embarrassing situation and caused it to make its first open break with the Communist Party of the Soviet Union in 1965. The tension between the Turks and the Greek Cypriots is so great that AKEL could be hurt by this turn of events, despite the fact that Soviet arms are among those being employed by the Greek Cypriot National Guard. As a result, in Cyprus today there exists another interesting example of a small communist party endeavoring to extricate itself from a detrimental decision on the part of Moscow, as its Greek counterpart (KKE) had to do in the 1940's on the issue of whether Macedonia should be independent, part of Yugoslavia, or part of Greece. There is little doubt that the Soviet Union would sacrifice its Cypriot comrades with no second thoughts if that served higher interests. Yet the Kremlin would not want a Turkish invasion of Cyprus to force its hand, and AKEL consequently realizes why it must bear the brunt of current Soviet policy toward Turkey. How this realization will affect the future behavior of AKEL is not altogether apparent.

When it has seemed opportune, AKEL has exploited the nagging Cyprus crisis as a logical continuation of its efforts to drive British bases from the island, to eliminate American involvements, and to weaken NATO's eastern flank. Such a campaign is in many respects consonant with the Soviet Union's own long-range ambitions in the Middle East—to remove Western influence in the area and strengthen the Soviet position there as much as possible. The U.S.S.R. has introduced a strategic naval consideration in this area recently, and this will probably have ramifications affecting Cyprus. The build-up of the Mediterranean squadron of the Soviet Black Sea Fleet is likely to present the Cypriot communists with new problems which could affect their relations with Moscow's ruling elite. The impact of these developments on the whole Eastern Mediterranean as well as on the larger matter of Soviet-American relations is in the process of unfolding.

Past success in controlling AKEL, coupled with the fact that the party does not profess revolutionary tactics, apparently causes the Greek Cypriot nationalists to perceive communism as less of a threat to the island's way of life than the West would prefer to have the Makarios government believe. The Ministry of the Interior and the island's police force feel they have AKEL under adequate surveillance and have set up other safeguards to prevent any sort of damaging leftist subversion. Though the infiltration tactics of AKEL, particularly in organized labor, seem to have been highly successful thus far, the political achievements of the party have still fallen decidedly short of its aspirations.

While admittedly not revolutionary in nature, AKEL has been an otherwise model communist party: highly authoritarian, bureaucratized, stable, and obedient to the Soviet Union. In practice, the party is oriented toward the working class and its problems, and shows little or no interest in arguing points of ideology. As long as the unity of the Greek Cypriot community is the paramount interest of the government of the Republic, AKEL can coast along as an accepted element of that community. But when national conditions allow peace to come again to Cyprus, a question will arise as to how long AKEL will be able to cling to its present pro-Soviet identity and survive. If the Soviet Union becomes the dominant power in the entire Eastern Mediterranean region, AKEL would certainly be in a favorable position in Cyprus. If the West is able to bring about a detente between Greek and Turk so as to pave the way for a smoothly functioning independent Republic of Cyprus, AKEL would undoubtedly be looked upon with a much more critical eye by whatever government is in power. While AKEL may enjoy a privileged position as a result of the current discord in Cyprus, it will only be a matter of time until it is forced by circumstances to reappraise its position and decide upon a new course of action.

Modern-day Cyprus is a neat microcosm of one type of communist activity. Considering the numerous revolutions or upheavals which have occurred within other communist parties of the world, AKEL is still a sleepy party ruled by an insecure and unimaginative group of old men, all of whom abhor change. Tracing the development of AKEL from modest cadres to a popular movement; dissecting the political strategy of the local communist leaders; investigating the operation of the present AKEL organization; and examining the party's interaction with Cypriot political forces in the light of debilitating international pressures are some of the fascinating areas which have thus far not been given adequate and objective attention by Western scholars. The intent of this study is to search into and describe some of these neglected areas, drawing on first-hand data from most of the political actors while they were still alive.

1: The History of Communism in Cyprus until 1960

Early British Impact

The Disraeli government's leasing of Cyprus from the Ottoman Empire in 1878 was the event which signaled a new epoch in the modern history of the island, but it also helped to perpetuate the dire socio-economic conditions which were ultimately to be exploited by the first Cypriot communists. England wanted a presence in the Eastern Mediterranean to offset any psychological advantage which Czarist Russia might gain in her designs to control the Dardanelles and occupy Ottoman Asia. The ever-recurring problem of how to fill the power vacuum of the moribund Ottoman Empire—the so-called "Eastern Question"—was a prime concern of the major powers at the end of the last century, and Cyprus attracted the British as a potential bulwark in the defense of her interests in the Near East at that time. Subsequent events, however, caused England to lose much of her initial desire to develop the island. By the first quarter of the twentieth century Cyprus had not moved far from the same impoverished conditions that the British had found after three centuries of Ottoman rule.*

Actually England had acquired Cyprus for purposes it could never fully realize, and this fact was recognized by the Liberal government of Gladstone within the first four years of British occupancy of the island. The 1878 Cyprus Convention with the Sultan entailed a virtually impossible British commitment to protect the vast stretches of the Ottoman Empire which bordered on Russia. Cyprus lies almost a thousand miles from the Russo-Turkish border in Armenia, and an attack from there onward to the Persian Gulf could scarcely have been prevented by

---

*The British penetration in Cyprus began as early as the end of the eighteenth century when the Royal Consul in Larnaca initiated a policy of encouraging the local population to demand freedom from both the sovereignty of the Sultan and the authority of the Patriarch in Istanbul. See Hill, *History of Cyprus,* Vol. III *passim.*

any number of British troops garrisoned on Cyprus. Therefore, the fundamental moral and defense problems that Disraeli wanted to solve with his Cyprus policy were handled by the passage of time. The British occupation of Egypt, after France gave up her role in the joint control of Suez in 1882, eliminated some of them; others were reconciled by the Anglo-Russian Entente of 1907 and the rest were set aside entirely.[1]

The tenuous conditions on which Cyprus was originally held—England was to evacuate the island if Russia restored to Turkey the Ottoman lands seized in Armenia—discouraged British investments to foster the island's economy. Moreover, the British knew that loyalty to the Empire would be difficult to obtain from the chauvinistic Cypriots, whose attachments were to Greece. Although much was promised for the island, little was actually accomplished. In fact in 1915 Britain even offered to cede Cyprus to Greece if she would join the Allied side in the war, but the offer was refused by King Constantine. Elizabeth Monroe, writing as late as the 1930's, claimed that England "allowed it [Cyprus] to degenerate into a Cinderella, and the Fairy Godmother, though announced two or three times, has not yet put in an appearance."[2] Despite the British failure to develop whatever economic potential existed on Cyprus, control of the island was considered to be a valuable, though far from indispensable, link in British imperial defense policy after the turn of the century.

At the outbreak of the First World War, Great Britain annexed Cyprus outright, though it was not until the 1923 Treaty of Lausanne that Turkey formally ceded the island to the British. In 1925 the British constituted Cyprus as a Crown Colony. In addition, with the defeat of Czarist Russia in 1917, and in view of Russia's relative weakness at sea during the war, Britain had grown indifferent toward Cyprus as a military base. Still there was little thought of relinquishing the colony, even after the indigenous movement for *enosis* finally erupted into violence.

Socio-Economic Conditions in the 1920's

Following the Bolshevik Revolution, Cyprus was ripe for socialist exploitation. According to a communist account of

11

the island's history, living standards were low, poverty was widespread, and education was poor. Peasant sons were leaving the farms to seek work in the cities, only to find frustration. Wages for a twelve- to fourteen-hour work day amounted to one or two shillings, and one shilling could buy only two and a half okes of bread at the time. In the government printing office, children were working nine and a half hours a day, with a mandatory night shift, six days a week, for four to eight shillings. The mines were owned primarily by British and Canadian capital and the best workers received two and a half shillings for a twelve-hour day. Through extraterritorial rights granted by the British government, these companies maintained virtual "states within a state" and had complete control over all their employees.[3]

It was within this framework of general deprivation that three restless young men began studying Marxist literature, which they started to receive from Greece in 1921. The three pioneers were Christodoulas Christodoulides, a bank employee; Leonides Stringos, a retail clerk; and Demetrios Christostomides, an accountant and journalist. These three were soon joined by others; within a year they headed a Marxist group of thirty men and women. The first communist newspaper, *Pyrsos* (Torch), was founded by this group. The paper was dedicated to a systematic attack on the British colonial government, which they accused of being responsible for the people's misfortunes. In 1923, with the coming to power of the British Labour Party. Christostomides optimistically sent a "message of greeting to the Labour Party," but this did no more than raise "false hopes" within the burgeoning communist party of Cyprus.[4] There was little the Ramsay MacDonald government could do to improve vastly or rapidly the conditions of the native Cypriots, and there were more pressing demands for the new government to apply its newly gained power to bettering the lot of the working class in England. Had the Labour government recognized, among the many demands for its attention, the clamors of a new left in the little faraway island, the course of the history of communism in Cyprus might have been quite different. Inasmuch as this was not to happen, the story of the Kommonistikon Komma Kyprou (KKK, the

Communist Party of Cyprus) and its successor organization, AKEL, must be told as it actually unfolded.*

First Stirrings of Communism: Dr. Yiavopoulos

Contrary to AKEL's newspaper *Haravghi* in 1966—and insofar as it is possible to trace the origin of communism in any country to a single personality or event—the founder of the movement in Cyprus was probably Dr. Nicolas Othon Yiavopoulos, a Greek subject who was born in the island in 1898. Dr. Yiavopoulos studied medicine (and obviously communism) in Athens between the years 1919 and 1924 and became a member of KKE (Kommonistikon Komma Ellas), the Greek Communist Party. In 1924, four years after the KKE was established, he returned to Cyprus and set himself up as a medical practitioner in Limassol. One of his first actions on his return was to form a "Laborers' Club" in the town for the ostensible purpose of bettering labor conditions. After the foundation of the club, communist literature was supplied to it free of charge from Greece and elsewhere. Moreover, Dr. Yiavopoulos kept up his correspondence with communists in Athens and in Moscow, from whence he surely received the party line. His club became "a single shelter" for all of the workers in Cyprus. The doctor, along with his physician son-in-law, Dr. Vassos Vassiliou, was also identified with the publication of a fortnightly Limassol newspaper *Neos Anthropos* (New Man), which openly declared itself to be the organ of the Cyprus

*Few authoritative works have been published in either Greek or English on the roots of communism in Cyprus. This present history of the early years of the movement has been reconstructed from lengthy personal interviews with former General Secretaries Kononas, Servas, and Ioannou during 1965, 1966, 1967, and 1969, as well as from various undated and unsigned American or British "information tracts." The small British pamphlet *Communism in Cyprus* (Nicosia: Government Printing Office, n.d.) was helpful for the period 1921–54. In many parts, it will not agree with the official version that AKEL published in its own newspaper *Haravghi* (Dawn) on November 27, 1966, in honor of the Fortieth Anniversary of the First Party Congress of KKK (Kommonistikon Komma Kyprou), the original communist organization in Cyprus. This same edition announced that an official history was being written—possibly by long-time member Minos Perdios—but as yet the book has not been published.

13

Communist Party. This newspaper, slavishly following the orthodox communist line, at once set about penetrating the peasant consciousness in rural areas. By June 1925 a group of peasants recently dispossessed of their lands by money-lenders had been formed into unions in three of the villages of the Limassol district (Yermasoyia, Kilani, and Episkopi). These unions worked in cooperation and consultation with the Laborers' Club in Limassol.

Dr. Yiavopoulos was deported from Cyprus to Greece on July 5, 1925, on the grounds that he was a source of potential danger to the peace of the island; he was later expelled from the party as a Trotskyist spy and was not mentioned in AKEL's 1966 history of communism in Cyprus. His place as leader of the local communists was taken first by Costas Skeleas and subsequently, upon his return to Cyprus, by Haralambos Vatiliotis (nicknamed "Vatis"), a Cypriot who had resigned his post in the Agricultural Department of the Colony in order to study in Russia.[5]

Under the leadership of Vatis, who had obviously learned the proper techniques of organizing a mass movement, major developments took place. In 1926 the Constitution of KKK (the Communist Party of Cyprus) was published. The party was therein declared to be dedicated to: (a) "the struggle for the organization and the economic improvement of the circumstances of the classes fettered by the present-day capitalists of Cyprus"; (b) "the struggle for the political independence of Cyprus from the imperialistic yoke of the United Kingdom"; (c) "the development in Cyprus of the international solidarity of the labor movement and the unification of the struggle of the laborers and peasants of Cyprus with that of their colleagues in other countries."[6]

The work of the communists was thus aimed primarily at solving the problems facing the working class and the farmers. The party constitution was formulated at the First Party Congress on August 14, 1926. Twenty-two representatives from the previously organized workers', youth, and women's organizations met in Limassol, formally established the KKK, and elected Costas Skeleas General Secretary. Five years later, in 1931, the KKK was officially recognized by the Comintern and was directed to report to the Greek Communist Party by the Eleventh Plenum.[7]

It was claimed in the 1966 *Haravghi* article that the founding of the working class party was the product of the social conditions that prevailed in Cyprus in the first quarter of the twentieth century. Thus, KKK's first task was to organize unions and improve working conditions. A resolution of the First Congress stressed the need for concentrating all workers, "particularly those working in the mines," into "conscious professional organizations." "These organizations," continued the resolution, "will unify to form a higher organization: an all-inclusive union of Cyprus workers." Also during the First Congress some important resolutions were adopted regarding the farmers of Cyprus: "The alliance of workers and farmers," reads the final resolution adopted, "is a historical consequence necessitated by the present social order and a necessary element for the liberation from imperialism." A resolution adopted for women stressed the equality of the sexes in relation to marriage and wages, as well as advocating the building of maternity clinics. For the young people, a resolution was passed against the hiring of children under fourteen and another was adopted demanding free tuition for needy students. Another resolution stated that communist youth must be "champions in athletic endeavors, which are becoming very popular in the island." The First Party Congress tried to be all things to all people and initially felt sanguine about its prospects for success in Cyprus.

Initial Reactions to the KKK

Communism did not have a strong and immediate appeal to Cypriots. Anti-British and independence slogans seemed to be countered by the *enosis* spirit and the belief that Cyprus one day would be ceded to Greece, as were the Ionian Islands in 1864. Moreover, the deep-rooted superstitions of the dominant peasant class and the influence of the Orthodox Church, which had an ingrained Hellenic nationalism, were powerful deterrents to international revolutionary preachings. But the submissive nature of the Cypriots was possibly the hardest obstacle the KKK had to overcome. Throughout its long history, Cyprus' people have succumbed to wave upon wave of conquerors with little or no resistance. On the contrary, they have often greeted the arrivals with an almost unrealistic hope that the new ruler would give the people better treatment. Rather than resort to revolution to throw off an "imperialistic yoke," the Cypriot has more often than not been known to adopt the opposite extreme. Even the issue of land reform proved to be of little use to the communists in the agricultural country of Cyprus, which had grown accustomed to an inheritance system which had produced small but equal landholdings. While the Greek Orthodox Church and the Muslim charitable foundation, the Evkaf, were the only vast landowners in the island, both the Greek and the Turkish peasants were accustomed to wealth in their religious institutions and did not look upon them as oppressive.

The communists had a hard job ahead of them, but they possessed sufficient determination to survive initial setbacks. Faced with Cypriot hesitancy about acceptance of the communist dogma, they soon introduced the "popular front from below" technique, as shown in the following pronouncement:

> Not until we obtain our freedom and cease to be the slaves of British imperialism shall we be able to breathe economically. All parties that recognize the need of saving Cyprus from the foreign yoke as the first condition for economic and national restoration should direct their endeavors in that direction. But, in order that such endeavors should bear fruit, they should be united. All the anti-British elements, whether they be townspeople or of the proletariat, whether they be Greeks or Turks, and whether they want Greece or autonomy, must cooperate in the struggle against foreign rule. All views meet on this point. The Communist Party, which was the first to suggest the idea of a united front, calls everybody to battle against British imperialism at this critical moment when the British threat looms as a dark cloud over the Cyprian horizon. It is only by means of such a united and tenacious struggle that we shall be able to resist decisively the blows of the English spurs and achieve our liberation. The united anti-British front must be our answer to the British threat. This front must include all Cypriots, all classes and all parties which, for one reason or another, do not want British rule.[8]

An ad hoc meeting of the KKK in 1927 gave special attention to the problem of creating a united front. A main objective was harassment of the British, and the patriotic ideas expressed during that meeting have a familiar ring today. "We shall achieve our liberation only with one united undivided struggle," one declaration said. "The United Liberation Front must include all Cypriots, all classes, all parties . . . who oppose English rule," ran another. From its beginning the KKK called on Cypriot Greeks, Turks, and Armenians alike to fight for the island's self-determination. The KKK hoped to limit ethnic chauvinism and instead promote a spirit of cooperation and united action "against the common enemy of all the people—imperialism."

With the passage of new legislation in 1928, the British soon tightened up internal security. The following New Year's Day the party went underground; its newspaper *Neos Anthropos* was forced to close down, but it was replaced by a biweekly publication called *O Neos Ergatis* (The New Worker). In 1930 the KKK leader Vatiliotis was tried in the assize court for distributing communist propaganda but was acquitted. This was the type of harassment the British began to levy at the communists, who were finally developing a following in the island. In 1931, a less violent individual, Costas Kononas, was elevated to the position of General Secretary. Kononas capitalized on the semi-free status of the party and accused the nationalists of not protesting restrictions that were placed on the "leadership of the people." Despite its difficulties, KKK gained members. Bold attacks on the British as well as on the Orthodox Church were encouraged by the KKE in Greece, which had paternalistic feelings toward the fledgling Cypriot party.

Early KKK Tactics

Although still young, and despite the police surveillance of many of its members, the new party was able to organize an important island-wide strike in July 1929: 6,000 asbestos miners left work the same day. They demonstrated in front of their company offices and shouted slogans demanding shorter work hours, higher wages, and freedom to buy bread from markets of their own choice. Two years earlier, a strike of 1,000 asbestos miners had succeeded only in reducing a ten-hour work-day to nine hours, but the strike of 1929 challenged the foreign company in control of the mines. (Their profits at the time allegedly came to 45,103 pounds sterling annually.)

The company's management asked the workers to return to work and promised to meet all of their demands, but the workers would not trust the company's promises and continued the strike. Consequently many workers were arrested, tried, convicted, and imprisoned; scores more were fired; and some communists were exiled. Even though the strike of 6,000 asbestos miners was not successful, it was a turning point for the entire labor movement in Cyprus, and the experience strengthened the KKK for its later struggles.

The communists soon realized that the Church and nationalist politicians were striving for the same ends as they were, though from totally different motives. Yet KKK's plan to overthrow the status quo in the island by means of a united front against British imperialism ultimately misfired. A violent quarrel broke out between the right and the left. On August 14, 1931, the acting governor recorded in a memorandum to the Colonial Office that the activities of the communists in Cyprus had caused so much ill-feeling between the two forces that it might "result in serious disorder involving loss of life."

The quarrel was probably instigated by the Communist Party of Greece, which sent to Cyprus a proclamation in which the Cypriot nationalist leaders were denounced for aiming at exploiting the workers in exactly the same way as British imperialism exploited them. The Greek communists, at that time violently against Prime Minister Venizelos, were no doubt concerned at the efforts of the Cyprus party to align itself with the local nationalists. Communist propaganda was therefore turned against the Church generally (and the Orthodox Church of Cyprus in particular), against Greek Cypriot agitation for *enosis,* and against the indigenous capitalists or middleman trader class (*emporomessitiki taxis*). KKK supporters were exhorted again to "defend the land of the Soviets and work for the liberation of our country from imperialism for a free Soviet Democracy of workers and farmers in Cyprus"; this slogan proved to be anathema to supporters of *enosis.*

The Church and certain nationalist leaders were solely responsible for the October 1931 pro-*enosis* riots which ended in the burning of the Government House. This event would have no place in the history of communism in Cyprus were it not for the fact that the communists—who initially called the nationalists "adventurous bourgeoisie"—readily lent their assistance in stirring up the trouble, once it had started, because it was obviously an anti-British protest. The communist leader, Vatiliotis, was arrested in Nicosia on October 25 while addressing a crowd; his comrade, Skeleas, was apprehended in Limassol the following day after his arrival from Nicosia with pamphlets announcing the KKK's decision to join in the protest but to demand "autonomy" rather than "union." Both men were tried and deported, along with other communists and nationalists. Later that same year the Comintern criticized the KKK for its inept handling of an anti-imperialist uprising, and as punishment ordered the party leaders to report to the British Communist Party rather than to the Greek communists, as it had been doing since its inception. The 1931 imbroglio was a costly mistake for the young Communist Party of Cyprus.

After the disturbances the government took firm action in many directions to restore tranquility in the island: the constitution was abolished, the activities of clubs and organizations were suspended, meetings of more than five people were prohibited, and a press censorship was imposed. On August 15, 1933, the Criminal Code was amended with the main object of enabling the authorities to deal effectively with the communists and with any other unlawful associations. The following day the Communist Party of Cyprus (KKK) and seven communist front organizations were proscribed. During 1933 and 1934, after years of investigation, twenty-eight leading Cypriot communists were convicted on charges of seditious conspiracy and received sentences ranging up to four years' imprisonment. Only a small, clandestine KKK hard-core was to remain in Cyprus.

In 1936, the Cypriot communists who were exiled in London displayed with action their solidarity for the Spanish Republic. After the call for help, sixty KKK members, including the current General Secretary, Ezekias Papaioannou, joined the International Brigade as part of the British Battalion.[9] During the fight against Franco in the Civil War none of the Cypriots were killed. For those who may have returned to Cyprus, the British reward for their anti-fascist activities was probably a prison sentence. This was the low point in the history of the KKK. The movement had suffered severely and it was purely the patient perseverance of two Greek Cypriot

19

brothers, Ploutis Loizou Savvides (known as Ploutis Servas) and Christos Savvides, which had kept it going, however tenuously, through the late 1930's.

The KKK Under Servas

Ploutis Servas, born in Limassol in 1907, is a most significant figure in the history of communism in Cyprus. He first emerged as a leader in the party organization in the year 1928. In 1929 he went to Greece, and from there to Moscow. In September 1935, he was deported from Greece by the Greek government as a subversive. Although he had been excluded from Cyprus under the 1931 Defense Regulations, the colonial government decided that under the circumstances of imposed deportation there was no reasonable alternative to allowing him to return to the island. The one pre-condition was that he sign a document which pledged that he would "undertake to abstain from communistic and political propaganda and activities" during his stay in the Colony of Cyprus. The affidavit, needless to say, was of questionable value even though signed.

Under British Colonial Governor Sir Herbert Richmond Palmer, the labor front was restive and was seen by Servas to be the Achilles heel of the colonial administration. In 1933, 800 striking builders had organized a demonstration in front of the Colonial Administration Building in Nicosia and were successful in having their demands met. In 1935, a disruptive general strike was organized by the workers of shoe factories in Nicosia. Still, trade unions were legalized in 1936, hours were reduced, and wages raised. These events were followed by a period of hard organizing by crypto-communist unions. Servas saw in a coupling of the communist cause with the labor movement a chance to gain the respectability and the broad base the KKK would need in order to grow and regain legal recognition. He urged KKK members to act as "holy as the saints painted on the wall" and give "no evidence of being revolutionaries."[10] Up to the outbreak of the Second World War, Servas (in Limassol) and his brother (in Famagusta) were to devote their energies primarily to the formation of trade unions and to labor matters in general.

In June 1937 the first issue of a clandestine "Bulletin for the Communist Party of Cyprus" came into the hands of the police. It gave some information about a proposed revival of the party and this was confirmed the following year by the Central Committee of the Communist Party of Great Britain, which claimed that the party in Cyprus had been reorganized and was being given every assistance. There were at this time about sixty KKK members, who paid monthly dues ranging between three and five pounds sterling. In 1938 Servas was prosecuted and fined for possessing communist literature, but this did not hurt his campaign to organize workers. Between 1937 and 1939, some 2,500 workers were organized into unions, and in 1941 the number of unionized employees exceeded 3,800. The union movement, when finally united under the Pan-Cyprian Committee of Workers (PSE) in 1940, changed the small hard core of dedicated KKK members into a powerful, broadly based political force. The creation of a legal crypto-communist party was all that Servas then needed to complete his plan to change the revolutionary image of the communist movement in Cyprus. By so doing KKK would stop being "a sectarian party" and the way would be open for the communists to begin competing gradually with the ethnarchy for the lead in the *enosis* struggle.[11] Servas' final requirement was to be met in 1941.

The Formation of AKEL

By the start of the war in 1939 the island was described as "not unprosperous, though chronic indebtedness and the stranglehold of the moneylender were a millstone around the farmer's neck."[12] The Cypriot communist proclivity for exploiting difficulty was apparent in the early stages of World War II, when there was temporarily a good deal of unemployment in the island. More resolute infiltration into the trade unions became the policy.

In October 1940, the war was denounced on the grounds that Greece (who had chosen to fight rather than accept the Italian demand for surrender), Britain, and the Axis Powers, all capitalists, were "cutting each other's throats but doing nothing to improve the conditions of workers throughout the world." At the same time a prediction was offered that the imperialistic nations would so exhaust themselves as to make it easy for Russia to usher in a new communist millennium. Such a forecast had to be revised in the summer of 1941 when the German attack on Russia began; this event coincidentally gave tremendous encouragement to the Cypriot communists and paved the way for the growth of AKEL (the Progressive Party of the Working People). Buttonhole devices consisting of a red star incorporating the hammer and sickle were worn in public, and photographs of Stalin not only hung in the majority of trade-union offices but were sold to the public to raise funds for various communist purposes.

The AKEL was founded on April 14, 1941, in the course of a private meeting in a taverna at Skarinou, a village half way between Nicosia and Limassol. It owed its origin to Ploutis Servas, who along with other labor leaders felt that their movement should play an important role during the coming municipal elections, the first since the 1931 disturbances. Servas invited forty to the meeting; thirty-six came, and twenty-nine actively took part. Those who attended are listed in the accompanying tabulation. Among these were idealistic intellectuals and a few politicians previously associated with outlawed nationalist movements. The latter hoped to win supporters in the elections by espousing the workers' cause; two of them, not communists, were elected to a small central committee.*
At the close of the meeting one of the non-communists allegedly remarked: "The right wing would not create a coffeeshop, but the left wing created a political party." [13]

The formation of the party was ridiculed in newspapers unsympathetic to the labor cause and was completely overshadowed by the war events in Greece. Little more was heard of the party until three months later, when members sought permission for a second meeting in Limassol "for the purpose of exchanging views on their position in view of present

---

*They were George Vassiliades, now a Justice of the Cypriot Supreme Court, and Zenon Rossides, now Cyprus Ambassador to the United Nations and the U.S. It was mainly the participation in AKEL of these two men, as well as Lefkios Zenon (now a retired district judge), which caused the British government to recognize the party. After it was clear that AKEL was communist-dominated, most of the liberal intellectuals resigned from the party.

PERSONS AT SKARINOU MEETING TO FOUND AKEL, APRIL 14, 1941

Name	Occupation, 1941	Occupation, 1969	Residence, 1969
1 Ploutis Servas*	Commission agent; Ex-Mayor of Limassol	Official of auto agency	Nicosia
2 Lyssandros Tsimillis	Journalist	Journalist, *Neoi Kairoi*	Nicosia
3 Miltiades Christodoulou*	Journalist	Chief, Public Information Office	Nicosia
4 Minos Perdios*	Commission agent	Newspaper, *Haravghi*	Nicosia
5 Costas Kononas*	Journalist	Newspaper, *Patris*	Nicosia
6 Stavros Pandzaris*	Textile merchant	Textile merchant	Nicosia
7 Nicolaos Stratos*	Merchant tailor	Merchant tailor	Nicosia
8 Tefkros Anthias	Poet	Deceased	
9 George Mannouris*	Barber	Coffee industry	Nicosia
10 Andreas Fantis*	Construction worker	AKEL Secretariat, 2nd in line	Nicosia
11 Lazaros Christophides*	Construction worker	Building materials producer	Nicosia
12 Pavlos Georghiou*	Shoemaker's worker	AKEL Secretariat, 3rd in line	Nicosia
13 Kypridimos*	Bakery worker	Deceased	
14 Savvas Ioannou*	Shoemaker's worker	Newspaper, *Haravghi*	Nicosia
15 Christos Savvides*	Merchant tailor	Deceased	
16 Costas Ioakim	Chemist and druggist	Deceased	
17 George Vassiliades	Advocate	Chief Justice, High Court	Nicosia
18 George Christodoulides*	Ex-Mayor of Larnaca	Private business	Larnaca
19 Charalambos Solomonides*	Barber	Deceased	
20 Demetrios Stephanides*	Commission agent	Artisan	London
21 Marcos Marcoulis, M.D.*	Physician	Physician	Czechoslovakia
22 George Christophorou*	Trade union	Deceased	
23 Vassos Vassiliou, M.D.*	Oculist	Oculist	Limassol
24 Phofo Vassou Vassiliou, M.D.*	Dentist	Deceased	
25 Lefkios Zenon	Advocate	Retired judge	Limassol
26 Achilleas Argyrides	Agriculture	Merchant	Limassol District
27 Zenon Rossides	Advocate	Ambassador to U.S.	Limassol
28 Phedias Kyriakides	Advocate	Retired	Limassol
29 Phaedon Kalodikis	Professor of English	Advocate	Larnaca
30 Michael Constantinides*	Professor of Literature	Retired	Nicosia
31 Adamos Adamantos	Ex-Mayor of Famagusta	Deceased	
32 George Ladas	Advocate	Advocate	Nicosia
33 Costas Shakallis	Advocate	Advocate	Larnaca
34 Andreas Stavrinos*	Clerk	Merchant	South Africa
35 Kyriakos Yerodiakonou*	Suitcase maker	Importer	Nicosia
36 Costas Carnaos*	Worker	Tailor	Limassol

*Indicates member of KKK.

Source: This list was prepared by Stavros Pandzaris from memory, Nicosia, May 1969.

circumstances created by the war." That meeting, on October 5, was to be the First AKEL Party Congress and marked the culmination of efforts to exploit the position created by Britain's alliance with Russia for the enhancement of the communists' own position in local affairs. The party was now truly launched. With Ploutis Servas elected as its General Secretary, its line was never again in doubt. Servas, in his inaugural address to the meeting, directed that speakers should use the term "collaborators and fellow strugglers" for addressing an audience instead of the usual "ladies and gentlemen"— the more orthodox "comrade" (*syntrofos*) was avoided because the communist party was still proscribed.

The story of KKK, AKEL, and Servas' role in them is more involved than it appears and should be explained more fully. After returning from the Soviet Union as a legitimate "Moscow-trained Marxist" he became the dominant leader of the Cypriot communist movement because of his charisma as well as his education. His so-called "infallible wisdom," however, was resented by some old members and came to the conflict point when he conceived the idea of a new party to succeed KKK. While his public purpose was to legalize the communist party and eliminate its sectarian image, he probably was equally as interested in ridding the Central Committee of members who challenged his authority over party policies and practices.

In preliminary discussions for the Skarinou meeting, Servas tactically backed hard-line Central Committee members in opposition to some "intellectuals" who felt that none of the well-known communists should participate at Skarinou, so that the gathering would seem devoid of a communist taint. Even though Servas was an intellectual himself, he supported the hard-line position in order to pave the way for his attendance at the conference and his ultimate election as the first AKEL leader. Servas' open objective was achieved, but his second purpose could only be gained by dissolving the KKK, or at least making sure that none of his enemies in the KKK would be on the Central and District Committees of AKEL. To carry out this plan, Servas was in an ideal position, for he was simultaneously the General Secretary of both the KKK and the AKEL.

24

From the time of the Skarinou meeting, Servas felt the hostile reaction of the KKK veterans who were not counted among the AKEL leadership. They did more than oppose Servas' efforts to dissolve the KKK; they tried to oust him and take over both the illegal KKK and the legal AKEL apparatus. In short, there were for almost four years in Cyprus two communist parties in keen competition for ascendancy. A case in point was the AKEL Central Committee's decision of June 6, 1943, to encourage leftists to volunteer in the Cyprus Regiment. In fact, this was Servas' own plan for sidetracking his opponents—both in KKK and in AKEL—by having them enlist in the army. He rationalized his position as part of the struggle against fascism, and as a basis for allowing AKEL to make claim after the war for the release of Cyprus from colonial domination, in accord with the Allies' "declarations for freedom."

Over ten of the AKEL Central Committee members served with the British forces abroad, and Servas took advantage of their absence to promote moderates such as Fifis Ioannou, Christos Economides, Miltiades Christodoulou, and others to the AKEL Central Committee to replace opponents and others who did not support his policies. The conflict between Servas and his opponents in the KKK Central Committee, on the other hand, lasted until mid-1944, when he finally compromised by including the KKK Central Committee members in AKEL's Central Committee. This was done in exchange for merger of the KKK into AKEL and the pledge that there would be only one communist party in Cyprus. The anti-Servas group, which became part of the AKEL Central Committee, was strengthened later by KKK leaders who returned to Cyprus in late 1944 and early 1945. These individuals were invited after the merger to join the AKEL Central Committee as honorary members. All of this activity set the stage for the Fourth Party Congress held in August 1945, which will be discussed in another part of this chapter.

Policies and Activities of AKEL

The formation of AKEL gave impetus to the workers' movement and strengthened their "struggle for national liberation."

By 1942, the trade and labor unions numbered almost 10,000 members and in the villages numerous agricultural and cultural organizations had been formed. Also, in the big and small cities new front groups sprang up and drew into their ranks shopowners and other middle-class Cypriots. Municipal elections were finally held in March 1943 and the candidates of the newly formed AKEL party were successful in Limassol and Famagusta, winning the mayor's seat and the majority of seats on the city councils in both cities. Immediately after this, AKEL encouraged a number of strikes and refused to support the colonial government as a protest against the lack of more popularly elected bodies in the island. The two other parties, which participated in these first elections in over a decade, were also formed at the same time as AKEL, since the British had eased restrictions on all shades of political organizations. Though certainly far less structured than the communist-dominated party, the nationalist groups—the KEK (Cypriot National Party for Enosis) and the PEK (Pan-Agrarian Union of Cyprus)—had managed to attract some support from various constituencies.

The War Years

One must go back to the early war years in order to uncover AKEL's attitude toward the British-led military service. A clandestine KKK party bulletin of February 9, 1940, had said:

> The Government of starvation, having created all the conditions for an extension of misery, now asks for the third time new meat for the cannons, the blood of our children. The most important duty regarding the new attempt is untiring and systematic propaganda against recruiting. We must explain widely amongst the working classes the real object of recruiting and the fact that the recruits are destined directly for the front. The miserable news from those who have already gone must be widely spread.[14]

This continued to be the AKEL line, despite Russia's entry into the war on the side of the Allies. But after the Comintern was dissolved on May 15, 1943, AKEL saw fit to change the line, probably on instructions from the Kremlin. In any case the party leaders seem to have realized by June that their new

26

policy was inconsistent with their past raillery against fascism, and that it could no longer be justified. According to the British view of this period, their change of heart in abruptly deciding to urge members to join the war effort "proved to be little short of calamitous to the Cyprus Regiment and later led to the formation of the Union of Cypriot Ex-Servicemen (EKA)."* This organization was ostensibly founded in order to protect the interests of ex-servicemen, though its activities could lead one to the conclusion that its true purpose was to spread disaffection and subversive propaganda amongst active duty Cypriot soldiers and to enroll them in the AKEL upon their release from the army. Eleven of the seventeen members of the party's Central Committee and 700 other AKEL members enlisted in the Cyprus Regiment, even though conscription was not imposed.

AKEL's early policy on labor matters was, and still is, governed by its desire to establish control over the workers. It was obviously essential to the success of the party that the government should not obtain the confidence of the trade unions. A deputation of trade unionists, which included the present labor leader Andreas Ziartides, specifically told the Colonial Secretary in the course of an interview on April 6, 1942, that AKEL directed the policy of the unions; Ziartides himself has been General Secretary of the PEO (Pan-Cyprian Federation of Labor) since 1947. This present organization is the successor of the old PSE (Pancyprian Committee of Workers). In 1943, Ziartides had become General Secretary of the PSE and was elected to AKEL's Central Committee. A self-taught Marxist, his early political predilections were demonstrated by the fact that he signed the following telegram sent to Stalin on January 20, 1942, which stated among other things:

The Nicosia Trade Unions on the occasion of the Anniversary of the death of Great Lenin do honour today the memory of the man

*Quoted in *Communism in Cyprus*, p. 11. The entry of Italy into the war and her invasion of Greece in October 1940 inspired Cypriots to take up arms and 6,000 (along with the famous Cyprus mules distinguished for mountain warfare) are said to have fought on the British side in the Greek campaign. A total of 19,000 were under arms—with 5,000 abroad—by October 1945. See *Cyprus, the Dispute and the Settlement*, p. 6.

who created the present Soviet Unions, the Greatest Leader of the Universal Proletariat and founder of International Communism. ... Our Trade Unions display their confidence for the final victory of the Soviet Army in the universal anti-Fascist struggle, a victory which will contribute to the predominance of the populo-democratic ideals in the whole world.[15]

During the war PSE labor leaders, in concert with AKEL, maintained a consistent propaganda campaign for lower and more stable prices as well as for the elimination of profiteering.

The PSE, which itself was not registered as a trade union, exercised the greatest power in the direction of the Cyrpiot trade-union movement during the Second World War. The various component elements were bound to obey the commands of the PSE Central Committee as a precondition of membership. With a total membership of nearly 13,000 the PSE thus had influence over a considerable body of the working class. In 1945, after a lengthy and rather revealing court trial that showed connections with AKEL, the leadership of the PSE (Ziartides and seventeen other officers) were imprisoned for being perpetrators of a seditious association.* The sentences ranged from 6 to 18 months for the various individuals, but all of them were finally released by the colonial government within 9 months of their imprisonment. Nevertheless, the PSE was declared unlawful and dissolved; it was succeeded by the PEO in 1946.

During the war there arose a unique problem which AKEL managed to exploit; this concerned the flow of Zionist immigrants into the British mandate of Palestine. Since her restrictions on Jewish immigration were not being obeyed, Britain resorted to severe control measures. Large detention camps were created on Cyprus to hold Zionists apprehended trying to enter Palestine illegally. The route of many a Jewish émigré led from Nazi concentration camps in Poland and Germany via a Greek or Italian ship to a British concentration camp in Cyprus. No one, including the Cypriots, liked the unpleasant task of prolonging the hardship of the pitiful Jewish refugees, but the communists on the island found fertile

*Assize Court of Nicosia, *Rex v. Ziartides et al.,* December 17, 1945 (transcript in English). See Appendix A for extracts from PSE documents which were used as evidence that the organization was part of a conspiracy which intended to overthrow the colonial government.

propaganda in the Zionist situation. They circulated a rumor that Britain was intentionally trying to weaken the Greek Cypriot population by allowing foreign immigration. AKEL also charged that shortages and high prices of foodstuffs were caused by the excess provisions required for the detention camps.[16] Then in 1946, AKEL circulated a report to the effect that British troops had been obliged to evacuate Egypt and would install a massive military base on Cyprus. These rumors caused much of the wartime good will between the British and the Cypriots to vanish rapidly.

The Postwar Strikes

The sequence of postwar election successes revealed the extent of the power and influence of the communist party in Cyprus. Then as now AKEL derived its principal strength from the communist-dominated trade union, the PEO. Recognition of the communist threat brought about an effort to counter the leftist domination of the trade union movement, and a rival nationalist union, the Confederation of Cyprus Workers (SEK), was created. Because many employers continued to cooperate with the better organized PEO, SEK's progress was slow and its continued existence at times was in doubt. However, the communists overplayed their hand with some bold moves against the capitalists in Cyprus.

PEO decided to call widespread strikes in an effort to exclude SEK members from work opportunities and thus force them to abandon SEK. The first five-day strike was called at the American-owned Cyprus Mines Corporation in the northwest village of Skouriotissa on January 13, 1948. This was followed by an island-wide general strike on February 9, also called by PEO. The Cyprus Mines management was convinced that the strikes were basically political and rejected PEO's demands. It soon became obvious that PEO and AKEL were staking their prestige on the effort to humble the American company. When it became apparent that the company and SEK workers would resist, PEO resorted to violence. They perpetrated rioting, arson, the bombing of residences, the throwing of hand grenades, and shooting and assaults against fellow workmen and the police. The consequent bloodshed

29

and destruction caused by PEO in the face of the firm stand by Cyprus Mines tended to turn the Cypriot people against the communists.

When the violence continued, Archbishop Makarios II (not the present Archbishop) issued a circular on March 20 urging the workers to terminate their strike immediately. PEO responded by instigating renewed violence. Power lines were dynamited, buildings burned, bombs thrown; riots ensued and people were severely beaten. Nevertheless, neither Cyprus Mines nor SEK was intimidated and PEO was finally compelled to retreat, with a severe loss of prestige. The strike formally ended on May 17, 1948, after a stoppage of 125 days. Cyprus Mines fired numerous employees who were connected with the violence and to this day has consistently refused to recognize the PEO.[17]

Despite the setback with the Cyprus Mines strike, and probably on instructions from abroad, AKEL decided to make another bid. Overestimating its power over the building workers' unions, PEO attempted to restore its lost position by calling a general strike in the building industry on August 26, 1948. Again the employers refused to cooperate with PEO's demands for a closed shop and the communists once more resorted to violence; large numbers of non-communist workers were severely beaten and some employers suffered similar treatment. Construction sites were dynamited and burned; riots and many other incidents of violence occurred. This time the government stepped in and many PEO agitators were arrested, convicted, and given sentences of up to seven years. Finally, PEO was compelled after four months to retreat again; the strike formally ended on December 18, 1948. The communists had to absorb another reversal and an additional loss of prestige. PEO's generally militant attitude during this period subsequently began to turn people toward SEK. While PEO's hostility toward its weak rival resulted in actions designed to terrorize SEK members, it was perhaps more as a result of these tactics than anything else that SEK made considerable progress in the late 1940's.

The building-strike humiliation led the party leaders to indulge in some self-criticism; an unsigned article in AKEL's philosophical magazine, *Democratis,* called the strike tactics "a wrong policy which has proven to be detrimental to the best interests of the party."[18] By miscalculating its labor strength, PEO not only suffered a rude awakening but caused the nationalists in the island to work harder to counter the growth of communism in Cyprus.

AKEL and *Enosis* in Retrospect

The *enosis* issue has always caused problems for AKEL, and it might have been a partial cause for the inclusion of a significant item on the agenda of the Fourth Congress of AKEL, held in August 1945—the "resignation" of Servas. In fact, Servas had already been suspended by the party on several grounds: (a) that he had refused to comply with party decisions regarding his transfer from Limassol, where he was the elected Mayor, to Nicosia; (b) that he had put conditions on his future stay in the party; (c) that he had neglected his duties towards both the Limassol District Committee and the Central Committee; and (d) that he had declined to be present at party meetings at which he was likely to be criticized. Servas admitted that he was guilty of disobedience, but charged that this was the fault of opponents who were trying to undermine his authority. The result was that he was reinstated in the party but excluded from its Central Committee. Still, the fundamental reason for Servas' problems with AKEL could well have been his intense belief in the *enosis* cause, which he managed to get adopted at the Second Party Congress in 1942. It was about three years later that some impatient AKEL members decided that the *enosis* bandwagon tactic had not produced sufficient gains and that it might be wise to cooperate temporarily with the new Labour government's efforts to introduce local self-government in Cyprus. This was probably something Servas could not abide, and led his critics to see that he was eventually eased out of the way.*

---

*Servas first fell from favor with the hard-core communists not over the *enosis* issue, but more likely when he proposed the elimination of the KKK at the same time the AKEL was formed. After many trials and tribulations, he was finally purged from the party in 1952. Because he still honestly wants *enosis,* he cannot help but be critical of AKEL's shifting policies. Nonetheless, he still fashions himself the "only true Marxist in Cyprus today"—undoubtedly meaning a student of the

31

Despite internal bickering, AKEL did feel secure enough in 1944 to declare itself the official "Communist Party of Cyprus," which belatedly rang the death-knell for the moribund KKK. To this day, however, *enosis* is a bone of contention both within the AKEL and between some Cypriot leftists who are no longer in the party. Of necessity, AKEL takes pains to define its position on *enosis.* According to AKEL's commemorative issue of *Haravghi* of November 27, 1966: "Ever since its formation, AKEL has championed the basic demand for national restoration, that is *enosis,* with Greece, by applying the principle of self-determination to Cyprus." But *enosis* was an issue much earlier with the KKK. While initially permitting lip-service support of *enosis,* the Comintern in actuality had directed the KKK to reject the idea of union with Greece most strongly. In 1928, for instance, on the occasion of the fiftieth anniversary of British rule over Cyprus, the KKK issued a manifesto which included the slogan "Long live the autonomy of the people of Cyprus." A manifesto which the Cypriot communists published in 1931 was even more explicit:

> The Communist Party will struggle for the fulfillment of the immediate economic demands of the workers and peasants, for the exposure of the betrayal of the "National-Unionist" leaders and their *counter-revolutionary* slogan (union with Greece), for the united front against imperialism of the toiling Turks and Greeks (over the heads of the Nationalist leaders), for the Free Workers' and Peasants' Soviet Republic of Cyprus. [19]

This indicates that the Cypriot communists were then not inclined to support Greek nationalist demands. Also it is curious that the manifesto should have mentioned the "toiling Turks" before it referred to the Greeks. Perhaps the Turkish minority seemed more important from the communist point of view than the Greek majority of the population; or perhaps this gesture was dictated by the friendly relations which existed between Soviet Russia and the Turkish Republic of Kemal Ataturk during the 1930's.

---

philosophy, not a practitioner, since he does work for an old established capitalist concern.

The communists probably realized that no political party in Cyprus would ever get very far unless it could appeal in some way to Greek emotionalism over *enosis,* which the Church had monopolized for so many years. Under the shrewd guidance of Servas, AKEL did switch to strong public support for union. When the Permanent Under-Secretary for the Colonies, Sir Cosmo Parkinson, came to Cyprus in 1944 he was met with demands for *enosis,* the abolition of strict laws, and the restoration of free speech and assembly. He answered that he was not authorized to discuss "the separation of Cyprus from the British Commonwealth." In response, AKEL, the trade unions, and the shopkeepers' unions proclaimed a general strike on August 28, 1944.

At that time AKEL claimed it was in a true battle for self-determination, "the apex of the numerous national demonstrations during wartime." Because of the strength of the communist forces fighting in Greece (ELAS, the National Popular Liberation Army) AKEL also began celebrating the 25th of March, Greek Independence Day, in cooperation with the nationalists. Servas thus seemed to have the *enosis* situation well in hand until he was challenged at the Fourth Party Congress in 1945. Communist activity in Greece in the winter of 1944–45 brought the right- and left-wing supporters of *enosis* in Cyprus into a confrontation. During celebrations of Greek Independence Day in 1945 the two sides fought in the village of Lefkoniko; the police opened fire and there were casualties. While the trade unions and AKEL were in sympathy and in close touch with EAM (the National Liberation Front) and other parties of the left in Greece, right-wing elements supported by the Orthodox Church took the lead in demanding union with Greece. On the other hand, a statement by the Colonial Secretary of the new British Labour government in the House of Commons on October 10, 1945, described the British policy towards Cyprus. It was:

> to develop representative institutions in the sphere of local administration . . . before extending them to the central machinery of Government. In accordance with this policy elected municipal councils were restored in 1943, and some months ago proposals for the extension to rural areas of a similar system of local administration through elected councils were made public. I am hopeful that these councils will prove so successful as to make it possible

to contemplate the institution of a Legislative Council with un-
official elected representatives as early as possible.[20]

The municipal elections of May 1946 give another example
of the strength AKEL had gained in its brief five years of existence. In 1943, when AKEL had won the mayor's seat and
a majority of the municipal council in the towns of Limassol
and Famagusta, many observers felt this was an election freak
which could never be repeated. The communists took advantage of the intervening years to build up their grass roots
organization, especially in the labor unions. Despite the fact
that AKEL had openly declared itself to be "the Communist
Party of Cyprus" the year before, the left-wing National Cooperation Front led by AKEL was victorious in all but two of
the chief towns. Possibly the admission of being allied with the
Soviet Union—who shared with the Western powers the victory
over the fascists—served to help the leftist cause rather than
hinder it. Still and all, it became clear in 1946 that AKEL was
an organized political force, with muscle and determination.

In the autumn of 1946, the Labour Party's Colonial Secretary, Creech Jones, decided to take certain measures to liber-
alize the regime and develop the economy. He proposed a
Consultative Assembly drawn from representative elements
in the island to consider proposals for constitutional reform,
and ultimately self-government. AKEL might have anticipated
this move a year earlier, and it had surely thought about the
best way to exploit such a development. If the communists
went along with self-government, they could quite conceivably
assume power in the island in a peaceful manner. Yet overt
support for this British proposal would be seen as a betrayal
of *enosis,* and AKEL knew it would have to make this departure deftly or risk losing much of the following it already had
built up.

The Fifth Party Congress convened in 1947, and a contrite
Ploutis Servas was given back his seat on the Central Committee, though simultaneously replaced as General Secretary by
Neofytos (Fifis) Ioannou. The new chief executive served two
eventful years before he too fell victim to a purge. The events
leading up to that dramatic development give a vivid picture
of the shifting tactics of a non-ruling communist party: from
enosis to self-government and back to *enosis.*

The First Conference of the Communist Parties
in the British Empire

The groundwork for the departure from the *enosis* line was laid at an extraordinary meeting held in early 1947 primarily for the various communist parties of the British Empire. This was held in London between February 26 and March 2, under the auspices of the British Communist Party, and attracted among others eleven of the Empire parties including AKEL. This gathering was possibly the most significant meeting of communist parties since the 1943 dissolution of the Comintern and its purpose was clear-cut: to consider future action, jointly and individually, in view of postwar developments and the new strength of the Soviet Union in Eastern Europe.

The AKEL spokesman, Fifis Ioannou, gave a speech which included solid endorsement of a pro-*enosis* position. He claimed that the communists had organized demonstrations in support of the union cause and castigated the nationalists for frustrating AKEL's efforts to develop a "national unity front" to achieve a minimum program.[21] Notwithstanding the AKEL leader's negative opinion of the Cypriot right wing, the admission that the leftists had even considered an alignment with the nationalists on the *enosis* issue provoked hostility among the other representatives. Apparently Ioannou felt he would witness resistance or confusion on his pro-*enosis* stand, for he offered the obvious counter-argument himself: since Greece was a country ruled by fascists, "self-government or autonomy" for Cyprus should come first, and the Cypriots should consider union when the motherland became democratic once again. In his own defense, he claimed that fascism in Greece was maintained by the British and that once this support had been taken away the dictatorship would fall. With a small gesture toward the communists fighting in the Greek Civil War, Ioannou urged unity "with our Greek brothers" who were then struggling for "freedom, peace, and Socialism." AKEL's case was seemingly accepted by the conference; its final resolution demanded "the British Government to withdraw their troops from Cyprus [not Greece] and grant to the people of Cyprus the right of self-determination—that is, the right to be united with their motherland, Greece."[22] While this resolution was a concession to AKEL, it was not a solid endorsement of the established Cypriot communist policy toward the *enosis* issue, and AKEL was thus probably given another incentive to come out for the British offer of self-government.

The attitude of the Greek Communist Party (KKK) in the postwar years on the *enosis* issue was in line with the nationalist desire to expand Greek rule over all those areas held to be Hellenic—that is, Northern Epirus, the Dodecanese, and Cyprus. Since the KKK "could not afford to appear less patriotic than their opponents . . . as far as Cyprus or the Dodecanese were concerned, the Communists faced no ideological or political dilemma." Thus the "Greek claims on Cyprus, a British crown colony, and the Dodecanese, a possession of defeated Italy, received the unqualified support of the KKK."[23] This same determination, however, did not hold true for Northern Epirus, since this was also being claimed by Albania, a country that was already destined to become communistic. The zeal which AKEL shared with the KKK for union of Cyprus with a Greek motherland which could have easily become a People's Democracy was thus understandable. But this was a risky policy, for it could be considered a move toward "national communism," independent of the international movement, and thus contrary to the dictates of the Kremlin. This is undoubtedly why the AKEL position at the Empire Conference in London met the reluctance it did. A combination of factors, not the least of which was the American intervention in Greece under the 1947 Truman Doctrine, was behind the retreat AKEL was soon to make from its all-out support of the *enosis* line to an expedient policy of "self-government."

The 1947—48 Consultative Assembly

AKEL's next conflict with the nationalists under the ethnarchy came over the British offer of a new constitution to replace the one suspended in 1931. The nationalists refused to consider any solution of the Cyprus question other than union with Greece, but the communists saw a chance to make their mark on a new form of government and decided to play along with the British offer. The Colonial Governor, Lord Winster, opened the Consultative Assembly in November 1947 with eight AKEL representatives, six Turks, two non-party Greeks, one Maronite, and twenty-three empty seats which were boycotted by the nationalists. The purpose was to write a new constitution and the British kept the door open for the ethnarchy, hoping that it would have a change of heart and ultimately join in the deliberations. From the start the Assembly floundered and AKEL soon must have begun to wonder whether it had made a mistake in deciding to deal with the colonial power. By March 1948 AKEL saw that it needed help and formed the National Liberation Alliance (EAS) as a front. The purposes of the new group—supposedly 20,000 in number—were outlined in an information bulletin issued on March 31. This stated in part:

> The formation of the National Liberation Coalition [Alliance] is a decisive step toward the unification of the Greeks of Cyprus in their struggle for liberation . . . and is augmented by workers, farmers, and a large number of progressive members of the middle classes and the intelligentsia. The immediate task of EAS is to receive a constitution granting self-determination to the people of Cyprus. This encounters the bitter opposition of the forces of local reaction, which are doing their best to sabotage the work of the Consultative Assembly. . . .
>
> The duty of EAS is to oppose and isolate the reactionary leaders who strive for perpetuation of the present regime, which allows them to exploit the people with impunity. At the same time EAS makes it clear that they intend to use it as a weapon in the struggle for union with Greece. At the same time they point out that in view of the servile attitude of the Greek Government towards the United Kingdom and its refusal to take up the question of Cyprus, the immediate chances of union with Greece are remote and that it is necessary in the meantime to secure a liberal constitution in order to safeguard the political and economic interests of the people pending a change of the international situation which would bring the question of Cyprus into the realm of practical politics.[24]

Reading between the lines one can sense that AKEL saw itself in the untenable position of backing an imperialist power while watching its opposition act defiantly. In May AKEL had had enough and withdrew from the Assembly, denouncing both the British and the Church-led nationalists. By August, the British also saw the futility of prolonging the talks and dissolved the Assembly, but it kept the offer of a new constitution alive, particularly for the ethnarchy and the nationalist leaders, to consider at some future date.

The day after the British abandoned the Assembly, 15,000 workers took part in a 24-hour strike, which was followed by a number of prolonged strikes in various industries, all in protest against the failure of the constitutional talks. It may be assumed that the communist-led PEO union engineered these strikes out of a feeling of frustration over their abortive efforts to gain the upper hand over the nationalists. The strikes and protests continued into the autumn of 1948 and reached their peak in October, when AKEL sponsored a rally in Nicosia which attracted 25,000. This rally, however, was not concerned with the constitutional issue but was to protest King Paul's offer to allow British or United States bases to be built on Crete in exchange for *enosis*.[25] This hardened AKEL's line in support of self-government, which remained firm until the municipal elections of May 1949.

The 1949 municipal elections were costly for AKEL. Its shifting line between *enosis* and self-government resulted in a loss of popular support while the ethnarchy, consistently for *enosis*, had increased its influence. AKEL opponents were victorious in Nicosia and in ten of the fourteen other towns, while the communists retained Limassol and Larnaca. In the final tally the rightists polled approximately three-fifths of the votes cast, and AKEL had the remaining forty per cent. This temporary defection from the *enosis* line to the self-government stand eventually caused a major upheaval among the communists. Since the Consultative Assembly had foundered and the results of the municipal elections were hard upon AKEL, it was considered necessary to purge the party leadership and to revert to orthodox and vote-catching political agitation after the Sixth Party Congress in August 1949. At the Congress, Ioannou was replaced by Ezekias Papaioannou, a London-trained communist who had come to the island after World War II to be editor of the AKEL journal *Democratis.* He allegedly was raised to the General Secretary's post on the insistence of the Greek KKE chief, Nicos Zachariades.[26] Immediately upon Papaioannou's assuming office, the AKEL line changed once again to the *"enosis* and only *enosis"* position. It was from this base that AKEL optimistically felt it could take on the ethnarchy in competing for the leadership of the nationalistic cause of the Greek Cypriot.

AKEL and the Ethnarchy

The competition of the communists with the Church re-asserted itself in the immediate postwar years. Buoyed up by the results of the 1946 municipal elections, AKEL the next year decided to make an all-island effort to broaden its base. First, it sent Ploutis Servas and a delegation to London to ask the British for self-government, without success; then it moved to participating in the archiepiscopal elections of 1947. The candidate AKEL supported won an overwhelming victory over the candidate nominated by the rightists. The established popularity of that candidate, Bishop Leontios, played an important role in his election as Archbishop for life, but this did not prevent AKEL from claiming much of the credit. But Archbishop Leontios died a few months later, and this served to awaken the nationalists. Overconfident from their earlier victory, AKEL decided to oppose in 1948 the election of Bishop Makarios of Kyrenia (not the present incumbent) and to support an outsider, Ioakim, the Bishop of Derkon from the Patriarchate in Turkey. Their tactic was unsuccessful this time and Makarios II was elected Archbishop. Nevertheless, the election was a close contest and Makarios' ascendancy to the throne was a result of the votes cast in his favor by the Church leaders, who saw the danger in letting communists dabble in the internal politics of the Orthodox Church. AKEL found it necessary to change tactics in the face of this turn of events.

Reverting to a united front approach, the communists offered to cooperate with the ethnarchy on *enosis,* but they were roundly rejected. So in 1949 AKEL, under the leadership of Papaioannou, addressed a memorandum to the United Nations demanding "national restoration" for colonial Cyprus—that vague phrase could mean anything from self-determination to *enosis.* This initiative was countered by the plebiscite sponsored by the ethnarchy in January 1950, in which 95.7 per cent of all Greek Cypriots over 18 years of age voted "in the Orthodox Church of their choice" for union with Greece.

In this conflict between the nationalists and the communists for leadership of the *enosis* movement, AKEL's aim was to provoke an international discussion of the issue. Failing to join the mission of the Holy Synod of Cyprus to the U.N. after the plebiscite, AKEL sent its own delegation to a number of European capitals. This communist delegation, representing AKEL's front, the National Liberation Alliance (EAS), was prevented from visiting America for discussions at the U.N., but it was able to travel within the Soviet bloc. The U.S.S.R. and all Soviet satellites refrained in 1950, however, from taking action at the U.N. on Cyprus. The following year AKEL sent another delegation to the General Assembly, which met in Paris, with the view of provoking the ethnarchy and the Greek delegation at the U.N.

The strong communist endorsement of *enosis* seemed to be unqualified, but at the Seventh Congress of the Cypriot communists in 1951 the attitude towards *enosis* was redefined somewhat. A resolution was adopted which pledged Cypriot communists to pay greater attention to those in the Cypriot Turkish minority who were still under the influence of the chauvinist (mainland-oriented) Turkish bourgeoisie and landlords. That the primary aim of the communists in supporting union was *not* to defend Greek national aspirations was implied in an article published in an illegal mainland Greek communist journal. It said: "The *enosis* slogan permits the strongest anti-imperialist mobilization under the present existing conditions."[27]

The failure of AKEL to discredit the ethnarchy through an independent course of action ultimately was to lead the communists to inaugurate a "United Liberation Front of Struggle." Coincident with a world-wide shift in communist strategy to broaden the base of its support, AKEL set forth its new program at the Eighth Congress in March 1954. Rejecting the view that *enosis* would soon be realized as "both ridiculous and misleading," the new program nevertheless stated:

Our demand is that we should be united with Greece without any conditions. . . . We do not demand to be united with a Greece ruled by the people [i.e., a communist-dominated government]. The people should in one body demand that the Greek government bring up the *enosis* question before the U.N. We are prepared to cooperate with any party, organization, or even individual person who agrees with [AKEL's new program].... The road to the national liberation of Cyprus is the road of the United Liberation Front of Struggle. [28]

This line of action, which was consistent with the eth-narchy's firm position, was formulated so that AKEL could begin infiltrating the *enosis* movement, which was strictly under the leadership of the Church. Though the ethnarchy had publicly rejected AKEL's cooperation on previous occasions, it saw some advantage in communist support in late 1952. Before leaving for the United States to attend the General Assembly of the United Nations in October 1952, Archbishop Makarios allegedly told a reporter: "If the Soviet Union raises the [Cyprus] question we shall not be displeased. We demand our freedom by all means." On March 22, 1953, he said in church on his return from the United States: "We shall seek the support [at the United Nations] of every nation and we shall accept support from every hand, even from dirty hands." On June 28, 1953, he again said in church: "We [the Cypriots] are prepared to knock on the door of the British and to knock again; but if the British do not open their door, we will then break it in." The Archbishop concluded his attack on the colonial government by saying: "We will put forth our hand for help to both the East and the West."[29] Though this last remark was interpreted in some quarters to indicate new leanings toward the Soviet Union, it was really an unfortunate use of an ancient Cypriot adage to the effect that help for the cause would be accepted from anyone.

The new relationship AKEL established with the Church and the good inroads the party had made with its pro-*enosis* campaign brought renewed strength to the Cypriot communists. This, plus the successful recruiting efforts by AKEL's arm in the labor movement, the PEO, put the party in a competitive position for the municipal elections of 1953. When the results were tallied, AKEL received 43 per cent of the vote, retaining Larnaca and Limassol while winning back Famagusta. This did not match the heights AKEL had reached in 1946, but it was a definite improvement over the debacle of 1949. The policy of supporting *enosis* in conjunction with the ethnarchy seemed to be paying off and AKEL was in no hurry to depart openly from it, regardless of challenges which quite likely came from both within and without its own ranks.

Papaioannou, General Secretary of AKEL, later rationalized the AKEL approach to *enosis* in a press interview printed in the *London Times* of April 29, 1954. He claimed:

> Some people abroad find it difficult to understand why the people of Cyprus should fight for the Union of Cyprus with Greece when Greece itself has a monarcho-fascist regime and is actually under American subjugation and control.
>
> The struggle of the people of Cyprus for national rehabilitation must be viewed in relation to the struggle of the Greek people for peace and national independence and not separately. It is part and parcel of the same struggle. Governments come and go in Greece but the Greek people are always there.
>
> When the people in Greece and Cyprus have achieved their national freedom, they will then be able to decide for themselves the type of regime they wish to live under—without any foreign intervention or influence.

The communist tactical advocacy of the popular and almost sacred cause of *enosis* certainly took into account the realization that Cyprus had taken on an even more important strategic importance to the British after their pullout from Egypt and the creation of their Middle East headquarters in the island. In fact it was in 1954 that Foreign Secretary Anthony Eden bluntly reminded Greek Prime Minister Papagos that as far as the British were concerned "there was no Cyprus question at the present time or in the future."[30] It would seem then, as today, that the communists could afford to support *enosis* openly, despite their true desire to have the island become independent, because the chances of union with Greece were remote.

The Second Conference of "British Empire" Communist Parties

After the death of Stalin, non-ruling communist parties saw the need and opportunity to reappraise their own particular tactics. London was the scene of a second conference of communist parties within the British sphere of influence; this opened on April 21, 1954. Eight such parties, including

AKEL, were represented, and the key reason for the meeting was to see how the various affected parties might find ways to accommodate themselves with the ruling bourgeoisie in a type of peace offensive. AKEL General Secretary Papaioannou spoke at the conference and indicated that he was in complete accord with the policy of peace, but that he had reservations about the desirability of cooperating with the Cypriot nationalists.[31] He claimed that the ethnarchy was pro-imperialist, supported by the big landlords and foreign rulers in Cyprus and subservient to a "monarcho-fascist" Greece which was in turn beholden to America. Despite all this, he again defended *enosis:*

> You will never understand why we fight for union with Greece if you look at the Greek problem and the Cyprus problem separately. It is all one problem. The struggle for a free Greece and a free Cyprus is one and the same struggle. The Greek government would be brought down within 24 hours after the Americans are kicked out. Governments come and go but the Greek people are always there. It is on the people that we lay our trust and confidence. Our struggle strengthens the struggle of the Greek people for national independence and vice versa.[32]

Papaioannou concluded by saying that the minimum program of "self-determination" thru peaceful means would be gained by a united front made up of workers, intelligentsia, and patriotic elements from the right wing, which would exclude most of the nationalists and ethnarchy supporters.

Later that year AKEL was still trying to ingratiate itself with Makarios, but with decidedly less success than the following slanted news piece tried to imply: "On the 4th of August a delegation of the Central Committee of AKEL consisting of the General Secretary of the Party, Mr. E. Papaioannou, and the Organizing Secretary, Pavlos Georghiou, had a meeting with His Beatitude the Archbishop at the Archbishopric and exchanged views on the best way of facing the situation. On many points there was agreement."[33]

AKEL's Attitude Toward the Turkish Community

If the Greeks were a major problem for AKEL in the early 1950's, the Turks in Cyprus were a totally different matter when it came to communist tactics. The preference of the Turkish community for continued British rule, and their opposition to Greek proposals for either self-government or union with Greece, presented the communists with a dilemma. The solution advanced in AKEL's 1952 program was a dialectical linking of the welfare of the minority community with future "liberation" of the Greek and the Turkish people, of which the communist-led *enosis* movement was the present stage. The paradox was phrased in these terms: "Only common struggle with the daily common problems of the Greek and Turkish working people, the mutual understanding and help of the Turks in their special problems, will forge an inseparable unity, and the Turks will be convinced that the right path to their own liberation is not with the aghas and the beys of Turkey, but with the common struggle and democratic movement of the Greeks."[34]

AKEL failed to win over the Turkish Cypriot community primarily because communism in Cyprus was Greek-dominated and was therefore patently alien to the Turks. From interviews with a number of Cypriot Turks other reasons were unearthed which may help to explain AKEL's frustrated hopes. First of all, most of the Turks were farmers, isolated from the urban centers in which the communists began their initial proselytism. Moreover, the Turks tend to live apart from the Greeks in Cyprus, even though there were at one time a good number of mixed villages. Hence, there was little opportunity for Greek Cypriot communists to meet openly with Turkish Cypriots in the normal course of everyday activities. This cultural distinctiveness became even more pronounced in the early 1950's as communists ostensibly pushed the *enosis* cause; it would have been awkward then for AKEL members from the Greek community to carry out overt campaigns among the Turks. In addition, AKEL's harangue against the British "imperialists" also served to estrange the Turks, since they usually regarded the colonial government as a buffer against the Greeks.

Lastly the Cypriot Turks, as opposed to those in the mainland, are stricter in their Muslim faith and this strong religious belief was a definite deterrent to the infusion of communistic secularism in that community. Turks in both Cyprus and Turkey still look upon the Russians as traditional enemies and undoubtedly resisted the Soviet-inspired philosophy of class struggle, even though class struggle was one of the few avenues which could possibly lead beyond the ethnic divisions in the island. On the other hand, many Turkish Cypriots did join the early communist labor-union fronts simply for economic benefits derived from membership. When the Turkish Trade Union Confederation emerged in 1943, most of the island's Turks soon left the Greek-dominated labor movement. In short, even with an ideology and material rewards that could potentially appeal to Greek and Turkish proletariat alike, neither KKK nor AKEL could make any significant inroads among the Cypriot Turks. Whatever political maneuvering or good will which may have existed between AKEL and the Turkish community in the 1950's was ultimately abandoned during the height of the struggle against the British by the underground EOKA organization. To this day, however, AKEL is still not willing to write off this temptingly large Cypriot minority community.

AKEL and EOKA

On the morning of April 1, 1955, EOKA terrorist bombs first exploded in British military and civil installations. AKEL's Central Committee issued a communique that day stating "the explosions were not connected with the Cyprus struggle." The communique added: "The people should strengthen their vigilance to the utmost degree and . . . isolate the troublemakers." PEO, the communist trade union, issued a release the next day stating that the struggle "would increase hostilities, thus separating Greeks and Turks." At the time, the communists claimed they boycotted the early revolt simply because EOKA pointedly "asked them to keep out."* This decision was most

---

*"Democritus" (George Cacoyannis), *The Leadership of AKEL and the Armed Struggle—A Marxist Critique,* the English Edition (Cyprus, privately published, June 1959). This passage was quoted in the critique's Introductory Note, p. ii, and was signed simply "S," which may be assumed to be the code name of another ex-AKEL member—not Ploutis Servas, however—who had also become an outspoken critic of the leadership of the Cypriot communists. AKEL also managed to find a Leninist justification for their actions as an answer to their Marxist critics. AKEL claimed EOKA was like a popular front in Czarist Russia

significant for AKEL, for it produced one of the few occasions when arguments over Marxist interpretation erupted within the party. The essence of the "Marxist critique" offered by one faction on the decision was stated this way: "AKEL should have taken a decisive stand for the armed rebellion, it should have taken up the front rows of the rebellion and entered into a steady alliance with the revolutionary sections of the classes, helping their rebellion and revolutionary war."[35] The logic of this criticism was apparently lost on the AKEL leadership at that crucial moment of history.

On April 22, 1955, the Communist Party of Greece sealed the "treachery" by revealing the EOKA leader "Digenis" (a legendary folk hero) to be Col. George Grivas, once the leader of "X," the wartime rightist underground organization in Greece. Similar intelligence was published in the Cypriot communist newspaper.[36] Thus it was clear that the Cypriot communists opposed the EOKA struggle from the start, and even tried to sabotage it. AKEL had reason to dread Grivas as the one who had fought communists as well as the Nazis during the Second World War; his fanaticism against the left had not waned, and could have potentially been directed at that time against the leftists in Cyprus as well as the British—and exactly that was to happen.[37]

The communists soon became involved in the intercommunal problem, which they undoubtedly knew would adversely affect relations between Greece and Turkey. In the eyes of the Greeks, AKEL's failure to support the Greek Cypriot cause was tantamount to supporting the Turks. Furthermore, AKEL's talk about the community rights of the Turks, a concession to the Turkish communists, began to create suspicion between the two communities. For example, AKEL published an article by the Greek Communist Party leader Zachariades suggesting the separateness of the two communities. An extract from it reads: "The liberation of the people of Cyprus can only be realistic if it provides for the liberation of the

known as Narodniks which was criticized by Lenin in 1902 as a threat to the revolution because "it substituted the struggle of the few heroes for the struggle of the masses." The Narodniks finally resorted to lone terrorism and spasmodic assassination in an effort to gain their ends, and that was the basis of AKEL's analogy of them to EOKA. *Ibid.*, pp. 29–33.

Turks as well. By demanding implementation of the right of self-determination we cannot refuse the same right to the Turkish minority."[38]

During the swelling tide of nationalist agitation in mid-1955, the leaders of AKEL did not abandon their struggle to induce the ethnarchy to collaborate with the communists in establishing a united front. Profound differences existed over such issues as the role of the Athens government and the future use of Cyprus as a British military base. It was understandable in view of the clash with EOKA that AKEL's pleas for cooperation with the nationalists found little sympathy.

In July of 1955, seemingly a most inappropriate time, AKEL launched a campaign to collect £10,000 and to increase its membership and the circulation of *Neos Democratis* by 3,000. According to the party's statements, the drive was remarkably successful; it claimed that by the beginning of September over £12,000 had been collected, and increases of 1,144 in membership and 1,113 in newspaper circulation recorded.[39] The charged political atmosphere helped AKEL rally its convinced supporters, but in influence over the population in general, it continued to lose ground to the nationalists.

During August of 1955, AKEL planned a number of protest meetings and a general strike, which were to be held immediately before the opening of the London Tripartite Talks with Greece and Turkey on the future of Cyprus. An appeal was submitted to Archbishop Makarios, offering to alter the date of the protest meetings to suit the nationalists if the latter would collaborate. The appeal was ignored and the protest meetings took place as arranged on August 28, but they were not well attended except in Famagusta. The theme at these meetings, "Cyprus demands *enosis* without conditions, without bases," was one that would be acceptable only to extremists among the ethnarchy's supporters. In September, after the failure of the London talks, AKEL's Politburo issued a communique condemning the talks, and particularly the Greek government's acknowledgment that Cyprus should continue to be used as a military base. Once again advocating a Pan-Cyprian United Front, it insisted that the Archbishop clarify his attitude toward the Tripartite Talks, and asked him "to call upon the people for unity and cooperation, and to condemn the policy of threats and terrorism against AKEL."[40]

Peaceful tactics were employed in AKEL's continued opposition to the use of violence as a means of furthering the policy of *enosis*.[41] During the latter part of August and in September a pamphlet war of accusation and denial was waged between AKEL and EOKA. (See Appendix B.) In September shots were fired into the house of the Secretary General of PEO, Ziartides. This incident widened, at least temporarily, the area of disagreement between communists and nationalists, for the shooting was generally believed to be the work of EOKA. Even though there supposedly existed a militant group in AKEL known as the "Red Hand" (composed mainly of miners who took part in the strikes in the 1940's), there is no evidence that communists themselves carried out terrorist incidents or even contributed as a party to the other outbreaks of violence and disorder which were becoming commonplace.

Toward the end of September 1955 British reinforcements came to Cyprus, the United Nations rejected the Greek presentation of the Cyprus case, and a "no-nonsense" Colonial Governor, Sir John Harding, was appointed. The supporters of *enosis* were forced to reappraise their situation. By all indications, in late 1955 the communists seemed to want to see the Cyprus question left unresolved. This would provide them with several opportunities: (a) to discredit the ethnarchy in Cyprus, showing it to be an ineffective leader of the *enosis* movement; (b) to continue their disruptive influence in Cyprus, a military base important to the defense of the Middle East; (c) to hold the U.S. responsible for the failure to resolve the Cyprus question at the U. N.; and (d) to attack the Greek government for its inability to promote its own national interests. Such propaganda themes were evident in the communist publications at the time and in the clandestine radio broadcasts of the Communist Party in Greece.[42]

Despite AKEL's calculations or desires, its active role in opposing the *enosis* movement was soon to come to naught. On December 14, 1955, after EOKA had begun all-out guerrilla fighting, the axe fell: in a surprising move Governor Harding proscribed, because of "the promotion of disorder and the spread of sedition within the Colony,"[43] AKEL and its front organizations—AON (Reform Youth Organization), EAK (Union of Cyprus Farmers), and PODY (Pan-Cypriot Organization of Democratic Women). In a single night, 135 high echelon party members were arrested and were sent to detention camps. Also, the offices of the party and the other organizations were raided, and records and documents were seized. (According to Kononas, all these files are stored in the British Sovereign Base Areas and are not accessible to scholars as yet.) The following communist publications were also banned: *Anexarititos* (Independent), *Theoriticos Democratis* (Theoretical Democrat), *Neos Democratis* (New Democrat), *Embros* (Forward), and the Turkish leftist newspaper *Inkilapci* (Progressive).

Even though the communist-controlled PEO union was not banned, a detention order was issued for its General Secretary, Ziartides, who had left for Vienna a few days earlier to attend a World Federation of Trade Unions (WFTU) meeting. He subsequently went to London in 1956 and stayed through 1957. PEO probably was not banned because the British authorities in Cyprus recognized the useful work of its patriotic noncommunist members; they hoped that the labor unions, of which PEO was the oldest and largest in Cyprus, would play an important role in promoting stability and prosperity in the island. Throughout this period, PEO leaders could maintain their contacts with international communists through membership in the WFTU. Party General Secretary Papaioannou was arrested by the colonial government in 1955 but escaped with suspicious ease the following year and paradoxically also turned up in Britain in 1957. He returned to Nicosia a year later and took over the party before the ban was lifted on its activities in 1959, just before independence. There is no evidence that he or Ziartides attended the Twentieth Party Congress of the Soviet communist party in 1956, even though both were free to do so.*

AKEL Goes Underground

The imprisonment of the leadership of AKEL and the illegal status of the party and its front groups drove the communist movement underground. Despite the enormous difficulties

---

*It is interesting that the old-line leadership of AKEL remained intact after the Twentieth Congress even though a number of communist party leaders, including the Greek KKE chief Nicos Zachariades, were deposed by direct order of the CPSU. AKEL's policy of non-cooperation

created by British martial law during the 1955–59 Emergency, coupled with the illegal status of the party and "the internal factionalism that resulted," AKEL still claimed that it "contributed with determination to the liberation struggle fought by the people. Many strikes and massive demonstrations were organized against the executions of many patriots . . . the imprisonment and persecution of others, and against the repressive measures of the British colonists. The victims which fell during this phase of the struggle are not few."[44]

While underground, AKEL maintained its estimated strength of about 4,000 Greek Cypriot members, its organization, and its strong position of control over organized labor. It took no part in the organized EOKA terrorism and little part in other forms of violence during the Emergency. In truth there was a left-wing element supporting EOKA, but these were among others made up of ex-AKEL members who left the party over disagreements at various times. Dr. Vassos Lyssarides was a leader of this EOKA group and their line still was "self-determination" first, even though EOKA invited these leftists to join its ranks only on the condition that they individually renounce AKEL's policy.

Evidence of AKEL's continued existence was to be seen in their newspaper, propaganda leaflets, letters, and declarations. AKEL probably maintained a fairly well organized second-level leadership which attempted to recruit new members and raise funds, but if so it had little success. British government investigations of the 135 leaders arrested in December 1955 did not dictate continued detention, and most of those detained were released under surveillance during the following year. Enough of the AKEL members were free by May of 1957 to make possible a secret meeting of a majority of the Central Committee. The purpose was to reappraise the party's position in light of its anti-EOKA stance and the events which followed that decision. The meeting concluded with agreement that the decision was right, since conditions in Cyprus could not yet support a revolutionary movement, and since neither Makarios nor Grivas was a spokesman for the masses.[45] This could be taken as further proof that AKEL's overt support of the *enosis* cause was based on a consideration of means, not ends.

---

with EOKA apparently sat well with the Kremlin since it was in essence directed against the fanatical anti-communist Col. Grivas.

The British probably recognized the folly of proscribing AKEL rather quickly, and hence allowed the party to operate rather freely from 1957 on. The communists in Cyprus were the only group, other than the Turks, who were opposed to EOKA, and it would naturally serve British interests to permit AKEL some independence of action even though it was officially outlawed. Not only did the British ostensibly fail to uphold their ban on the communists, but it was alleged in the American press early in the struggle that PEO leader Andreas Ziartides, as well as three other important leftists, had been receiving a subsidy of 65 pounds sterling per month from the British.[46] Grivas thus perceived that the British, while offering plans for self-government, were really employing their traditional "divide and rule" technique among the Greek Cypriots by playing off AKEL against EOKA. It was not surprising that Grivas wrote during this period that his task was "to fight three enemies, the British, the communists, and the Turks."[47] More than once during the Emergency, the EOKA leader warned the communists that he would retaliate severely if ever AKEL were to get in the way of the Greek Cypriot liberation drive. Grivas finally concluded that whatever opposition AKEL did show against EOKA resulted from "simply taking orders from behind the Iron Curtain."[48]

The propaganda which emanated from AKEL centered on two key themes: "complete liberation, without any fetters," to be achieved by the tactic of a "mass, open, united democratic struggle," and denunciation of EOKA. *Haravghi* (Dawn), the Greek-language daily newspaper (first edited by the poet and AKEL Central Committee member Tefkros Anthias) which in February 1956 took over the role (and circulation) of the party organ, *Neos Democratis,* consistently defined AKEL's program during the Emergency Period as follows: (1) A complete truce and end of "all kinds of military action and persecution of persons" should be proclaimed. (2) The Archbishop should be freed. (Makarios had been deported in March 1956.) (3) All political prisoners should be freed. (4) "Political and democratic rights of the people should be restored." (5) All pending executions should be "abandoned" as a first step toward final agreement on the question of amnesty.

AKEL did not exploit opportunities for trouble-making because it saw more to gain in the situation by identifying itself, in fact as well as in public statements, with "peaceful" tactics. There were, however, continued vituperative exchanges in which EOKA and AKEL bitterly denounced each other. The main publication along these lines was a 69-page Greek-language tract entitled, *The Communist Leadership Against the Cypriot Struggle,* which was dated 1958 and probably written in part by Grivas' lieutenant, Antonios Georgiades. The thrust of the attack on AKEL's collaboration with the British was contained in the first 44 pages and the remainder was made up of documents: affidavits of ex-AKEL members; evidence of complicity with the British on the parts of Ziartides and Partassides, the mayor of Limassol; and a critical letter to Moscow Radio by Pavlos Modinos, an advocate, who felt EOKA had been praised in one broadcast. The EOKA pamphlet stated at the end: "In connection with these events, as well as any possible future treacherous acts, a supplementary bible will be published." The necessity for the verbal sequel was obviated by the actual outbreak of open conflict between AKEL and EOKA forces at a remote mountain village in August of 1958. This was more than likely precipitated by the assassination of certain PEO leaders marked for their pro-British activities.

Archbishop Makarios, who by this time had been released from his exile on the Seychelles Islands, made an appeal for calm between the two Greek Cypriot factions. AKEL had arms hidden away for possible use in a crisis and the "Red Hand" militants in the party urged the leadership to begin an all-out campaign against the EOKA terrorists, who never had more than 300 full-time active participants within their ranks at any one time.* Makarios was apparently worried about a war within the Greek Cypriot community, but his tone of moderation with the communists incensed Grivas. The EOKA

*Obviously 300 fighters was merely the hard core of the EOKA organization in the mountains. In addition there were some 750 OKT (shotgun troops), who worked on their own with little direction from Grivas, and there was an organized "Young Stalwarts" network (ANE) made up of teenagers. The chief element of EOKA's effectiveness was the passionate support of an overwhelming majority of the Greek Cypriot citizenry, and this was undoubtedly the main deterrent against the leftists ever getting into an open war with the right-wing militants.

leader later wrote in his memoirs: "When I went on to execute a few left-wing traitors, the communist mayors rushed to Athens to protest to Makarios. . . . I learned that the Archbishop had shown sympathy toward the mayors, but I saw no reason why traitors should be protected by a communist trade-union card."[49] The truth of the matter was that this was one of the first times Makarios used the communists in Cyprus to play off extremist elements within his own following. It was true that the Turks had begun their own campaign against the EOKA forces and, as today in the face of a common enemy, Makarios did not want to split the Greek Cypriot forces. Nevertheless, an equally important rationale in the mind of Makarios undoubtedly was that he saw Grivas' growing strength and popularity as a threat to his own leadership. Since AKEL was still in control of a sizeable proportion of the Greek Cypriot populace, it would serve temporarily as a counterweight to any overly ambitious designs on the part of the EOKA mastermind. Ziartides even met with Makarios in Athens, which resulted in "an appeal for peace among the Greeks."[50] This was to bring AKEL and the Archbishop closer together than they had ever been; but it was simultaneously the beginning of an intense, long-lasting hostility between Makarios and Grivas, which could be the cause of some of the difficulties with the right wing in Cyprus today.

AKEL took advantage of its newly found good will with the Archbishop, who soon began giving indications that the battle for *enosis* was proving costly for any number of reasons and was not progressing rapidly enough toward its goal. The communists urged Makarios to begin direct talks with the British to achieve by diplomacy what EOKA could not do with terrorism. Moreover, EOKA was having extreme difficulty fighting off raids by the Turkish terrorist organization (TMT) while still trying to keep up its hit-and-run attacks on the British. Grivas grudgingly must have recognized the need to keep the Greek community intact and supposedly made overtures to the leftists to establish "joint defense associations" in certain areas to ward off impending Turkish attacks.[51] With the front virtually everywhere, and the Turkish position against *enosis* hardened, the situation in Cyprus had indeed become grim by the end of 1958. The long-awaited break in the crisis was to come early the next year when the Greek and Turkish prime ministers and foreign ministers met in Zurich to begin diplomatic negotiations in hopes of resolving the dilemma.

The Road to Independence

The Cyprus question was settled at long last by the London Agreement of February 19, 1959, which followed the compromise in Zurich between Greece and Turkey. The Zurich-London Agreements (basically articles to be included in a Treaty of Establishment, a Treaty of Guarantee, a Treaty of Alliance, and the Republic's Constitution) provided that one year from the date of signing, Cyprus was to become an independent republic with a Greek Cypriot President and a Turkish Cypriot Vice-President.[52] The Agreements specifically prohibited the union of Cyprus with any other state (the former Greek position) and also prohibited any future partition of the island (the former Turkish position). In addition, British sovereignty over the two areas (Akrotiri and Dhekelia) where she maintained military bases would continue. During the last year of British control of Cyprus, Britain agreed to modify her internal Cypriot policy, to release all political prisoners, and to grant amnesty to all members of EOKA and TMT. The burning issues which had caused the loss of more than 600 lives in a four-year period were thus amicably resolved in less than two weeks' time.

The maintenance of the independence of Cyprus was provided for in the Treaty of Guarantee, which was signed by Great Britain, Greece, Turkey, and the Republic of Cyprus. Article 4 of the treaty allows any of the guarantor nations to consult together and act jointly in the event of a breach of the provisions of the treaty. In fact, if joint action to guarantee the status quo is not possible, then any one of the guarantor nations may act unilaterally. It could be noted that there must necessarily be a three-nation decision at all times on what constitutes the status quo and on what constitutes "indirect subversion" of it.

The provision in the Zurich-London Agreements regarding security forces on the island was most interesting. In the section Treaty of Alliance between the Republic of Cyprus, Greece, and Turkey, definite arrangements were made for the stationing of Greek and Turkish troops and the training of a Cypriot army. Articles 4 and 5 of the treaty state that "Greece shall take part in the [military] Headquarters . . . with a contingent of 950 officers and soldiers . . . and Turkey with a contingent of 650 officers and soldiers [which] shall be responsible for the training of the Army of Cyprus." Further provisions of this treaty allow the Greek President and the Turkish Vice-President (who jointly share veto power of all defense legislation) to request an increase or a decrease in the size of the Greek and Turkish troops. The command (held by a general officer) of the tripartite military headquarters was to rotate yearly among a Cypriot, a Greek, and a Turk.

Other provisions agreed to at the London Conference concerned the legislature and the public service agencies of the new Republic. Each of the two communities was to hold separate elections and choose its representatives to the legislature in the ratio of seven Greek Cypriots for every three Turkish Cypriots. The public service was designed to operate with the same proportion of employees.

Finally, the Zurich-London Agreements established separate Communal Chambers for the Greek and Turkish communities on Cyprus. These local representative bodies were given control of the religious, educational, cultural, and certain economic affairs of their respective communities. Moreover, each of these Chambers was given the authority to impose taxes and levies on its own constituencies to provide for operational needs. This proposal, coupled with the provision creating separate Turkish municipalities in the five largest towns, caused Archbishop Makarios, who was representing the Greek Cypriots, to balk initially and for a time refuse to sign the Zurich-London Agreements.[53]

The "agreed foundation for the final settlement of the problem of Cyprus" was initiated by the representatives of Greece, Turkey, the United Kingdom, and Cyprus on February 19, 1959, in London. The greater task of implementing the Zurich-London settlement was still ahead, however, for the nations concerned. The colonial government of Cyprus, under the leadership of Governor Sir Hugh Foot, launched immediate attempts to bring the island back to the normality of the pre-Emergency period.

While the Cypriot communists had definitely been in favor of "self-determination," "self-government," and independence at various times in its history, the Zurich-London Agreements were not greeted enthusiastically. In fact, the news of independence came "like a shock to Cypriots" and the members of AKEL were apparently no different on this score than their fellow countrymen.[54] Moreover, since independence for Cyprus was "against the aspirations of generations of Greeks,"[55] AKEL did not care to find itself in the position of supporting the Agreements too loudly. There were also imponderables in the Agreements which made the communists uneasy. The stationing of Greek and Turkish troops and the retention of British bases in the island could not have furthered AKEL's strategic interests in any conceivable way. Finally, the general divisiveness of the two communities, which was built into the Constitution and reflected in the governing institutions, did not promise to be the ideal form of government under which AKEL could function. But obviously there could have been worse alternatives, such as partition, and the members of AKEL prepared to reconcile themselves to their fate.

All these matters must have been discussed at the party's Ninth Congress, which was held on September 12, 1959, in an undisclosed location (AKEL was still officially proscribed). Reportedly over 200 delegates attended the Congress and cast their votes for elected officials by "secret ballot." Papaioannou was re-elected to his post, but the names of the Central Committee members were not released at this time because AKEL protested that there was not a free press on the island as long as the proscription order against AKEL was in force.[56] This order was finally lifted on December 4, 1959, when the Emergency was ended.

The presidential elections were held nine days later. In the meantime, two political factions had formed while AKEL was still officially outlawed: one was the Patriotic Front (PM), made up of those loyal to Makarios and the Zurich-London Agreements; the other was the Democratic Union (DE), formed by a pro-Grivas faction which still wanted to hold out for *enosis* with Greece. AKEL was virtually caught in the middle and could do little more than ask Governor Foot that the elections be postponed. Foot refused. It is alleged that

AKEL then proposed to make a deal with the Makarios forces, trading their support for the presidency for a sizeable share of the seats in the parliament, as well as in the Greek Communal Chamber; and that Makarios turned down the offer, since he was sure he did not need the support of the communists to win. But the election was closer than expected. The DE Party, in fusion with AKEL, managed to win one-third of the vote. This result has since nourished the myth that the communists control over 30 per cent of the Cypriot electorate; in fact, the vote was drawn from all shades of political opinion who just happened to be against Makarios or the Agreements at that time. For the follow-on elections in 1960 AKEL settled on a deal which provided for five seats in the House of Representatives and three in the Communal Chamber, since it did not want to risk another confrontation with Makarios. After all the extensive preparations were made, the Republic of Cyprus was formally established on August 16, 1960.

Summary of the Pre-Independence Period

Only a devout communist could believe that AKEL played a part in gaining the independence Cyprus was granted in 1960. Though it was guided by motives unconnected with Cypriot national interests, AKEL's failure to participate in the EOKA movement was a tactical blunder: its withdrawal from the EOKA struggle lost it support, some of which it will never regain. By the time the Republic was formed, the position of the communists had deteriorated to one of the lowest points in their long history on Cyprus.

In the long run, it could turn out that the British may have helped the communists by banning the party during the Emergency. Some communist organizations are more skilled in underground activities than in the open, and AKEL took a page from the book of the illegal KKE in Greece and managed to keep going during its dark period. Generally speaking, and through the wisdom of hindsight, had the British followed a more enlightened policy toward the Cypriots during the 82 years in which they controlled their "Cinderella Island" many of today's problems in Cyprus might have been avoided. Reality, however, was otherwise.

The 1959 Zurich-London Agreements establishing and guaranteeing an independent Republic of Cyprus were agreed upon first by Great Britain, Greece, and Turkey, and then presented to the Cypriot people, who really had no choice but to accept. The settlement may have been a "success" in the eyes of the British, but it certainly was no victory for any of the peoples most vitally concerned. To most Greek Cypriots, as well as to the AKEL members, complete liberation had not been achieved, and that realization was to remain an issue in Cypriot politics throughout the following decade.*

---

*The Soviets felt—along with Makarios, so it turned out—that the Zurich-London Agreements were only half the loaf, so to speak. The Soviets characterized the Agreements as a renunciation of "self-determination" and the "establishment of a condominium of Greece, Turkey, and Britain against the wishes of the Cypriot population." The U.S.S.R. also insisted that Cyprus would be nothing more than a NATO strategic base and raised the specter of U.S. missile sites there. In a comment directed to Turkey, it asserted that the Agreements were not the final word since the Cypriot people have the right "to liberate themselves from foreign rule by whatever means available." *Tass International Service,* February 20, 1959. Andreas Fantis, Deputy General Secretary of AKEL, stated AKEL's view on the impending independence: "Under the regime imposed by the Zurich-London Agreements and since we are far away from having gained true independence, the basic goal of the Cypriot people continues to be: real independence for Cyprus, democratization of its Constitution, and demilitarization of the island." *Neos Democratis,* April 1960. An initial Soviet assessment of the independence of Cyprus may be found in M. Ivanov, "Cyprus: A New Republic," *International Affairs* (Moscow), September 1960.

2: AKEL's Role and Organization

The Status of AKEL Since 1960

The communists in Cyprus have been legally active since independence and AKEL is still the most effectively organized political party in Cyprus. Legal status has permitted AKEL to develop and maintain its current sizeable mass of followers by appeals on the social, cultural, and political levels. AKEL leaders are forced by circumstances to accept the overwhelmingly strong nationalist position on major issues, and they voice nationalist slogans in order to keep their present well-organized following in line. AKEL has come a long way since its dark days during the Cypriot guerrilla campaigns of the late 1950's.

The party quickly recognized its mistake in opposing EOKA's popular struggle and has consistently tried to improve its political image among the Greek Cypriots. AKEL lost many supporters when by its own admission it mistakenly chose to sit out the armed struggle against the British, in direct violation of Leninist doctrine. Later, one AKEL leader regretfully cited Lenin's *Left-wing Communism: An Infantile Disorder,* which expressed approval of cooperation with non-communist elements and criticized those communist parties which, "through poor maneuvering," placed themselves outside the main political currents because of their inability to "shift, make agreements, and compromise."[1]

The communists in Cyprus had greater opportunities to expand their influence under British rule than after independence; since then AKEL has felt constrained to employ tactics and follow policies that would not irritate the nationalist majority. The communists can no longer depend on British opposition to the nationalists who had held the banner of *enosis,* nor do they now see much advantage in opposing the leadership of the Church, as they did under British rule. In general, since 1960 the Greek Cypriot national environment operates against communist expansion. The island has largely a peasant economy under the strong influence of the Church, which is one

59

branch of the Eastern Orthodox Church with all its dynamism, wealth, and prestige. On the other hand, Cyprus has a sophisticated and influential entrepreneur class with a strong preference for a free economy as opposed to communistic socialism. Communism has virtually no appeal to the middle class in Cyprus, and the middle class has provided the leadership for the Greek majority in all areas of public life—particularly in national education.

In two areas, however, communism has found acceptance: among intellectuals disaffected with the dominant Church, and in labor organizations, which found AKEL more effective with the colonial authorities in achieving trade-union objectives. But AKEL is still largely dependent for new intellectual leadership on the youth it sends to the Soviet Union for training, and in the case of labor, AKEL is faced with a growing government-supported anti-communist labor organization (SEK), which is now five times the size it was under British rule.

More than half of the labor force is now organized with a strong loyalty to the Church, which in Cyprus under Turkish and British rule provided national leadership under the ethnarchy. The influence that the communists might have over labor is counter-balanced by the fact that there is no depressed urban class and the rural areas are still religious, traditional, and highly conservative. It should be recalled that in the Near East, Cyprus has a standard of living second only to Israel. Given this environment, the communists are hard put to convince the youth of the island that the East will give them a better future. As the popular feeling for *enosis* recedes, AKEL may hope to gain more respectability. So long as the Cyprus problem remains unresolved, however, and Archbishop Makarios—who was re-elected President in 1968 with AKEL support and a popular vote of over 95 per cent—remains at the helm, AKEL's influence will remain contained. In political action, AKEL as a minority party has a technical problem under the constitution provided by the Zurich-London Agreements. The Constitution provides a majority electoral system with large electoral districts, which would virtually exclude a minority party from gaining representation in the House of Representatives. Moreover, a party that has less than 12 per cent of the House seats cannot have the status of a party, which is now the case with AKEL.[2]

AKEL's leadership follows the expedient of cooperating with and even supporting President Makarios. It refrains from attacking any of the Cabinet members, many of whom are former EOKA fighters. The communists have no representation in Makarios' cabinet and their position in the House is too weak to have any significant impact on legislation. AKEL, then, can hardly take an independent course in the intercommunal problem in Cyprus, although the Greek communists in 1955 did advocate the "separateness" of two communities, which was taken by the Cypriot Turks to mean advocacy of "partition" of the island. In AKEL's terminology "the liberation of the people of Cyprus" can only be realistic if it provides for the "liberation of the Turks" as well. Thus, by demanding implementation of the right of self-determination, AKEL now "cannot refuse the same right to the Turkish Minority."[3] Currently, AKEL attributes the troubles between the Greeks and the Turks on the island to "foreign imperialists"—a phrase which is meaningless to a people who feel that they have already successfully forced the "imperialist" British to give Cyprus independence. Within an inimical national environment, AKEL has adopted an opportunistic policy based on popular front tactics, giving priority to developing its labor front and party membership.

Membership

AKEL's claimed membership is currently at four per cent of the country's adult population, which is proportionately the highest among non-ruling communist parties. The absolute figure available on its membership is 14,000, which was announced by the General Secretary of the party, Ezekias Papaioannou, in March 1966. Four years earlier, at the Tenth Party Congress, AKEL claimed 10,432 members.[*]

[*]*Haravghi,* March 3, 1966, and *Neos Democratis,* May 1962. If this increase is real, it can probably be attributed to relaxed criteria for the qualifications of new recruits, i.e., the termination of the 3-6 month probationary period. See *Neos Democratis,* December 1967.

Assuming these public figures are accurate, it is still impossible to come up with a certified account that they represent the actual, up-to-date, dues-paying membership. The reliability of these public figures should be judged in the circumstances of a military emergency in which the nationalists have been dominant. Since November 1963, Cyprus has become an armed camp within which the anti-communist military are more in control than at any other time. Within this militarized situation AKEL's rising membership cannot be understood, unless there is in Cyprus a strong unobservable public resentment of Makarios' policies—but this could hardly be the case in view of the presidential elections of 1968. AKEL would find it difficult to recruit members from outside its traditional family, particularly among the youth, which have come under right-wing military indoctrination within a system of obligatory national service. The withdrawal of Greek troops from Cyprus in early 1968 must have eased the situation for AKEL, but still the Cyprus National Guard continues to have a depressive effect on communist expansion. Thus, it is difficult to explain why AKEL's membership should in fact rise during this period of intercommunal strife from 10,000 in 1963 to 14,000 in 1966, especially when AKEL offers no alternative to Makarios' policies.

AKEL's membership is overwhelmingly Greek, although the Cypriot communists tried energetically to recruit among the Turks of the island. During the Emergency of the 1950's AKEL sought a tacit alliance with the Turks to oppose the nationalists in labor affairs and on the national issue of independence versus *enosis*. Since independence, however, and particularly after the intercommunal strife in Cyprus, AKEL has been cautious about seeking Turkish cooperation. When Makarios introduced his "pacification" policy, the communists resumed the line of "peaceful coexistence." AKEL has had an insignificant number of Turkish members, particularly in the trade unions, but the 1962 murders of two communist journalists, Mustafa Hekmet and Muzzafer Gurkan, along with the assassination in April 1966 of the Turkish trade unionist Dervis Kavazoglou, who cooperated with AKEL, were disillusioning. London-based Ahmed Sadi attended the Eleventh Party Congress in 1966 and two other Turkish communists came to Cyprus in 1967 from Britain and Bulgaria (N. N. Seferoglou and Ibrahim

Hassan Aziz) to win Turkish support for AKEL, but they were effectively blocked from making inroads into the Turkish labor movement.[4]

AKEL has also been weak in recruiting members from the civil service and police. Most of the new appointments since independence to these services have been made on the applicant's record during the EOKA struggle. The composition of the bureaucracy as well as the Cabinet reflects application of this "rule of thumb." The communists are therefore excluded from the public administration for political reasons, and also for security reasons under the practice of the former Minister of Interior, Polykarpos Georghadjis. This procedure of discrimination has discouraged civil servants from joining AKEL and its front organizations. (It is interesting, however, that graduates of Eastern European universities are being hired by government agencies without any stigma.)

Just as the labor arm of AKEL is finding it increasingly difficult to expand, in like manner the communist effort in the rural areas—which have been traditionally conservative under the influence of the Church—has failed to compete with the nationalist rural organizations. At rural party meetings AKEL feels obliged to pay tribute to Archbishop Makarios almost as if he were a patron saint! While it promotes village recreation and social activities, the basic village feeling toward the Church strongly militates against AKEL.

Voting Strength

A good indicator of the strength and influence of the communists can be obtained by studying the results of the Cyprus municipal elections before and after independence. Prior to 1960 the only elections in Cyprus were in 16 municipal centers covering largely the urban centers of the island, which consisted of about 25 per cent of the population. In these municipal elections, AKEL, with a minority vote, played a leading role in the electoral coalition of the left, but the nationalists, without the organization and financial resources of the communists, held their own supremacy under a British administration hostile to their cause. In the 1946 elections, AKEL won over 50 per cent of the votes, but the May 1949 elections revealed a decline in the communists' influence. In the 1949 tabulation, the nationalists polled 60 per cent of the votes and won in 11 out of the 15 municipalities (one of which, Lefka, was won by the Turkish right-wing party). Of the larger and more important urban centers, AKEL lost Nicosia, the capital, and retained its control by a very small margin in Limassol with the election of Mayor Costas Partassides, in Larnaca with Mayor Lyssos Santanes, and in Famagusta with Mayor Adamos Adamantos. Morphou, another fairly important town, elected a leftist but a non-communist. These elections resulted in a leftist urban vote of only 40 per cent and the elimination of AKEL's control over five of the towns which they had gained in the 1946 elections—Nicosia, Karavas, Lapithos, Lefkoniko, and Lefkara.

While it is clear that a decline in communist strength began in May 1949, the 40 per cent vote is nevertheless misleading in estimating the influence of the communists in Cyprus. The total population of the districts in which the municipal elections were held was only about 125,000 out of the 455,000 residents of the island, which was the population after the 1946 census. Moreover, only about 30,000 of these were qualified voters. Hence, the total number of urban voters influenced by communism numbered only about 12,000, chiefly workers. In 1950 there were probably not more than 4,000 hard-core members throughout the island capable of influencing about 20,000 of the 105,000 Cypriots who would have qualified to vote—that is, about 19 per cent of the electorate.

In the municipal elections of May 1953, the nationalist vote was 11,057 in the six principal municipalities (and brought nationalist control over the crucial municipal council of Nicosia) as against 8,483 votes for the communist-led coalition ticket, which won control of Limassol, Famagusta, and Larnaca. The independent vote of 5,256, which elected only one councilman, would have been devastating to the communists if it had gone to nationalists. Without taking into account the Turkish vote, which was cast separately from the Greek, the communist-led coalition represented one third of the total vote in the hard-core urban area—that is, only 12 per cent of the total population.[5]

Politically, there is no reason to believe that the true communist vote increased after the municipal elections of 1953. In fact, the anti-EOKA position of AKEL during the nationalist struggle against the British should have caused the non-communist protest voters of the leftist coalition to have swung over to Makarios. For this reason, despite the Greek dissatisfaction with the Zurich-London Agreements, Makarios won the 1959 presidential elections against the opposition of AKEL allied with other traditional ultra-rightist advocates of *enosis*.

The "Patriotic Front" of Makarios polled 67 per cent of the popular vote and the Democratic Union of which AKEL was a part received only 33 per cent on the Zurich-London opposition issue. It is hard to discern the communist vote in these presidential elections. Educated estimates have AKEL's contribution anywhere between 15 and 25 per cent of a vote that covered for the first time the whole island, including the 12 per cent hard-core urban vote. In the elections that followed for the House of Representatives, AKEL felt obliged to accept the five seats offered by the nationalists on their Patriotic Front multi-seat district ticket rather than run as an opposition party and risk electing no deputies at all under the majority system. An indication of the vote-getting power of four of the five AKEL deputies in 1960 is revealed in the following figures: in the Nicosia district Papaioannou obtained 22,346 votes of a total of 53,771, while Ziartides obtained 22,580 votes; in the Limassol district, Potamitis obtained 13,860 of a total of 29,995 votes; and in the Famagusta district, Hambis Michaelides obtained 15,396 votes of a total of 35,807. A curious feature of the overall elections was the low poll, which was due in part to mass leftist abstentions in constituencies where there were no AKEL candidates.[6]

Neither the presidential nor the House elections provide a firm basis for determining the communist vote. AKEL is the oldest and best organized party in Cyprus, but is likely to remain a political minority under the present international balance of power. Therefore, under the present electoral laws and constituency divisions, it is unlikely that the minority communists could come to power through the ballot box unless they worked through an effective coalition.

It is perhaps true that the number of ideologically convinced communists does not exceed ten per cent of AKEL's claimed strength, or an estimated 1,400. The remainder of AKEL's supporters, roughly 65,000 people, are not communists within this definition at all but are members of the AKEL front groups or the trade union (PEO) for reasons of expediency, need of trade-union support, or related materialistic motives. At the same time these followers continue without abatement to discharge their religious obligations and to think and often act in a national and patriotic way. AKEL does not have a hold on them sufficiently strong to influence them politically, or to lead them by a dynamic policy into a militant confrontation with the right wing.*

A retired Greek Army officer and former commander-in-chief of the Cyprus National Guard had this rather optimistic opinion of Cypriot communists in 1967:

> A people with intense and prevalent patriotic feelings could not be communist. The power of AKEL in no way proves that its followers are communist. AKEL has been a trade syndicate of workers and farmers since colonial days, and it never specified its attitude as a communist one. If this were specified, the majority of the members of AKEL would withdraw from it because they are good Greeks, honest family men and genuine Christians.[7]

The wish could be father of the thought, but it does portray the kind of nonchalant attitude many non-communists have about AKEL's influence. It has been explained that contrary to the attitude in the mainland of Greece, the British sense of fair play and tolerance of dissent exists in Cyprus. Hence, the members of AKEL are certainly not considered outcasts, and many of the leading Cypriot nationalists claim that "some of their best friends are communists." Of course, there are others who feel that even one communist in Cyprus is one too many, but this is a minority opinion.

Structure of the Party

The hierarchy and organization of AKEL follow the standard communist model. The highest continuing body is the 30-member Central Committee, headed by the General Secretary, all of whom are elected at each Party Congress (the top of the

---

*When one professed communist was questioned about the rather lavishly materialistic life he was leading on the island, his answer was classic: "Why should I have to suffer for what I believe in?"

hierarchy), which meets every four years.[8] The Central Committee meets in plenary session every two or three months. To carry on day-to-day activities, there is a four-member General Secretariat appointed from the Central Committee, all of whose members are permanent, salaried employees. The Central Committee also appoints a 12-member Politburo which meets every two weeks, deals with concrete political matters, and serves as the policy-making instrument between congresses.* The secretaries of the five AKEL district offices are also members of the Central Committee and are full-time, salaried workers in their respective districts: Nicosia-Kyrenia, Famagusta, Limassol, Larnaca, and Paphos. District conferences are held every two years, at which time the District Committees are elected.

The three members of the Central Committee which form the Control Commission are outside of the hierarchy structure. Though the Commission supposedly has never functioned as intended, in theory this group watches over the Central Committee to see that party policies are carried out properly, exposes anyone who violates the Constitution or program, and controls party finances. The two appointed Central Committee members who make up the Vigilance Bureau are responsible for oversight of other members of the party as well as for collecting information from those who work in government offices and other places of interest.

Other offices which function under the Central Committee, and are appointed by it, include those responsible for Organization, Training, Education, Finance, Minorities, Labor, and Agriculture. Each of these entities have peripheral structures (*grapheia*) in the island's administrative districts and towns to carry out their duties in a highly disciplined manner as defined by the Central Committee. There is no enlightenment or propaganda office *per se,* but these activities fall under the Education Office and include the control of the main organ of the party, the daily newspaper *Haravghi,* and the other weekly and monthly journals. AKEL's subsidiary organizations are its numerous front groups which are concerned with labor,

---

*The 12 members of the Politburo in 1969 were: the four General Secretariat members—Papaioannou, Fantis, Georghiou, and Katsourides—along with Ziartides, Petas, Varnavas, K. Christou, Michaelides, Z. Fillipides, Pombouris, and Sophocles.

youth, women, students, farmers, and so on. (This aspect of communist front activity will be treated in Chapter 4.)

The base of the party structure is the so-called party group or "cell" (KOB is the Greek acronym), which is made up of as few as three and as many as ten people determined either by geography or, in the larger cities, by professional interests—e.g., one for journalists, one for civil servants, one for shopkeepers, etc. These groups meet once a week, usually in someone's home, and discuss the party line. Every party member is a member of a party group and it is from these groups that delegates to the congresses are selected. As small as Cyprus is, it is not unusual for members of the Central Committee to exercise direct control even as far down as the individual cells, as well as on other day-to-day activities.

The Leadership: Social Composition, Decision-making, and Stability

The biographies of 34 communist leaders show that one was over 65 years old and the average age was 50. Top leadership of AKEL originates from lower middle class tradesmen or workers who joined the party at the median age of 27.5 years; very few of the older members are university trained. The principal occupation of this leadership is the business of AKEL on a professional basis, salaried from the treasury of the party. (For sketches of AKEL personalities, see Appendix E.)

Since the leadership of AKEL arose during World War I under British rule, it is emotionally out of date with the young nationalist leadership that was seasoned in a struggle against the British between 1955 and 1959. The basic question is whether AKEL has the capability of developing dynamic leadership under the present challenges and rivalries in Cyprus. The two principal leaders of AKEL, Papaioannou and Ziartides, who have been at the helm since the 1940's, illustrate the quality and personal motivation of the communist leadership in Cyprus. Both have come up through the ranks without formal training and neither one is an outstanding Marxist theoretician. Both are hard workers, and make a living from AKEL or PEO. Both are property owners, attend church on occasion, and have a penchant for travel. Their wives are active in the women's communist front group (POGO) as much for social as for ideological reasons, and their children work in young peoples' clubs in much the same manner. This suggests that the drive for keeping leadership in the party is closely linked with personal vested interests, family prestige, and material rewards. Under Papaioannou, the "collective leadership" or "democratic centralism" principle has given way to a veritable "cult of personality"—which is something the General Secretary would certainly deny.

Consequently, the maintenance of strict discipline in the party hierarchy is due as much to the desires of the incumbents to preserve what status they already have as it is to the political necessity of developing and fostering consistency in the party line. The orderliness and cohesiveness of the party organization is a fact that cannot be overstressed. Positions on the Central Committee and district units are jealously guarded and given only to the most loyal members. The Deputy General Secretary once said: "AKEL is a monolith, from its leadership to its followers, because of its correct line and cool-headed and nonextremist handling of the serious problems it has had to face, and because of the application of the Leninist principle of collective leadership and democratic centralism."[9]

It might also be noted that membership on the Central Committee is so important because of the elite status connected with each individual's position and the power he can exercise. The majority of Committee members do not always attain influence in top-level AKEL decision-making simply by being elected to this body. They are usually chosen because they have already become elite members of their various occupational groups. Consequently, by selecting members on the basis of previously established achievement, the Central Committee has become the primary coupling between the top level of the party hierarchy and the functional groups in which the party seeks influence. Hence, the membership of the Central Committee represents a connection between the social structure and the decision-making process. In such a way the membership of the Central Committee can be a means for determining which critical occupational groups the party authorities wish to infiltrate. Unfortunately, the occupations, not to mention the names, of Central Committee members are not always publicly disclosed.

The leadership of AKEL follows the orthodox communist concept of "indoctrination" in contrast to the "enlightenment" process of its nationalist adversaries. The labor union and the youth front (EDON) are the principal areas for indoctrination. Some 100 party members received this type of "education" at the Central School of AKEL in 1961, the year it was founded. By 1964 the party had seven such schools for adults in various parts of the island.[10] Since that time, the number of communist schools has grown steadily, as has the number of members attending.

AKEL's select youth, including the sons of the party's leaders, however, are trained within the Soviet bloc. On the average it is estimated that about 600 young Cypriot men and women are receiving training in communist countries in contrast to some 4,000 Greek Cypriot students receiving university training in Greece within a strongly anti-communist climate. (See Chapter 4.)

The Rank and File: Social Composition, Responsiveness, Autonomy, and Discipline

AKEL's membership apparently depends greatly on the trade union PEO, which is three times as large as AKEL and provides a more or less captive membership for party work. In an article published by *Neos Democratis,* the occupational breakdown of AKEL's membership in 1961 was revealed by Christos Petas, district secretary for Nicosia-Kyrenia, to be as follows: 66 per cent workers, 8 per cent farmers, 8 per cent middle class, 16 per cent women, and 2 per cent intellectuals. Petas was critical of this membership composition although he reasoned that AKEL "maintains the party's proletariat character." Nonetheless, he characterized this unevenness as a "considerable weakness" and noted that even in the "most industrialized countries, one rarely encounters such high percentage of workers in party ranks." Petas cited the communist parties of France and Italy as examples.[11]

The extent to which the party members are responsive to AKEL's leadership might be measured by the assertion of

Giannis Sophocles, the district secretary of Paphos, that about 50 per cent of the party's members fail to read *Haravghi* and other communist publications. Furthermore, he noted that "certain members of the district leadership" are not utilizing *Haravghi* "despite the superiority of its contents."[12] In another area of the party's membership, Mrs. Androula Christophorou discussed the position of the 2,000 women "who hold the honorable title of party members." She condemned, in a 1962 article, the party's "reactionary position that women are inferior to men," claiming that "over 20,000 women are now enrolled in the various mass [front] organizations."[13] A revelation of the difficulties encountered in attempts to recruit young women was given in an article on the duties of women who must "ignore old customs and restrictions on their activities," and not allow such customs to prevent their joining EDON (the youth front). It also called on the young women to "ignore gossip, and work together with the young men of EDON for the progress of the organization" and to persuade their friends and neighbors "with democratic ideas" also to become members.[14]

The usual view is that AKEL as a communist party is eclectic in recruiting new members, but exercises a strict discipline and indoctrination. Evidence, however, suggests that while the party hierarchy is highly centralized it has a kind of indifferent attitude toward rank-and-file members, most of whom joined the party when AKEL simply needed members while Cyprus was under British rule.

Apparently, there is little autonomy within the framework of AKEL. In his article on organizational matters, Petas warned against the "bureaucratization" of the party and against the preoccupation of its leadership with work that could be handled by special groups. He stressed as essential the establishment of a "party base in every village, community, and place of work." He recommended the *"aktives"* (regular meetings to do business) as tools "at all stages of the party hierarchy," asserting that an *"aktive"* serves to inject new enthusiasm into party work. Petas urged the establishment of *"aktives"* in the Nicosia-Kyrenia district, which covers about 40 per cent of the land and "where the greatest political and economic activity" of Cyprus is concentrated. He goes on to say that since 1950 regional committees have proven their effectiveness in transmitting the party program directly to the people, although "during the early years of the party there were constant changes from regional committees to liaison offices until the committees finally received constitutional approval." In Petas' opinion, the leadership of the various regional committees has contributed greatly to the "expansion of the party into a large number of formerly unorganized villages."[15]

The problem of continually funding cadres is being faced by all the rural organizations of the party. The district committee is confronted with the problem of staffing its auxiliary groups, particularly the district political-education office and the district farm office. In addition, the rural committees, as well as the district committee, need "leader cadres" to supervise the liaison offices, and certain areas do not have a committee because of a lack of cadres. This problem also troubles city offices and is particularly serious in young peoples' organizations.

In the same article, Petas further stated that the growth of the party had made the creation and training of cadres a matter of urgency. He proposed that this be done through the establishment of "special educational circles." His qualifications for a capable cadre included "unlimited love for the people, unlimited devotion to the party and to socialism, respect for the constitutional principles of the party, and a willingness to struggle." Any other necessary qualities are to be acquired "through the course of party life." The educational program adopted by the underground Ninth Congress in 1959 was to be the "richest and most complete" in the history of the party. A complete grasp of theory "is as necessary to an Akelist as is technical mastery of the skills of his occupation," declared Petas. The danger to the party and the people in inadequate theoretical training and departures from the correct line and tactics was cited as a possible "rupture to party unity with the party losing its authority among the masses."

Labor Supporters

While the communists in Cyprus have organized a network of front groups, AKEL's principal support today comes from its trade-union structure, which has about 25 per cent of the 150,000 workers in Cyprus. It is not, however, stable support inasmuch as membership in PEO is not doctrinal or ideological. Membership in PEO is predicated on trade unionism and the ability of this union to get good results. Since the nationalists gained control of Cyprus in 1960, PEO has refrained from engaging in politically motivated strikes. Strikes have been used as a last resort in labor disputes, and PEO's leadership has been more circumspect than the communist-controlled labor unions in Western Europe. Out of PEO's estimated 35,500 members, about 3,000 are thought to be members of AKEL. Any militancy on PEO's part, however, will work against it. Communist members of PEO would run the risk of splitting its non-communist labor structure with overly partisan tactics.[16] (See Chapter 4.)

Financial Support

AKEL's operating funds are derived, according to its leaders, from voluntary dues of the members and annual fund-raising drives. While inability to pay dues may not be a barrier to membership, AKEL naturally encourages up-to-date payment because the party has "no other income than the dues of its members and the contributions of its friends," and funds are needed to "neutralize and defeat the schemes of the imperialists."[17] It is never revealed where the money raised in fund-drives comes from, though the party newspaper carries a coverage of the amounts. Through such an anonymous system, it is most easy for crypto-communists, sympathizers, and foreign embassies to contribute. In 1968 the AKEL Central Committee announced that its appeal for funds to strengthen the party's financial resources was exceptionally successful: the target was achieved by 137.2 per cent. The total amount collected in 1968 was 35,281 pounds sterling compared to 34,300 in 1967 and some 25,000 in 1965. Success of the AKEL Central Committee's appeal for funds under present conditions is also of particular importance from its political aspect. According to an official report, the drive "shows the Cypriot people's confidence in the party which has always struggled tirelessly and consistently on the front lines for the correct solution of the Cyprus problem, for the rights of the working elements, for the interests of all the people, and for the solution of all this country's major and minor problems."[18] The 1969 amount dropped to 27,315 pounds sterling, even though the target was exceeded by 109 per cent.[19]

For a party that has a long list of paid officials these sums are far from adequate. There are, however, no indications that AKEL is applying any substantial funds to efforts that would subvert the nationalists and undermine Makarios' regime. The product of these drives is less significant than the opportunity it offers its members to work at the grass roots and keep the party's program alive. Undoubtedly there is a degree of financial support which comes from the Cypriot communist adjunct in England; there are some 1,250 members of a group called the Union of Cypriots in England and individuals show their close ties with AKEL by sending remittances, particularly during the fund-raising drives.

Business Interests

AKEL has relationships with several business concerns in Cyprus. The most important of these are the People's Spirit Company of Limassol (LOEL); the People's Coffee Grinding Co-operative (Laikon Kafekopteion) in Kaimakli; Maxlo, Ltd. (importers of Soviet bloc electrical appliances); and the Delta Trading Company of Nicosia. These business concerns are not owned by AKEL as a party but by shareholders, the largest of whom are AKEL cadre members. By virtue of these major shareholders the businesses are effectively under the control of AKEL, and these concerns employ almost exclusively AKEL party members. While this may appear capitalistic, every investor in LOEL has only one vote regardless of how many shares he owns. There are approximately 3,500 votes now.[20]

According to the 1960 annual report on LOEL financial activities, presented by manager Georgios Minas at the annual stockholders' meeting in Limassol on August 14, LOEL profits for 1960 came to 9,398 pounds sterling; to this amount was added the remainder of the 1959 profits, which made a total of 10,094 pounds. Of this, Minas reported that 4,000 pounds were to be set aside as a reserve, 2,795 pounds to be distributed among the stockholders in the form of dividends, 3,200 pounds to be paid in the form of income tax, and 99 pounds to be transferred to the 1961 account. The dividend distribution amounted to a profit of 15 per cent on the investment of each shareholder.

At the 1960 meeting the decision was made to adopt the name "LOEL, Ltd., Importers, Exporters, and Industrialists." It was also decided that each stockholder might appoint a representative (or proxy) to attend the stockholders' meeting and vote in his stead. The proxy need not be a member of the company. At the second special meeting, it was decided to modify the company charter to authorize members of the company executive board to borrow sums for the operation of the company, and to commit as security for their repayment all or any portion of the liquid or fixed assets of the company.[21] These "borrowed funds" are surely some of the operating capital which AKEL enjoys.

These businesses support AKEL and the other communist organizations by contributing heavily to collection campaigns sponsored by AKEL. When AKEL has financial needs it calls on these business concerns for monetary support. These contributions are covered in some manner in the company books so that the boards of directors of the concerns do not reveal the expenditures at the yearly stockholders' meetings. Of all the AKEL front groups, the PEO labor union draws most heavily on the business concerns, particularly when it needs funds for labor strikes.

PEO has considerably more reported income than AKEL. In a 1961 report, which followed the two-year build-up period after communist organizations (not including PEO, however) were proscribed, the following statement was made:

> The receipts from dues and extra sources during the period of 1959, including collections of PEO dues, were over £65,000. During 1960, although the audit is incomplete, we believe we have collected a larger sum of money, considering the Pancyprian collection of PEO. During 1959-1960 more than £130,000 were collected.
>
> Taking into consideration this enormous amount of money collected from members and officers of our union movement during the difficult period of the last two years, we must say without reservation that a very good job was done in the field of finances. We must also say that our members and officers

worked with enthusiasm and devotion, contributing generously toward maintenance of the union mechanism as a whole.

On account of the lack of a sufficient number of collectors to cover all areas of work, we do not contact our members regularly and, therefore, considerable amounts from dues remain uncollected, although it is proven that our members always are ready and willing to pay.[22]

AKEL's viability is, thus, based to a large extent on its substantial financial resources. There is no public estimate of the amounts AKEL receives directly from the Soviet Union, but the income from its controlled businesses could be considerable as a result of trade with the bloc countries. In short, these businesses serve as mechanisms for international communist support.

Soviet Bloc Assistance

Overall Cypriot trade with the Soviet bloc has not been impressive. Out of a total 73 million dollars' worth of exports in 1965, the share of the Soviet bloc was only 7 million, and out of 148 million worth of imports only 9.7 million was the value of the goods imported from communist sources.[23] It is doubtful if AKEL businesses have the capability to compete for these communist markets against the well-established and shrewd Greek Cypriot merchants, even though AKEL is favored by the satellite countries. Cyprus' marginal trade with the Soviet bloc provides only a limited opportunity for significant income to the Greek Cypriot communists from commercial activity. It is nonetheless a channel through which international communism could clandestinely pour substantial funds into Cyprus for subversion. Cyprus security authorities are aware of this situation and are presumed to have taken measures to counter such a flow of capital from communist sources.

General Secretary Papaioannou is very sensitive about accusations that AKEL has received direct financial assistance from the Soviet bloc. During a speech in 1962, he found an occasion to express his anger against one such attack in particular:

A certain imperialist writer under the pen name of Dymyr wrote in the *Lausanne Journal* considerable nonsense, lies, and slander against our party and its leadership. Among other things, he wrote that our party receives funds from behind the Iron Curtain through the Bulgarian Embassy in Cyprus. I am sure that today's meeting will give him an answer to silence him even in Lausanne where he is now staying. Our party is extremely proud of the fact that every mil we spend comes from the Cypriot people. As you know, our party is supported by contributions from its members, by contributions from friends outside the party, and through the annual collections organized by the Central Committee.[24]

He then went into the goal for the 1962 annual collection and gave a rousing charge to the "comrades," which was probably intended to show the public once and for all that AKEL was financially self-sufficient from its island resources:

I also wish to appeal to all comrades and party members to enhance their endeavors with a view to exceeding the amount of £35,000, which is the new goal of the collection of our Central Committee.

Our Central Committee is convinced that this new goal will be attained within a very short time, and it will constitute the hardest slap in the face of Dymyr and all the other Dymyrs who slander our party. LONG LIVE AKEL!

(Dymyr's rejoinder was not found, but he must have felt some pleasure in provoking so vigorous a denial from the Cypriot communist leader.) The goal for this particular drive was rather high for the period and it is not known for certain what amount was ultimately collected. Three months later, in an article, Central Committee member Giannis Katsourides contradictorily stated: "A target of 25 thousand pounds has been set for collections [in the 1962 plan]."[25]

The Formal Organization Contrasted to Actuality

AKEL is a communist party that is dominated by ordinary individuals who have a financial stake in remaining at the helm of the organization. Even though the full-time paid members of the Central Committee must be elected to their offices, there is seldom any concerted effort to purge the leadership. The last AKEL purge was carried out in 1952 when the first group of intellectuals was ousted. In 1956 the journalists Christos Katsambas and Diomides Galanos submigted resignations along with a number of others over the AKEL's failure to participate in the EOKA struggle. Most of these disaffected members are much better educated than the present leadership, and they may have tried to challenge Papaioannou on ideological matters. The entrenched ruling body was undoubtedly threatened by the activities of younger, more intelligent members and saw to it that such people were put in their place or banished from party ranks.

There have been unverified reports that some dissension exists over the high living standard exhibited by the AKEL's General Secretary. Papaioannou not only earns a salary for being a member of Parliament but also receives a stipend and liberal expense allotments from his party position. Some members would like to see the General Secretary serve the party without compensation, but he has thus far refused to do so. Prior to every Party Congress, rumors are rife that Papaioannou will be defeated and Andreas Ziartides will replace him, but "Pappy" (as he has come to be known by Western journalists) has always withstood the storm and stayed in office. Supposedly he is well liked in Moscow and can usually count on support from the Communist Party of the Soviet Union if he ever needs it. Papaioannou is a comparatively affluent man who, together with his wife, has extensive real property holdings. When it comes to AKEL fund-raising drives, however, he has a reputation for being not overly generous.

Other struggles within AKEL occur between the hard and soft liners on the matter of cooperation with President Makarios and the nationalists. The hard line is supposed to be represented by Papaioannou and the soft line by Ziartides. With his base of support solidly in the labor movement, Ziartides has been one of the few people capable enough to compete in a struggle with Papaioannou. Because of that, as well as his personal ability, his seat in the Parliament, and his membership on the Central Committee, he has been able to exert a considerable amount of influence on party policy. If it is true that a controversy between hard and soft liners does exist, the Makarios issue is one hard-liner Papaioannou lost.

Reportedly in 1956, while it was banned, AKEL decided to become a communist party devoted to the dictates of the Soviet party. (No member of AKEL will have anything to do with Peking.) Central Committee meetings are said to be frank, free-swinging affairs, but after hours of discussion, and often heated debate, the vote on an issue is nonetheless always unanimous. Papaioannou is known as an emotional person disposed to violent outbursts. However, when he sees that he may not be getting his view across, he backs off and lines up with the sense of the meeting. Due to the apparent need for unanimity in the party's highest councils, members are often not sure of one another's true beliefs and are thought not to trust each other completely. If such suspicions do indeed exist, there are never any outward expressions of anything but complete discipline and agreement. Thus, there is complete centralization of authority, which is reflected in every echelon of the party hierarchy. One fact which stands out in press reports on the congresses held by AKEL, whether on the top level or on the district level, is their manner of combining open and closed sessions. As a rule, the general political situation and various economic and other local problems are discussed at the open meetings, with speeches from Papaioannou, or Deputy General Secretary Fantis, or another member of the Central Committee. The agenda at the closed meetings generally includes discussions of financial and organizational activities reports, the party program, and the election of new officers. Much of what happens in these latter meetings is apparently excluded from coverage in communist organs.

Effectiveness of Communication

Nationalists who have had a continuing interest in AKEL believe that communication between the Central Committee and the lower organizational units of the party is generally conducted through personal contacts by members of the Central Committee with the responsible officers of the respective units. There are no written, recorded, or radio broadcast systems established for communication between party units. Papaioannou is aware that the party has been criticized for this and has spoken in public about the stand taken by some of the conservative newspapers, particularly the English-language, pro-Makarios *Cyprus Mail.* He once said:

> AKEL has nothing to hide from the people, no masks to cover its face, no guns and secret orders to its members.
>
> Our policy is declared to the people, and the party seeks to enlighten the people on our policy. The *Cyprus Mail* does not tell the truth when it says that "the Secretary General of AKEL says one thing in Nicosia and another thing in Moscow."
>
> What the Secretary General of AKEL wrote in *Pravda* is what had been decided by [our] Tenth Party Congress and nothing else. We do not conceal the fact that our ultimate objective is socialism, and if the *Cyprus Mail* writer takes time to read our party program approved by our 10th Party Congress and circulated to thousands of people, he will see that we say exactly that. He will also see that AKEL now places the struggle for completion of independence for Cyprus, together with other people, as its immediate aim.
>
> But even for the party's ultimate aim, which is Socialism, AKEL emphasized in its program that it could only be achieved if the majority of the people desired it. Is there anything more democratic than this?
>
> *There is no communist danger for Cyprus. There is only imperialist danger.*[26]

It may be that the General Secretary is protesting too much about the candor of the AKEL process of communication. In any case, AKEL's communication within Cyprus appears to be less effective than it is with the outside world. The international press often gives headlines to AKEL's presumed capability to dominate the island, and Cyprus is occasionally referred to in the West as a possible "Cuba of the Eastern Mediterranean."[27] AKEL, however, has not been able to communicate this threat to the nationalists in Cyprus. As long as the intercommunal struggle overshadows everything else politically, Makarios in effect isolates communism by effectively keeping the Greek Cypriot rank and file united under the Orthodox Church.

The communist press has refrained from assuming an aggressive position against the nationalists. In fact, the most recent political position taken by AKEL reflects its worries about the forthcoming House of Representatives elections. It advocates the preservation of Makarios' "Patriotic Front" rather than accepting the challenge of political splintering, which the nationalist majority has begun to do. While the party's principal daily newspaper has stressed this line in reference to the formation of new parties, it cannot openly oppose their formation.[28] The communists know full well that the existence of right-wing and moderate parties at the next parliamentary and local elections will render impossible another "deal" with the nationalists.

The circulation of the communist press might reflect the measure of AKEL's influence in Cyprus, but the figures alone are misleading since all communist publications are subsidized. Unlike the regular press of Cyprus, which is principally commercial, AKEL's publications have a large margin of free circulation for party work. The 1968 declared circulation of *Haravghi* of about 15,000 copies daily placed the paper first among the other dailies in Nicosia, but the total circulation of the three non-communist newspapers in Nicosia amounted to 40,000, not taking into account the weekly press. Considering the declared party membership of 14,000 one could get the mistaken idea that *Haravghi* is published chiefly for party members.

Haravghi's managing editor, Chrysis Dimetriou Dimetriades, appeared in 1967 as the proprietor of the paper, but actual ownership belongs to AKEL. Under the directorship of Andreas Neophytou Fantis (the Deputy Secretary General of AKEL's Central Committee) and the newly appointed principal editor, *Haravghi* is the best-edited newspaper in Cyprus. All of its personnel are well-trained communists, some of them educated in Prague and Budapest. Most of the reporting staff, in addition to putting out the paper, are also involved in collecting information for AKEL's private use. Communist editors do not have a secure tenure in office. Stellinos Jacovides was fired as editor of *Haravghi* and removed from the Central Committee in 1962. His successor, Stavros Angelides, was relieved in January 1969 because of a "policy difference" over the Czech invasion. Nominally the current editor is Andreas Fantis, but this may indicate that AKEL is having difficulty finding a trained and experienced man who is also trustworthy; it is said that Andreas Kanouras is really serving as the main editor, though his name does not appear on the masthead.

The cost of AKEL's publishing operations, which include pamphlets and books, has not been estimated, but it must be a drain on its resources, as it is far above what any other political party in Cyprus has ever been able to invest. AKEL's other publications are designed for the hard core of the party's workers. Its weekly *Neoi Kairoi* (New Times), edited by Lyssandros Michael Tsimillis, and the monthly *Nea Epochi* (New Epoch), edited by Andreas Fantis, have a small circulation mainly for party purposes. The other communist organs are: *Politiki Epitheorisis* (Political Survey), which is a theoretical journal; *Ergatiko Vima* (Workers' Forum), the PEO labor weekly, which has a circulation of only 15,000 (small compared to the union's membership) and is edited by Georgios Tsirponouris; and *Neolaia* (Youth), which is the weekly organ of the youth front EDON. Another afternoon left-wing newspaper, *Democratia* (Republic), began publishing on March 3, 1970. *Neos Democratis* is still published monthly, but not as a philosophical journal because there does not seem to be a need to discuss ideological or theoretical matters any longer. All communist publications write in the everyday *demotiki* (the language of the people) rather than the official *katherevoussa,* which is much more difficult. AKEL was particularly interested in early 1970 in securing more mass media for propaganda in view of the announced elections and the political rivalry.

One strong advantage the communists have in the mass media field is the fact that the "closed shop" printers' and linotype union is under PEO, and many of these workers are fanatic party members. The largest private printing plant on the island is Printko, Ltd. (located in the Nicosia suburb of Kaimakli), which publishes all of the communist organs. While there are nationalists among the members of the printers' union, only trusted party members are allowed to work on the communist publications. Theoretically AKEL and PEO could close down any newspaper by calling a printers' strike; the profession is a small one and extremely well paid. It is doubtful if SEK's non-communist printers could or would fill the gap of a work stoppage. There is no government censorship or control of newspapers and they are the most influential means of communication in Cyprus.

While the Republic's radio and television facilities are government regulated, clandestine communist radios from Eastern Europe send a steady stream of propaganda in both Greek and Turkish to Cyprus. One of the island's book shops, the "Sputnik," is also under communist auspices, and Soviet literature is believed to be channeled through this outlet into Israel and the Arab countries as well.

The non-communist newspapers employ a good many ex-AKEL members and also undoubtedly have crypto-communists on their staffs. Whether this should be considered a conscious "penetration" of the island's press by AKEL is a moot question. It may well be that the particular individuals have the requisite training or experience to put out a newspaper, and may have very little to do with actual editorial policy. Nevertheless, the following rundown of newspapers that employ active or ex-communists may be of interest. *Patris,* strongly pro-*enosis* and anti-communist, is edited by Costas Kononas, former General Secretary of the KKK. *Phileleftheros,* a pro-nationalist organ, employs ex-communist Christos Katsambas on its principal staff; Katsambas is still considered a socialist intellectual if not an ideological believer in communism. *Machi,* owned by the nationalist and ex-EOKA member Nicos Samson, employs as a chief editor Neofytos ("Fifis") Ioannou, former General Secretary of AKEL, who is now regarded as a communist opponent. *Agon,* owned by the ex-EOKA member Nicos Kossis, employs Diomides Galanos, an ex-communist, who previously was employed on the staffs of *Haravghi* and *Neos Democratis. Tharros,* a weekly paper, is put together by the staff of *Machi. Kypros,* a weekly regarded as pro-government, is put out by the ex-communist Christakis Katsambas.

The Journalists' Association *(Enosis Syndakton)* consisted in 1969 of an ex-communist president, Diomides Galanos, a communist vice president, Stavros Angelides, a nationalist secretary, P. Petrides, and an ex-communist treasurer, M. Pantelides. Of the remaining members of its executive board, two, A. Lykavghis and Glafkos Xenos, were nationalists; the other, Panikos Peonides, is an active AKEL member. Thus, 2 of the 7 members are active communists, 2 are ex-communists, and 3 are nationalists. One might not be surprised by the fact that the government's present Director of Public

Information, Miltiades Christodoulou, was also once an active member of AKEL. And some time ago the present editor of the Greek News Section of the Cyprus Broadcasting Corporation, Andreas Kyriakou, was employed by the communist youth paper *Neoi Kairoi.*

Whether the fact that these ex-members of AKEL are now in key opinion-producing positions has aided or embarrassed AKEL is not known for certain. But the fact that so many ex-AKEL members—not to mention party members themselves—are now behaving in respectable capacities at almost every level of Greek-Cypriot society lends reinforcement to the widely held belief in the island that AKEL is not a foreign-directed apparatus and offers no threat to the island's accepted way of life. Still, even communists must eat, and they often must work to do so.

3: The National Environment

The unique physical outline of Cyprus—mythical birthplace of the love goddess Aphrodite—has been likened to a dried-out deerskin, a "heavy helicopter traveling west," a cannon pointing at the heart of Turkey, and a haughty tadpole swimming away from the Levantine coast. In point of fact, it is the third largest island in the Mediterranean, stretching over a distance of some 140 by 60 miles at its extreme length and breadth. Its land area of 3,572 square miles makes it about the size of Puerto Rico or half the size of the state of New Jersey.

The last official census of 1960 found 577,615 people on the island, of which approximately 80 per cent were administratively in the Greek community, 18 per cent claiming allegiance to the Turkish community, and the remainder being largely expatriated Englishmen.* The population in 1970 is estimated to have increased by 100,000 in the same proportion, and the density of 140 people per square mile is roughly the same as that of Greece and nearly twice that of mainland Turkey. Since the outbreak of internecine warfare in 1963, a new census as well as some other essential governmental activities (notably parliamentary and local elections) have been put in abeyance pending the settlement of the current political problem.

Resources and Strategic Location

The island is believed to have derived its name from the Roman word for copper, *cuprum.* Today, as thousands of years ago, copper and iron pyrites, though being depleted, are still the most important minerals to be found. Topographically, Cyprus has two almost unbroken mountain ranges along the northern

*The figures for the Greek population also include 2,708 Maronites, 3,628 Armenians, and a small Roman Catholic (Latin) element who chose to come under the Greek Communal Chamber after the island was granted independence in 1960.

coast (the Kyrenia range) and along the west-southwest shore (the Troodos range). In the middle lies the Mesaoria, a dry treeless plain flooded by winter rains and arid in the summer. Most of the minerals are mined in the foothills of the Troodos mountains; the American-owned Cyprus Mines Corporation is one of the principal firms in this enterprise. Asbestos and chrome are found on the higher slopes of the Troodos, and marble and gypsum lie in the Kyrenia range and elsewhere. Traditionally Cyprus has been one of the principal pyrite producing countries of the world. In this area, according to one official report, "it is surpassed only slightly by Japan and Spain, but is unfortunately unique in exporting all its mineral products."[1] Mining has been most important to the Cypriot economy, providing employment for some 2 per cent of the total labor force, contributing about 8 per cent of the gross national product, and usually accounting for almost half of the country's total exports.

The rich ore deposits in Cyprus, along with her strategic location off the coasts of Asia Minor and Syria, have made the island a prize sought by expansionist powers since 1500 B.C. The first foreigners to arrive on the island were Mycenean Greeks, who established colonies and introduced a Hellenic culture. Later, Phoenicians and Achaean Greeks set up independent city-states. Since then, Cyprus has been fought over or dominated by Egyptian Pharaohs, Persians, Macedonians, Romans, Byzantines, Arabs, Crusaders, Frankish Kings, Genoese, Venetians, Ottoman Turks and, most recently, the British. The current political controversy between Greece and Turkey over the island has not yet erupted into warfare between these two mainland powers.

The geographic coordinates of 32° to 34° east longitude and 35° north latitude make the island coveted for other reasons. Cyprus is approximately 40 miles south of Turkish Anatolia, 60 miles from the coast of Syria, 260 miles from Port Said at the mouth of the Suez Canal, 500 air miles from the Dardanelles, and 565 air miles from Athens. Lacking an adequate deep water port and sources of fresh water, Cyprus is not ideally suited to the needs of an important defense base. Yet it is irrefutable that vis-à-vis crucial sections of Europe, Asia, and Africa, the island occupies a uniquely strategic location under present world conditions.

As a center of operations directed toward the Soviet bloc—presuming over-flight rights with Turkey—Cyprus has great potential. Moscow is only 1,500 air miles from Cyprus airstrips; Baku, the Soviet oil center on the Caspian Sea, lies only 1,000 miles away; Rostov, a main industrial center on the Don River, is 900 miles distant; Sverdlovsk, a center of Soviet heavy industry, is situated at a distance of 2,000 miles, and the oil fields of Rumania are as near as 800 miles. In fact, Batum, the nearest point in the Soviet Union from Cyprus, is only 830 miles away and the nearest city in the Soviet bloc, the Bulgarian port of Akhtopol, is a mere 550 air miles. Cyprus thus occupies a peculiarly strategic location as an air base.

It has been said that the British refer to the island as "an unsinkable aircraft carrier," and this may explain why the United Kingdom was particularly keen on keeping two Sovereign Base Areas on the island after independence was granted to Cyprus in 1960. It should not be forgotten that it was from Cyprus that the combined British-French expedition against Egypt was launched in 1956, and from the island the British landed commandos in Jordan to complement the American intervention in Lebanon in 1958.

The British bases in Cyprus today provide AKEL a standing issue which they never fail to exploit whenever opportunity arises. In October 1968, for example, the General Secretary of AKEL summed up the party's attitude:

> The Anglo-American imperialists are using Cyprus as a base for their own aggressive and adventurous activities in the Middle East as well as for those of their Zionist puppets. We hail President Makarios' recent statement that any use of the British bases against neighboring countries would face the Cypriot people's opposition. The Cypriot people will not remain indifferent toward the fatal danger of total annihilation as a result of the conversion of their country into a nuclear base.
>
> The best guarantee for the Cypriot people's security is the abolition of the bases and the complete demilitarization of Cyprus. There cannot be an independent, territorially integral, or sovereign Cyprus while the "sovereign" British bases exist. The bases must go; they are not a "spring of prosperity" as the imperialists have devilishly described them, but a spring of death.[2]

Such attacks have continued since the inception of the

Republic. As long as the British choose to maintain their Sovereign Base Areas in the island, they will undoubtedly be a key propaganda target for the Cypriot communists.

Origin of the Current Political Problem

The communal unrest in Cyprus is essentially a resumption of the unsettled pre-independence struggle between the divergent stands of *enosis* (union) and *taksim* (partition) held respectively by the Greeks and Turks. Independent Cyprus was created in 1960 by three concerned, though external powers for a four-fold purpose: to end the fighting between Greek and Turkish Cypriots which began anew in 1958; to provide a means for the two ethnic communities to live together on the island and to govern themselves; to protect the national interests of Greece, Turkey, and the United Kingdom; and to restore and maintain peace and stability in the Eastern Mediterranean. The Zurich-London Agreements of 1959 established a series of compromise safeguards for guaranteeing the rights of Greece, Turkey, and the two major communities on Cyprus. These guarantees were spelled out in great detail in the Constitution of the Republic, as well as in three treaties signed by the four parties concerned. In truth, the Republic of Cyprus, with a government whose powers were divided in proportion to the ethnic composition of the population, was a bold experiment designed to heal a serious breach in intercommunal and inter-national relations. The experiment was destined to fail—and three years later it did just that.[3]

The Constitution provided that Cyprus would be governed under a central executive system, the President to be a Greek Cypriot and the Vice-President a Turkish Cypriot, elected separately by their respective ethnic communities. The Greek community was defined as those citizens of the Republic who were of Greek origin and had linguistic, cultural, or religious ties to the Greek community. The Turkish community was similarly constituted. Matters of a purely communal nature were left up to two subordinate but autonomous Communal Chambers, whose members were to be elected by the Greek and Turkish Cypriots respectively. Other constitutional provisions allowed for a 70 to 30 proportional participation of the

88

two populations in the legislative functions, the Executive Cabinet and the Public Service. Thus the structure of the Republic's Government was designed to protect the separate community interests of the Greek and Turkish Cypriots. This arrangement, unfortunately, served to institutionalize and perpetuate the historic cultural cleavage on the island. Obviously, independence in 1960 made Cyprus a political state, but not a nation.[4]

The months prior to the December 1963 outbreak of violence saw a worsening of relations between the two Cypriot communities. No talks were held between the leaders, who instead exacerbated the situation by argumentative public statements. An irresponsible press aired increasingly extreme views on both sides. In November 1963, Archbishop Makarios put the Greek case in writing in the form of thirteen suggested amendments to the Constitution, which he then proposed in a memorandum to Vice-President Küçük as a basis for discussion. Information copies were sent to Ankara and Athens.

The first answer Makarios received came from Ankara: it was a flat rejection. The Turkish Cypriots would probably have reacted negatively, too, after they had studied the memorandum, but their formal reply was made unnecessary when violence broke out. No one has been able to pinpoint the blame for this breakdown in communications. Perhaps it was the result of a self-fulfilling prophesy, since both sides had expected open warfare sooner or later and were ready when the flash-point arrived.[5] The United Nations peacekeeping force which landed in March 1964 to cool down the temperature of the conflict has remained on Cyprus ever since.[6]

As a result of the compelling circumstances, both communities have constituted themselves as virtually independent operating governmental bodies: the Government of Cyprus (Greek) and the Turkish Cypriot Provisional Administration, both headquartered in the capital city and both separately performing the necessary services for their respective populations. Since early 1968, as a result of a crisis the previous November, inter-Cypriot talks are going on in hopes of finding a solution to the chaotic situation that has brought Cyprus so often to the brink of civil war. In such a fluid context, a lasting political settlement for Cyprus might be produced by cooperative international effort assisted by the good offices of the

United Nations or a combination of the major powers. But with each passing year it becomes less likely that another detente can be imposed upon the Cypriot people from external sources, as was done in 1959. The Greek Cypriots particularly want to solve their internal problems by themselves. It would appear from past performances, however, that the most unlikely method for peaceably resolving the problems of Cyprus would be to leave the settlement up to the Cypriot people themselves.

President Makarios has hinted that Cypriot general elections would take place in 1970 and has expressed the hope that talks with the Turkish Cypriots could produce a new constitution before then. In an optimistic moment, he stated: "Eight years is too long a time for a parliament to sit; we must have elections this autumn—preferably under a new constitution, but if that is not possible, then with the old one." He added that a solution to the conflict required peaceful conditions under which negotiations could be conducted. In response the Turkish Cypriot leader Dr. Küçük was quoted as saying that a settlement might take anything from a month to two years to work out, but that the Turks would also like a settlement as soon as possible.[7]

It would seem that "genuine *enosis*" or "pure *taksim*" are unreal solutions for the future of Cyprus. Even the mild forms of union with Greece, such as a "commonwealth" relationship, are opposed by Turkey. This would seem to leave independence as the only alternative. If only guarantees for the Turkish community could now be reconciled with Greek majoritarian rule, the path would be open.

The Greek Cypriot Ruling Structure

Like many post-colonial countries, Cyprus today is ruled by a coalition of the most influential parts of its society, which is 80 per cent Greek Cypriot. This coalition reflects the power of the Greek Orthodox Church, economic interest groups, and the administrative bureaucracy. The intelligentsia, which is not represented in the Church, is not part of the Greek Cypriot ruling elite (which is unlike that of most other nations which have emerged into statehood since the end of World War II).

The other groups outside the Greek Cypriot ruling scheme are the peasants and the labor unions; the great majority of these persons are under the domination of the Church.

The coalition in power is charged with supervising the still-continuing Greek Cypriot "national liberation" or "self-determination" struggle which independence in 1960 failed to resolve completely. Each of the three elements in the coalition seems indispensable for the successful outcome of the Greek Cypriot community's aspirations, but each interprets the struggle differently. The Greek Orthodox Church sees the campaign as a national issue, a struggle against possible domination by the Turks—which seems to be in conformity with the traditional ecclesiastical conflict of Christian versus infidel. The bourgeois interest groups, which adhere to the British Commonwealth system, do not clearly define what they mean by the national liberation struggle. Some of the business interests in the island do not seem to care if the outcome would be the formation of an independent Cypriot "nation" composed of Greeks and Turks cooperating in a regional arrangement without the interference from their respective mainland governments. Lastly, the third power element within the ruling coalition, the bureaucracy, tends to identify itself with the state. Thus any resulting form of government which protects and preserves their individual positions would be acceptable to the bulk of career civil servants. All of the factions of the ruling elite are obliged by the sentimentality of the Greek Cypriot population to support in some way or another the demand for *enosis,* but all of the groups could stand to lose part of their historically entrenched power positions if that possibility were realized.

The Church appears by some of its actions to be creating more questions than answers so far as its position on the national liberation struggle is concerned. Some clerics are openly backing *enosis,* but some others behave as if they do not want to take a stand which would alienate themselves from other powerful elements in the ruling scheme. The Church, as the island's wealthiest landowner, has an obvious economic stake in Cyprus. Also, its historic role of national leader (as the ethnarchy), coupled with the tactical needs of the struggle it leads, requires the Church to act as a balancer between the divergent tendencies within its own body and among the other

91

ruling interests. Unlike the Cypriot Church, the Orthodox Church in Greece has evolved in varying ways over the centuries and has had to accept subordination to the state. Thus some of the fluctuations in the attitude of the Cypriot Church toward *enosis* over the past years may be explained as a natural consequence of the clash of two separate social systems—mainland Greek and Cypriot Greek—which have developed independently of one another.

The advent of British economic interests in Cyprus is usually dated 1878, when the island was leased from the Turks. In reality, the British infiltration—as in other colonial cases—began much earlier than the actual occupation by imperial troops. At the end of the eighteenth century the British vice-consul in Larnaca, by ingratiating himself with the *dragoman* and other Greek officials, paved the way for the introduction of British financial interests in Cyprus. The indigenous social class most favorable to cooperation with the British Crown was that of the middleman traders (*emporomessitiki taxis*), which later developed into the Cypriot bourgeoisie. In 1878, the merchant families welcomed the arrival of the British Empire to Cyprus, and to those wealthy merchant families, then as today, belong the best friends of the British. The descendants of these same families are the strongest proponents of the island's ties with the British Commonwealth, and some members still keep the honorary title of "Sir" which was conferred for services rendered to the Crown in times past. If Cyprus were united with Greece, Commonwealth ties would be severed and the centuries of economic advantages would vanish for this class of British clientele.

During the uprising of 1931, the British finally realized that the alliance they had enjoyed with the wealthy merchant families in Cyprus was not sufficient to assure British supremacy in the island. In the fifty years since their occupation, the British through no design on their own part saw the emergence of other social classes which did not share fully in the economic rewards possible under the colonial government. After 1931 the British therefore tried to create their own loyal bureaucratic intelligentsia by granting English university scholarships to the bright sons of middle-class families. In this manner, the British created in addition to the wealthy families a specialized Cypriot colonial apparatus which was well paid and beholden to the Crown. The members of this administrative class continued the British tradition after independence in 1960 by virtue of special transitional agreements which guaranteed them positions in the new government. In the event of *enosis,* the jobs of Cypriot civil servants would probably be in grave jeopardy.

With the formation of the Republic, the bourgeois economic interests became vitally interested in political life, and promoted the integration of ex-EOKA members into the administrative class. It was only natural that many of the fighters, mainly from lower-class families, who were rewarded with good jobs in the new government were promptly co-opted into being allies of the heretofore established interests. By such means, the revolutionary element (EOKA) did not form a unified power bloc after independence but became by and large part of the pre-existing system. Those members of EOKA who were not so rewarded by the established interests are now considered to be the backbone of the pro-*enosis* terrorist groups (e.g., the *Ethnikon Metapon* or National Front) which harassed the Makarios government throughout 1969. The widely accepted belief that there are more guns in Cyprus than people does little to discourage militancy among any frustrated elements of the population.

Obviously the three distinct currents of Greek Cypriot society find their coexistence and cooperation within the dynamics of the so-called "national liberation struggle." Every time the intensity of the national struggle diminishes, the parallel connections between the elements of the establishment weaken. However, should another national crisis erupt, the centripetal trend of the Greek Cypriot community would again manifest itself. It is not easy to say to what extent the ebb and flow of the intensity of the national question is serving the instincts of self-preservation of some of the major elements in the Greek Cypriot ruling structure.

Esoteric Tendencies of the Cypriots

To understand better the Greek Cypriot society, and to some extent that of the Turkish Cypriots as well, one must consider the isolation in which the islanders live. This is a natural phenomenon, both physical and cultural. First, Cyprus is surrounded by a wall of water and the parochial personality of its population reflects this fact. Second, the countries near Cyprus belong to different cycles of civilization, most of which are alien to the European traditions adhered to by the majority of the Greek Cypriot population. Third, the centuries of different invaders in the island have provoked xenophobic attitudes in the indigenous population. Consequently, feelings were directed inward to preserve the national ethnic and religious character of the island, which is traditionally Greek. For example, there has seldom been intermarriage between Cypriot Greeks and the Turks, who represent the next to the last invaders of the island. The fact that there is such a substantial Turkish community in Cyprus may also be proof that the Turks also desired the opportunity to exist culturally apart from the Greeks. Regardless, there has never emerged any unique Cypriot identity, nor have there been any superordinate goals which may have helped this phenomenon. Rather there are two distinct communities in Cyprus, one majority and one minority, which have tended to develop independently from one another.

The esoteric character of Cypriot society is also partly attributable to the island's physical character: its central plain is shut off almost entirely from the sea by two mountain ranges. The capital and cultural center has always been inland and the usual seaward channel of communication was cut off from the vital center of the island. Thus the dominant institutions and customs were formed in something like a sealed environment. The passions of the people boiled in the cauldron between its protective mountain ranges, continually heated by the hostile fires lit by foreign elements coming to its periphery.

Like most small countries, Cyprus has had to develop special defense mechanisms in order to survive its continuous invasions. In many Mediterranean islands, clandestine life was often the response to external challenges. In some of the islands, secret societies emerged and worked as independence movements against the foreign intruders. It is therefore not incidental that Cyprus produced EOKA, which in many ways could be considered the best organized and most successful of recent underground movements. Furthermore, the natural inclination of the islanders toward clandestine life is manifested in their chosen means of expression, which usually operate on two levels simultaneously. Language in Cyprus generally has cryptic symbolism. Politics in the island also has its mysterious overtones with secret leaflets, death threats, and overt acts of terrorism. In short, Cypriot inner social life—both Greek and Turkish—is often unintelligible to most foreigners.

This hermetic, insular environment has even contributed to the development of an indigenous system of exploitation of its own people, which escapes notice and explanation by the Cypriots themselves. This system is based upon two pillars: (1) the high monopolization of land ownership, and (2) the exclusivity of the importation and distribution of manufactured goods in the island. In the case of land, ownership belongs to a limited number of organized interest groups among which are some of the Greek Orthodox religious institutions, particularly the Kykko Monastery, and some private development companies. The land is usually sold to individuals, at prices the government intentionally overvalues, through certain agent banks that act as creditors. Practically every ordinary citizen who wants private housing inescapably ends up paying a life-time tribute in the form of interest to these agent banks.

In the second case, an island the size of Cyprus, which is too small to be self-sufficient and too big to be totally dependent from abroad, has created a special status for a few importers in its system of commercial exchanges. Since Cyprus does not have its own factories, it must import from highly industrialized countries in exchange for raw materials or agricultural goods. The product of this exchange (what the Yugoslavs have been known to call "superprofits" for the benefit of the Russians) is shared between the British exporters and the exclusive franchised importers. This system creates a real economic tie between the British bourgeoisie and their Cypriot correspondents rather than between the user and the supplier in the island's population. This situation seems to be perpetuated because the British Commonwealth trade advantages do not permit equal commerce with other countries, nor does the size of the island readily lend itself to extensive industrialization.

Thus Cyprus is a small, democratic country which has developed monopolizing institutions of unusual size. The physical and financial barriers around the island consolidate to create a sophisticated system of inner exploitation which is characteristic of many such closed societies. (Sicily, for example, has been characterized as suffering from an "invisible sickness" because of its inability to be revitalized.) The resulting fossilization of society is seldom changed by foreign invaders, as has been the case with Cyprus, and often only an upheaval can release the grip the system has over its people. AKEL recognized this traditional malaise that was so much a part of Cypriot society, but has not been able to sell its brand of proletarian revolution. EOKA, on the other extreme, was an abortive and unintended attempt to renew Cypriot society from within. The British may have been removed from Government House as a result of the EOKA struggle, but it is doubtful whether British economic domination was changed very much by this.

Police and Military Forces

Under the terms of the Constitution of the Republic, the division between the police and gendarmerie was made on a territorial basis with a proportion of seven Greeks for every three Turks. The police were in charge of public order and safety in the six principal cities of the island—Nicosia, Famagusta, Limassol, Larnaca, Paphos, and Kyrenia—while the gendarmerie were responsible for the outlying villages and rural areas, excluding the British Sovereign Base Areas. Relative strengths of the forces were about 1,150 for the police and 850 for the gendarmerie. Both forces were to contribute to common services, including the Training School, the Communication Branch, the Criminal Records Office, and the unusually small Port and Marine Branch. The Fire Service, though not charged against police strength, was administered by the Force Headquarters.

Under Article 130 of the Constitution, the gendarmerie also came into being on Independence Day, August 16, 1960. Taken from the former colonial police force, the gendarmerie was well trained and, after redistribution in the six administrative districts, was ready to enter upon its responsibilities for maintaining law and order in the villages and rural areas. The original strength of the force was 842, approximately 62 per cent Greek and 38 per cent Turkish.

Both of these security forces were well paid and well trained and had been developed in the British police tradition of impartiality and justice. They were perhaps somewhat less inclined than other parts of the government to divide loyalties along racial lines, and it was the general belief that they were not noticeably infected with any degree of communist subversion.

During the years 1960 through 1963, the forces made excellent records in preserving order and combating crime. However, no organization composed of men with divided ethnic origins could be expected to surmount the violence of the civil strife which developed between Greek and Turkish Cypriots in 1963. The police and gendarmerie in the affected areas obviously split along racial lines. Only the British military personnel from the Sovereign Base Areas, and now the United Nations peacekeeping force, could be depended upon to act impartially.

The 2,000-man army on a 60 to 40 ratio of Greek over Turk provided for in the Zurich-London Agreements and in Articles 129 through 132 of the Constitution of the Republic of Cyprus never came into being because of a conflict over the level at which Greeks and Turks would be integrated. While the need for security forces of police and gendarmerie was unquestioned, the role of an army for Cyprus was not so apparent. Since Britain, Greece, and Turkey have guaranteed Cyprus' independence and Britain's military bases and garrisons are present for defense of the island, some members of the new government initially questioned the expenditure of scarce funds for a seemingly unnecessary army.

AKEL, for instance, has deplored the expenditures for a national army from the start. The 1962 party platform stated: "The establishment of a Cypriot Army is totally unjustified, and moreover places a serious burden on the heavily taxed people of Cyprus. The defense of Cyprus is not safeguarded by an army of 2,000 men, but by a policy of peace and friendship with the other people of the world. For this reason, the constitutional provision for the establishment of an army must be revised."[8] Still, AKEL always insists that once "genuine democratic parliamentary institutions are realized, they must be defended against foreign intervention." Their paradoxical position on this issue possibly reflects their hostility to the erstwhile commander in chief, General Grivas, who had followed a policy of distributing communist-indoctrinated youths among different units in the Greek Cypriot National Guard and keeping them under scrutiny by security officers.

After violence finally erupted in December 1963, the then Minister of the Interior, Mr. Polykarpos Georghadjis, was put in charge of all armed forces, including irregular and private armies. These were to be uniformed and incorporated into the National Guard of the Republic as an auxiliary police force for the emergency. The National Guard became the virtual, although extra-constitutional, military arm of the Greek Cypriot controlled government. General George Grivas was in command until December 1967, when Ankara demanded that he be exiled and the force dismantled.

It is not known to what extent the National Guard and the various local Turkish Cypriot *mucahit* (freedom fighters) have been disbanded. Some action by the Greeks has been taken, but there is little doubt that virtually overnight both sides could mobilize practically the full strength they had under arms at the end of 1967 (about 15,000 Greeks and about 5,000 Turks), with an additional local mobilization potentially double this.

The U.N. peacekeeping force (UNFICYP), with a strength fluctuating between 4,000 and 6,000 men, has continued to maintain an unsteady peace in the island, with its precarious existence being extended every six months by the U.N. Security Council. This uncertainty darkens the clouds still obscuring the current military situation and future military developments in Cyprus. The national contingents comprising UNFICYP are battalion-sized units, plus supporting elements, from Britain, Canada, Denmark, Finland, and Sweden. A 175-man civil police unit, the UNCIVPOL, has aided in the development of the police force in the island and has assisted the military peacekeeping force in some of its investigations of ceasefire violations.

Britain maintains a 1,000-man ground force consisting of a battalion group (rifle battalion plus supporting arms) and the Near East Air Force, consisting of one squadron of Lightning F3 all-weather fighters, four squadrons of Canberra light bombers (40 planes), one transport squadron, and one battalion of Thunderbird surface-to-air missles. Missions for the bombers include support of CENTO. All are based at Akrotiri, the larger of the two British areas.

Following the terms of the 1959 treaty, Greece was allowed to maintain 950 military instructors (the ELDYK) and 650 for Turkey's (TOURDYK). During the crisis of 1964–66 these contingents swelled to combat forces of some 10,000 and over 2,000 men respectively. By a December 1967 agreement between Greece and Turkey these units were reduced to the treaty-authorized sizes in early 1968 and have been stable since.[9]

The Economic System

The underlying philosophy of the Cypriot economic system is, essentially, free-enterprise capitalism. The Cypriot economy is comparatively well developed but prosperity stems mainly from three conditions, all of which are far from permanent: high prices for copper ore, membership in the British Commonwealth (resulting in a protected market for agricultural products, and an advantage for tourists), and a high level of expenditures at the British Sovereign Base Areas, including sizeable employment for indigenous labor. Still, the economy is fairly well developed by Mediterranean standards. The average Cypriot is better off than his opposite number in Turkey or Greece. In 1960, Cyprus had the highest annual per capita income (equivalent to U.S. $415) in the Mediterranean area, with the exception of Israel. This was about the same as that of Malta, nearly double that of Turkey and Portugal and somewhat the same as that of Greece. It is estimated that the 1969 per capita income will approach $750 despite the past devaluation of the pound and the continuation of intercommunal tension. This per capita income ranks Cyprus in about 35th place among the nations of the world while on a population basis she would be 125th.[10]

Agriculture is the mainstay of Cyprus, not only because it contributes to the national product and provides employment for the majority of Cypriots, but also because local industry and exports are largely based on it. About 25 per cent of the gross national product is produced by agriculture, chiefly from citrus farming, viticulture, and forestry, and also from the export of vegetables to the European market. Mining contributes significantly, though at a declining rate, to the island's revenue and to the export trade. Commerce occupies primarily the urban population. Some light industry has been established since World War II, and the construction industry has been expanding. Income from the military forces, emigrant remittances, and particularly tourism provide major economic support.

The government has followed an agricultural policy of maintaining and increasing the productivity of land and livestock. While agriculture is the backbone of the Cypriot economy, it is also the chief economic problem. Cyprus does not produce enough food to feed her own people, nor does she export enough farm surplus to offset the cost of imported foodstuffs. Productivity is hampered by natural and cultural factors: the scarcity of water, under-fertilized land planted in the same crops year after year, and land inheritance practices. Land ownership continues to be fragmented into small scattered holdings by the division of inheritance among many sons and daughters for generation after generation. Nevertheless, with approximately one-half of her total land area under cultivation (out of a potential of 66 per cent), Cyprus ranks first in the Near East in utilization of land for agriculture.

There are a few wealthy industrialists on the island who have profited from the liberal tax structure in the Republic. Most of the capital invested in the island, apart from that of the large mining firms and one or two industrial groups, is provided by local businessmen and goes into small industries. There is, however, a tendency toward a collectivistic cooperative system among the lower income groups, which serves to undercut some of the appeal of communist economic plans. The cooperative movement in Cyprus has served as a model for other countries. Originally established during the 1930's to enable farmers to escape exploitation by money-lenders and middlemen, the cooperatives now number over 850 with a membership of 175,000, and they play a vital part in the economic life of both producers and consumers.

Mining has been important to the economy of the land, providing employment for 2 per cent of the total labor force, contributing about 8 per cent of the GNP and accounting for 40 per cent of the total exports. The most important mineral groups are copper and iron pyrites, followed by asbestos, chrome, and gypsum. The largest and richest of the known ore reserves will be depleted in a few years, according to present estimates. The major mining concern is an American firm, the Cyprus Mines Corporation, which has been a chief target of communist attacks.

There has been some growth in animal husbandry and manufacturing, but larger increases have taken place in electric power, transportation, and services. While the capital invested in mining is almost entirely of foreign origin—American, Greek, and British—most of the capital going into other enterprises is Cypriot. Capital formation is relatively high and has been rising steadily, although industrial development is still comparatively limited.

The greater part of Cyprus' external receipts come not from exports but from the provision of services to foreign governments in Cyprus, from tourism, and from emigrants' remittances. There are more than 100,000 Cypriots in London alone, and many thousands more throughout the Middle East, Egypt, Turkey, and Greece. The flow of capital back to the island from Cypriots residing abroad and others returning home after acquiring substantial wealth in Africa and elsewhere is one of the "invisibles" which alleviates the chronic trade deficit. Other important factors which work toward the same end are the incomes derived from the presence of British forces in the Sovereign Base Areas and from the U.N. troops.

A large part of Cyprus' trade deficit has been caused by adverse balances with Great Britain, but the economy of Cyprus benefits to the extent of several million pounds each year from the activities of the British bases. British expenditures in Cyprus have grown tremendously over the last ten years: from 1.4 million pounds sterling in 1950, they rose to 6.1 million pounds in 1954, reached a peak of 19.3 million in 1956 (a figure equal to that of the whole agricultural income), and since then have remained at around 15 million pounds a year. These expenditures loom large in relation to both the gross national product and export earnings. About two-thirds of them are spent locally and the other third directly on imported goods.

After independence, the Cypriot government sought and obtained United Nations technical assistance in formulating an economic development program for Cyprus. Subsequently, in August 1961 the President of the Republic presented a Five-Year Development Plan of public investment for the years 1962 to 1966. Still, Cyprus continues to suffer from a chronic trade deficit. More than 90 per cent of her exports consist of minerals and agricultural products, items subject to wide price fluctuations in world markets. In an effort to increase exports, the government has entered into bilateral trade agreements with the U.S.S.R. and other Soviet bloc countries.

The Cypriot economy showed an impressive average growth rate of 5 per cent per year from 1950 through 1957, with the GNP at constant prices (1950) rising from 39.5 million pounds in 1950 to 58.5 million pounds in 1957. The outbreak of violence in April 1955 and subsequent events retarded the island's progress until 1961, when the economy again showed positive gains. The GNP registered 57.8 million pounds in that year and rose to 62.9 million pounds in 1962. Between 1962 and 1966 (the first Five-Year Plan), the annual growth rate averaged 5.7 per cent and the GNP rose by over 40 per cent from the beginning of independence to 1966. Despite this favorable growth, the need for improvement in the agricultural sector and the artificial factors which induced past expansion (but which may not be permanent) have been given major consideration in the restructuring of the economy, which is the main objective of the second Five-Year Development Plan begun in 1967.

In spite of its political problems Cyprus is prospering: trade continues to thrive, building activity has reached a record level, and government revenues in 1969 reached an all-time high. But this impressive growth has been achieved under the protection of the United Nations force, whose withdrawal could likely result in a fresh outbreak of violence. The vast majority of Cypriots on both sides are hoping for a breakthrough which may bring return to normality. In other words, concern for material prosperity since 1960 has been unable to surmount political conflicts which grew out of the pre-independence struggle in Cyprus. While economic viability should logically be of vital concern to every citizen of the Republic of Cyprus, the two major ethnic communities on the island have not been able to resume the former spirit of cooperation and to work toward this mutually beneficial, superordinate goal.

The Cypriot Turks have not enjoyed the fruits of prosperity on Cyprus, which has achieved a truly amazing record for a newly independent state. Mainland Turkey has provided her ethnic brothers in Cyprus with approximately $16 million in direct assistance, and this constitutes the main source of revenue for that beleaguered community. While the Turk generally has not excelled in the business world in Cyprus, he has indeed made significant contributions to the economic gains of Cyprus over the years. One can only speculate as to how much greater the economy of the island would be today if the Greeks and Turks had learned to cooperate from the beginning in running the Republic of Cyprus.

Socio-Economic Structure

A valid characterization of the Cypriot population is one of two distinct societies existing side by side, each containing a set of social classes comprising the elite, the middle sectors, and the lower echelons. The comparable social classes of the two societies in better times displayed many similarities in terms of such objective criteria as occupation, income, and residence, and thus previously formed a single Cypriot socio-economic structure. However, there are many differences in the values and attitudes of otherwise similar Greek and Turkish social classes.

The increase in governmental functions and in economic development which took place under the British administration and the independent Republic of Cyprus resulted in the growth of urban centers and urban populations. As governmental and economic activities centered in the towns, so did foreign dignitaries and residents, tourists and educated Cypriots, making the towns centers for the dissemination of Western European influences. Thus wealth, power, and education were concentrated in the Cypriot towns, particularly in the capital city of Nicosia. Where these elements are found, so also are found the elite who possess them. In both the Greek and the Turkish societies of Cyprus, the elite upper classes are composed of high government and political functionaries, successful professional men and entrepreneurs (including large landowners, of which comparatively few are left), bankers, industrialists, and men of commerce.

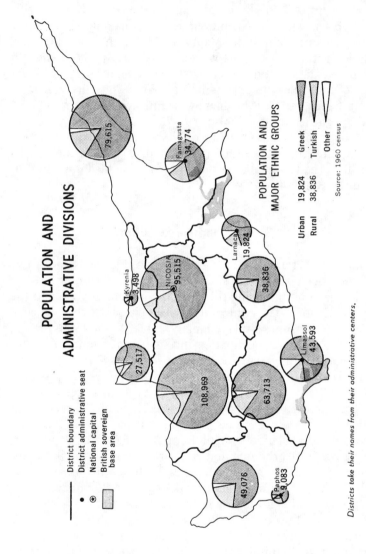

POPULATION AND
ADMINISTRATIVE DIVISIONS

District boundary
• District administrative seat
⊛ National capital
☐ British sovereign
  base area

POPULATION AND
MAJOR ETHNIC GROUPS

	Greek	Turkish	Other

Urban 19,824
Rural 38,836

Source: 1960 census

Famagusta
34,774

Kyrenia
3,498

NICOSIA
95,515

Larnaca
19,824

79,615

27,517

108,969

Limassol
43,593

63,713

49,076

Paphos
9,083

Districts take their names from their administrative centers.

104

ECONOMIC ACTIVITY

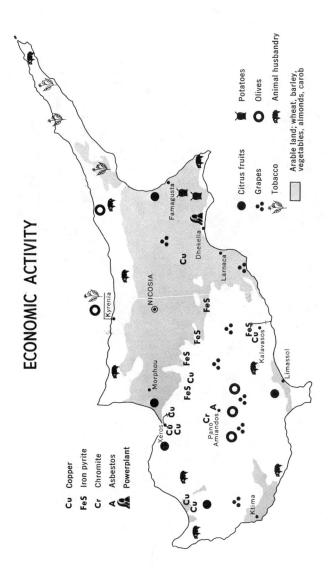

Cu Copper
FeS Iron pyrite
Cr Chromite
A Asbestos
Powerplant

Potatoes
Olives
Animal husbandry

Citrus fruits
Grapes
Tobacco

Arable land; wheat, barley, vegetables, almonds, carob

Famagusta
Dhekelia
Larnaca
Cu
NICOSIA
Kyrenia
FeS
FeS
FeS
Morphou
FeS Cu FeS
FeS Cu
Cu Kalavasos
Limassol
Cu Cu
Xeros
Cr A
Pano
Amiandos
Ktima
Cu Cu

LAND UTILIZATION

Dense to sparse evergreen forest, including orchards

Grazing on sparse forest and brush

Vineyards

Cultivated field crops

Irrigated area

Famagusta

Larnaca

Kyrenia

NICOSIA

Limassol

Paphos

The middle sectors of the Turkish and Greek societies also are located mainly in the urban centers. They are composed of persons who have been able to improve their standard of living and social status through one or more of the following: increased income and greater occupational opportunity resulting from economic and technological development; increased opportunity for primary and advanced education; and increased political participation and influence resulting from participation in revolutionary movements. The struggle of EOKA against the British, for example, formed a vehicle for many lower-class Greek Cypriots to elevate themselves in the social order.

In Cyprus, both the Greek and the Turkish middle sectors are composed of white-collar workers employed mainly in the civil service, teachers and professors, minor political functionaries, persons in the service trades, professional men and technicians, and small businessmen. Although most of the groups in the middle sectors are found in urban areas, some, such as village teachers, local religious leaders, minor political functionaries, and community leaders, are also located in the countryside.

The lower social strata, which constitute the majority of the population, consist of a small urban proletariat and the mass of rural peasants—both Greek and Turkish—who characteristically derive a minimum subsistence from agricultural and pastoral pursuits. Most of the individual farmers produce very few cash crops, or none at all, and usually dispose of their surplus through cooperatives. Some rural peasants work in the mines or find work as laborers in the towns and villages. In general, the rural lower classes have less education and maintain a lower standard of living than the lower classes in urban areas.

Both the Greek and the Turkish Cypriots, therefore, are divided into similar socio-economic strata which could form a single Cypriot social structure on the basis of objective criteria such as income, occupation, and residence. Nevertheless, Greeks and Turks of the same socio-economic echelon do not share a conscious identification in regard to class, values, or status symbols. Such identification does not cut across racial and cultural lines in Cyprus; it occurs only within the two separate societies, Greek and Turkish. Neither community has a landed aristocracy or a nobility, and movement between the various levels of society is based upon individual performance. Hence to understand the dynamics of the Cypriot social structure, one must examine the attributes and values which contribute to status within both the Greek and the Turkish societies.

Greek Social Structure

Because Greek Cypriots tend to stratify their society on the basis of achieved rather than ascribed criteria, urbanization has not proceeded to such an extent that class distinctions cut across family ties or racial lines. The Greek's sense of *philotimo* (literally meaning "love of honor"), his ingrained individualism, and his belief in the equality of all men mitigate against the formation of a rigid class structure. This belief in equality and stress upon personal achievement gives the Greek social structure extreme mobility. Any Greek, ideally, is believed capable of raising his status through his own accomplishments. Neither wealth nor power awe a Greek or create in him an attitude of servility. It is more important to him to be thought of as clever and cunning than simply to be thought of as wealthy.

All Greeks are extremely proud of the artistic, legislative, and cultural accomplishments of ancient Greece, and as a result they have a great respect for their elders and for those who have distinguished themselves by education. However, one is not considered an equal by a Greek unless one is Greek by descent; thus distinctions between racial or cultural groups become more important to Greeks than class distinctions.

The Greeks on Cyprus are predominantly rural, and status in the small villages is defined primarily by education, community interest, and qualities of leadership. Traditionally, the two most respected positions in the village have always been those of the teacher and the priest. For generations past, both have bridged the gap between the illiterate people of the village and the written mass media. All Greeks seem to be avid followers of politics, both national and international, and the teacher and the priest have acquired importance as disseminators as well as evaluators of the news.

However, in the twentieth century, the diminishing prestige of the local priest has become very noticeable, largely because many villagers equal or surpass him in education. Today the priest could be a man with little formal education, chosen by his fellow villagers. He continues his basic activities— usually farming or a craft—in addition to his ecclesiastical duties. A certain amount of respect is accorded his office, but otherwise he is no different from the rest of the villagers. The Church has recently made efforts to upgrade the training of priests.

In contrast, the traditional Greek Orthodox teacher, who is adviser to all the villagers as well as the local political "boss" *(muhktar),* remains an important political force in the village today. However, more and more teachers are former urban dwellers and their teaching posts tend to resemble political appointments. They usually have closer ties with the urban centers than with the villages, and they introduce urban political interests at the village level.

In urban areas there is a greater emphasis upon commercial and industrial activities than there is in the villages, as well as greater contact with Western influences and a more marked division of wealth. The social structure, accordingly, exhibits greater class differentiations, in the manner of urban centers of Western Europe. Class distinctions in the city, as in the rural areas, place greatest importance upon educational attainments. In addition, wealth appears to receive more attention than it does in the villages, as does political or literary eminence. The middle sector of urban Greek society is composed mainly of small shopkeepers and white-collar workers, who are able to raise their status by using their increased cash income to improve their standard of living and by taking advantage of increased educational opportunities.

In summary, the Greek social system focuses upon three central values: individualism, family loyalty, and nationalism. Individualism is the most highly prized among the Greeks. Underlying all the values and institutions of Greek society is a highly developed sense of individual self-esteem, which the Greeks call *philotimo.* This traditional belief is in *no* way equivalent to the Oriental conception of "face," since there is no element of public shame involved; rather it stresses the positive aspects of dignity and pride.

Turkish Social Structure

Most of the traditional socio-economic values of the Turkish Cypriots have been affected by the forced migrations and other disruptions which have resulted from the political problems since 1963. Nevertheless, some lasting characteristics have persisted despite the unusual environment in which the Turkish Cypriots have had to function. For example, within the villages the social distinctions are as narrow and lasting as ever. The household is the basic unit of production and consumption, with each family unit exploiting its own land and animals. The division of labor is based principally on age and sex, and each household is organized much like every other. Persons of like sex and age generally have the same kinds of rights and duties. The village *imam,* as schoolteacher and prayer leader, is probably the only full-time specialist aside from the policeman. The *mukhtar* (headman), the *azas* (council of elders), court officials, and skilled artisans are usually only part-time specialists.

Personal status in village society is measured by piety and other personal qualities, within the narrow limits established by the circumstances of birth: sex, age, relative strength of one's lineage or kin group, location within kin group, and inherited wealth. Males have higher status than females, and one usually defers to one's elders.

Wealth is the most important single factor in social ranking. It not only carries prestige, but it permits a man to underwrite building and repairing, well-digging, celebrations, and other village projects, as well as to extend charity or employment to his needy fellows. While inherited wealth usually consists of land and animals, personal frugality and industry have less to do with its accumulation than does the operation of the inheritance laws on succeeding generations of households.

Since the Kemalist revolution in Turkey in the 1920's, the traditional pattern of village life presented above has been subjected to calculated assault from the Turkish national authorities. Far-reaching government directives, an accelerated movement of peoples and educational reforms, along with other by-products of modernization and industrialization, have varied the basic patterns of village life. Although a majority of the villagers live in the traditional fashion, a number of others are taking on the basic values and attitudes of the urban centers. Village solidarity is becoming a thing of the past. There are relatively few Negroes living in Cyprus, but those there are members of the Muslim faith.

In the urban areas, political policies for the Turkish Cypriots are shaped by groups constituting an elite founded on education, social prestige, family connections, and wealth. The position of this elite has been bolstered by a tradition in which the ordinary Turkish people have come to expect rule from above. Under the Ottoman Empire the ruling groups were distributed among three parallel hierarchies: the civil, the ecclesiastical (religious-legal), and the military. Every rank within these three hierarchies had its equivalents in the other two. Individuals tended to move up and down within a single hierarchy but, except at the very top levels, seldom crossed from one to another. The leading families, however, usually were represented in all three hierarchies. Between the hierarchies, and therefore between the leading families, there was little conflict of interest.

Most of the landed wealthy have come to urban centers as absentee landlords and have been incorporated into the elite, mainly through marriage. Families with money and prestige from trade and industry also have been gradually incorporated. Although the law remains one of the principal avenues to political advancement, highly trained professional men and technicians in industry, banking, finance, and other economic and technological specialties have moved into top positions as policy-makers and administrators of government agencies. On the outer edge of the elite, and below it, are Turks of humbler origin and families which have gained wealth and prestige in business, education, or the professions. From these groups come the most articulate nationalistic statements and the most forceful pressures for economic, political, and social democracy.

In summary, the traditional values of Turkish life derive from the heritage of a society based on family ties and are often influenced by the Islamic religion. The strength of Islam is being eroded by secular trends, but it remains vital in rural areas, not only in determining behavior but also in explaining life itself. The social system and the values associated with it, which had remained static for centuries, began to change

111

slowly at the end of the nineteenth century. The pace quickened under the Kemalist reforms of the 1920's, and increased still more after World War II. Possibly social change has been more rapid on the mainland than on Cyprus, but in varying degrees it has affected all groups and threatened many long-held values.

Communal Nationalism in Cyprus Today

The Greek Cypriot community passionately loves and identifies with the motherland of Greece but does not regard her as a universal provider, protector, and source of strength. Rather, Greece represents the classical heritage, and the Greek Cypriot feels that he owes her a debt of kinship. Many a Greek Cypriot wishes to return himself and his island to the parent country, but his political views are his own and not necessarily those of the present junta government at Athens. Greece might be expected to support the Greek Cypriot's views but not to dictate them officially. In addition, the Greek Cypriot, if he emigrates, tends to go to England, Australia, or Africa, but not to Greece.

On the other hand, modern Turkey, after the Kemalist reforms, represents to the Turkish Cypriot the source of his worldly as well as his spiritual inspiration and strength. By necessity, Turkey is the authority and guardian whose word is law. The Turkish Cypriot generally will do what he is told by Ankara, for he believes in Turkey, not in Cyprus. Until 1953, when Turkey banned further immigration from Cyprus, the Turkish Cypriot emigrant most often went to Turkey. The "Mecca" of Turkish Cypriots is still Ankara, and "Medina" is Istanbul.

In summary, the Greeks and Turks both have displayed a strong identification with their motherlands for many centuries, and each considers the other a national rival. Nevertheless, until the 1930's the two communities appeared to have adjusted to living together in relative tolerance and good will. Nationalism was an emotional, sentimental, and spiritual attachment to the homeland, not the violent political passion it became in the 1950's and again in 1964. In many respects the "apron strings" from the two mainlands have held back the emergence of lasting cooperation and harmony between the island's two communities.

Religious Beliefs

Approximately 80 per cent of all Cypriots, including the communists, are at least nominal members of the Orthodox Church of Cyprus, and nearly 18 per cent are adherents of Islam. The remainder is divided among a number of Christian denominations and churches, of which the most important are the Armenian Apostolic Church of St. Gregory, the Uniate Catholic Church of Saint Maron (the Maronites), and the Roman Catholic Church.

The Orthodox Church of Cyprus is an autocephalous member church of the Greek Orthodox Communion, which is under the spiritual leadership of the Ecumenical Patriarch of Constantinople. An autocephalous church is entirely independent with respect to its internal government and its relations with other churches. The Orthodox Church of Cyprus regards itself as *isotimos* (of equal rank) with the four ancient Patriarchates of Eastern Christianity: Constantinople, Alexandria, Antioch, and Jerusalem.

During the period of Muslim Turkish rule, the native Greek Cypriots could maintain their cultural and national identity only through the Orthodox Church. The Muslim practice of governing subject "People of the Book" (Christians and Jews) indirectly through their religious leaders, with each religious group considered a separate people, a distinct *millet* (community), made the Church the center of corporate social life. Making no distinctions between secular and religious spheres in their own lives, the Ottomans did not draw such distinctions for their subjects. They considered the religious leaders of the monotheistic communities to be the natural political leaders as well. These leaders, or ethnarchs, were made responsible for the maintenance of law and order in their communities and for the collection and payment of the annual tribute or tax levied on "People of the Book." Although the people of the *millets* had only second-class citizenship, as long as they remained loyal and paid their taxes they were relatively undisturbed by the Imperial Government. It logically follows that

113

the Primate of the Church today, Archbishop Makarios III, is also President of the Republic. He is the last ethnarch—the traditional political leader of the Greek community on Cyprus.

Despite the fact that they were no longer part of the Ottoman Empire and were not citizens of republican Turkey, the Turkish Cypriots voluntarily, although unevenly, accepted many of the secularizing and modernizing reforms promulgated by Mustapha Kemal Ataturk. Since these reforms did not have the force of law behind them on Cyprus, however, certain Islamic institutions, such as the *evkaf* (religious property and charitable foundations and the officials controlling them), continued to function without interruption or suppression by the colonial government.[11]

The attitude of the religious establishment toward the communists in Cyprus has not been one of open hostility, despite the fact that the secular nature of the communist movement is antithetical to the dogmas of both Christianity and Islam. The relationship of communism and the Orthodox Church is a particularly interesting one. The Moscow Patriarchate of the Orthodox Church has been a vehicle of Soviet foreign policy ever since the Bolshevik Revolution. The Soviet Union has customarily used the high stature of the Russian Orthodox Church and its prelates to infiltrate the Orthodox following in the free world, in hopes that the Greek Orthodox Church, as well as other independent oriental Christian Churches in the Middle East, would be gradually drawn into the communist sphere of influence. For example, the Moscow Patriarchate has been in rivalry with the fifteen-century-old primacy of the Ecumenical Patriarchate of Constantinople (Istanbul) for leadership of the million-and-a-half Orthodox Christians under its control. In this respect, the perpetuation of the Orthodox Patriarchate in Istanbul—even though the Turks have often suggested that it be moved—is connected by some scholars with the security concern of the West against the intrusions of the Russians in the Middle East.[12]

That the Orthodox Churches of metropolitan Greece and Russia have been in close communion since the days of the czars is not a surprising revelation. In 1877, Czar Alexander II took the pretext of mistreatment of the Orthodox Christians in the Ottoman Empire to intervene in the affairs of the Porte and fought a brief war over it. The use of the Church in furtherance of Russian policies in the Middle East did not stop with that venture, but carried over after the Czar was deposed by the communists. One contemporary observer wrote about current Soviet exploitation of the Russian Orthodox Church:

> It is worth noting, therefore, as a sign of the times, that Moscow has quietly dusted off some of its surviving Orthodox prelates and dispatched them to inter-faith conferences around the world. They appear in berobed splendor at ecumenical councils, for example, and make pilgrimages to Jerusalem. It is hardly likely that the Kremlin's interest in such peregrinations is related to religion. Nor is it unduly sinister, I suppose, for the Soviets to employ these bearded *pappas* as contact men to keep a finger on the pulse of latent Pan-Slavism, linked with Orthodoxy. The end, as Lenin put it, justifies the means.[13]

An obvious manifestation of perhaps unintentional cooperation between the communists and the Orthodox Church in Cyprus came after the pro-*enosis* disturbances of 1931, in which both the prelates of the Church and the communists, for different reasons, took an active part. The British colonial government took punitive measures, after the violence, abolishing the constitution, deporting Church and political leaders, and banning meetings of more than five persons. After Archbishop Keretios died in 1933, the Bishop of Paphos, Leontios, became de facto leader (locum tenens) of the Church. Election of a new archbishop would not be permitted by the British except under conditions unacceptable to the Greeks, and the Archiepiscopal See remained vacant until 1947.

During this period, when the Greek Cypriots were without the services of an official ethnarch other than the senior Bishop Leontios, the communists tried to fill the vacuum created by the absence of strong national leaders. The cadres of the Communist Party of Cyprus (KKK), which had been proscribed in 1933, had developed some important inroads which began to serve the party well during this period.

Leontios saw the communist movement spreading among his flock, but seeing the good that it was doing had no fear of it. Leontios in reality did not have the vaguest idea of the theoretical mooring of international communism, but as a humanist saw only how it aided the poor and oppressed. He felt that the aims of the communists were the same as those of Christianity and claimed often that he was a "Christian Communist." After he was attacked by right-wing nationalists, Leontios stopped using the appellation openly, but he never lost his rapport with the communists. A few weeks before his death, in 1947, Leontios was elected Archbishop of Cyprus with strong support from the factions of the left led by the resuscitated communist party, AKEL. Leontios was never known to repudiate his organized communist following.[14]

The obvious tactic of the communists in Cyprus is to support any and all nationalist leaders who willfully, or unwittingly, do their bidding. In some ways, this may explain the current, though tacit, pact that AKEL has made with Archbishop Makarios. The advantages of this tactic to AKEL are apparent: If the Church does not openly come out against communism, the pious peasants and workers will see no harm in accepting overtures from the Communist Party or its dominated labor union, PEO. Yet Makarios seemingly feels that by this very means he controls the activities of AKEL without causing a cleavage within the Greek community. One conclusion that could be drawn is that the Orthodox Church may see communism as a threat, but perhaps not as the mortal enemy in the same way the Roman Catholic Church views the secular religion of Marxism-Leninism.[*] In contradistinction, as demonstrated by the peculiar manner in which the Arab countries treat communism, Islam makes no allowances to any earthly movement as a competitor for the allegiances of its followers, even though declared Muslims are also declared communists in some cases.

---

[*]Archbishop Makarios III has had a long and curious relationship with the AKEL in Cyprus. Possibly the following unverified incident, which allegedly occurred during the British occupation, may shed some light on it. On June 28, 1953, Makarios supposedly said during his sermon in church: "We, the Cypriots, are prepared to accept assistance from both East and West in our efforts to break away from our imperialistic rulers." This remark so delighted the predominantly communist congregation that day (many right-wing nationalists had stayed away for fear of trouble resulting from uninhibited communist enthusiasm for this particular service) that it provided the first known occasion when the communist "Internationale" was sung, spontaneously and unrehearsed, in a Greek Orthodox Church in Cyprus. (This story comes from a British propaganda tract and is vehemently denied by the

The Communist View of Cypriot Class Dynamics

AKEL's perception of the "class dynamics" of Cyprus follows dogmatic Marxist-Leninist lines on class war, even though the situation in the island does not obtain in the pure theoretical sense. Well before independence in 1960, AKEL stressed the need for the "unity of the working class," a slogan which also appealed to certain intellectuals. After the AKEL Party Congress in October 1952, the program of the day called for the linking of the welfare of the Turkish minority with the future liberation of both the Greek and Turkish people under a communist-led movement for *enosis* with Greece. Despite such pleas, the Cyprus communists notably failed to win over Turkish Cypriots in their campaign during the national liberation struggle against the British.

When the revolutionary *enosis* movement ensued in 1955, the Turks were similarly unsympathetic to the AKEL position of non-violence, since the minority's leadership preferred British rule and the guarantees it provided for them. AKEL's condemnation of the extreme measures of the EOKA fighters did not endear the party to either Greek or Turk. One prominent Marxist intellectual wrote that the communists missed a good opportunity to gain any advantage from the revolutionary movement against the "bourgeoisie's exploitation and colonial oppression" which affected both the Greek and Turkish proletariat. He lamented:

> Undoubtedly the absence from the armed struggle of the organized working class and its party (the only party that does not stand for national exceptionalism and national prejudice, the only party that could accept in its ranks Greeks and Turks without discrimination of race or religion) left the Turkish working class exposed to the demagogic commands of the Turkish leaders. . . . Taking advantage of the political backwardness of the Turkish minority, the Imperialists and their local agents strove to shut the eyes of

---

nationalists in Cyprus. It is difficult to confirm the event now.) See *Communism in Cyprus*, p. 13. After the 1960 elections in which Makarios made a deal with AKEL for 10 per cent of the parliamentary seats, the American press viewed the result in the following way: "The Cyprus Republic, due for independence August 16, will be the world's first state governed by churchmen and communists operating as partners." *Washington Post*, August 2, 1960.

the Turkish proletariat and peasantry, leading them to their political disaster.[15]

Even after Cypriot independence, efforts were made to show that mutual problems were shared by both Greek and Turkish workers. The AKEL program which emerged from the Tenth Party Congress in 1962 took great pains to say that the goal of "democratization of public and political life" had not been achieved through independence. In a subsequent speech, Secretary General Papaioannou paraphrased the AKEL program as follows:

The motive forces in the fight to achieve this goal are the workers, peasants, office employees, handicraftsmen, intellectuals, and the national bourgeoisie: in other words, the entire people—Greeks, Turks, Armenians, everyone, except those who have linked their interests with the interests of imperialism. All these forces should unite in a single anti-imperialist front. The basis of this front, which will unite the overwhelming majority of the people, will be the alliance of workers and peasants. . . . Under favourable international conditions, this front can win the full independence of Cyprus.[16]

This position was consistent with AKEL's line since the outbreak of violence in 1955 and probably represents the true, though tacit, line today. While the communists undoubtedly believe that there is an ultimate reward in pushing for the "unity of all the working class" in Cyprus, they have been significantly silent on the plight of the Turks and the dire conditions in which many have lived since 1964. The most effective tactic that AKEL feels it has at this point is to support Archbishop Makarios, even though this may run counter to the tactics of the Soviet Union. Consequently, AKEL has in recent years soft-pedaled its traditional "open-door" policy toward the Cypriot Turks, but without ever openly denouncing them as rebels or traitors in the fashion of the ruling Greek Cypriot government. The communists know that they may one day need the Turks and now are far ahead of Makarios in understanding the Turkish position. This present attitude toward the Turkish community may be taken as a tactical retreat rather than a permanent policy.

Foreign Relations

The internal political dynamics of Cyprus are difficult to separate from its foreign relations. The vested interests which the Zurich-London Agreements give Britain, Greece, and Turkey in the country have the effect of making each domestic problem an international issue. Consultations between the two communities, which may originate with either the Greek-Cypriot President or the Turkish-Cypriot Vice-President, often change from localized discussions into a diplomatic exercise involving the governments in Athens and Ankara. This is the sort of framework in which one must view the current discussions between the two communities in Cyprus.

The underlying element of the foreign policy of Cyprus is neutral nonalignment which by tradition has a pro-West orientation. The government of Cyprus has declared its desire to maintain friendly relations with all members of the United Nations, but not to belong to any military bloc. Its independent pursuit of foreign policy objectives is thus similar to that of many of the newly emergent nations who now speak with a majority voice in the United Nations General Assembly.

By the terms of the Zurich-London Agreements, Cyprus has special treaty arrangements with Great Britain, Greece, and Turkey. The terms of the treaties limit the sovereignty of the Republic in some respects and keep the government obligated to the three Western guarantors. President Makarios has openly expressed his dissatisfaction with the limitations of the Republic's sovereignty, and has sought support among the neutralist Afro-Asian nations in his efforts to alter the basic structure of the Republic. The Turkish Cypriots feel that the policy of nonalignment works to the detriment of the country. They would prefer to see Cyprus follow the Turkish government's policy of avowed anti-communism and alignment with the West in either the Central Treaty Organization (CENTO) or NATO alliances. The Republic's foreign policy is essentially set by the Greek Cypriots, as the controlling majority, and is another of the many areas in which the two major ethnic communities fail to agree.

Although Makarios has termed Cyprus "the golden bridge" between East and West, he seems to use the "bridge" himself to cross from side to side whenever it suits him. At the 1961 conference of nonaligned nations at Belgrade, Makarios expressed shock that the Soviet Union had resumed nuclear tests. He also supported the West, and thus became one of the few neutral statesmen to oppose the theory of coexistence between separate East and West Germanys. Instead, Makarios supported the plan for a free plebiscite on German reunification under the United Nations. (The West German government "rewarded" Cyprus with a long-term economic aid grant later that year.)

On the other side of the coin, Cyprus was unofficially represented at meetings of the Afro-Asian Peoples' Solidarity Organization (AAPSO), a neutralist group sponsored by Nasser and the U.A.R. and actively supported by Russia and Communist China. This group generally adheres to the position that agreements imposed under pressure by departing colonialists should not be recognized after the independence of a nation. On the other hand, Makarios favors the development of friendship and wholehearted cooperation with the Soviet Union. In the past, he has wished Mr. Khrushchev "great success in his exceptional activity which aims for the support of peace and prosperity of all humanity." The Soviet Premier supported Makarios' drive for "self-determination" in spite of the "imposed London-Zurich Agreements." Moreover, Makarios and the Russians currently seem to share almost the same attitude about the manner in which the problems of Cyprus should be resolved—that the Cypriots be left alone to work out their affairs peacefully. Early in 1964, the Russians established a 1,500 mile Nicosia-to-Moscow air route with the approval of President Makarios and his followers.

The two aims of U.S. foreign policy toward Cyprus have remained essentially the same since 1963: (1) the Greco-Turkish conflict in the island shall not become the cause of a larger war; and (2) the current political disorder shall not be the most important factor in the conduct of U.S. bilateral relations with either Greece or Turkey. The U.S. has had to play the "honest broker" in the present dispute between two of its NATO allies, but this posture often results in making no friends and two enemies. Thus, each time the U.S. contemplates a positive action toward one side, it must also run the risk of alienating the other. Yet both countries being equipped as they are with American-supplied NATO armaments compels the U.S. to be actively involved in peace-seeking efforts, as was demonstrated by the mediation attempts of Dean Acheson in 1964 and Cyrus Vance in 1967.

While there exists residual resentment toward the U.S. for failing to support *enosis,* the radio relay and communications monitoring facilities on Cyprus—the continued operation of which is vitally important to American Eastern Mediterranean interests—have not been affected by the Greek-Cypriot controlled government. United States relations with the Makarios regime are also strained for reasons of the Vietnam war. Not only do the island's communists attack America's role there, but "runaway" Greek ships flying the Cypriot flag have been observed unloading arms and supplies in Haiphong. Despite strong U.S. protests in the past, the practice still probably continues without interruption.

The negative attitude the two ethnic communities in Cyprus now have for Americans is therefore based first on the inability of the U.S. to favor one side over the other, and second on the unacceptable peace overtures which the U.S. has thus far made. Curiously, the Soviet Union has found itself in a similar quandary. By trying to back its Greek Cypriot communist brothers and their "self-determination" goal for the majority, while concurrently searching for ways to patch up an age-old feud with the mainland Turks, who insist on rights for the Cypriot minority community, the Russians have also experienced some embarrassment from sitting on the fence.

Summary

The coming of independence in 1960 created more problems for the people of Cyprus than it solved. The historic ethnic division between the island's Greeks and Turks was too firmly entrenched to bring about the trust needed to allow the delicate political structure to function properly. Those in the Greek community who favored independence could not openly advocate this position without running full face into the sentimental and emotional appeal of *enosis.* In like fashion, the moderate Turkish Cypriots who saw advantages in working with the Greeks and were willing to yield from the *taksim* stand were soon looked upon as turncoats by the other members of the minority community. Extremists in both camps demanded satisfaction of their conflicting demands and the result was the outbreak of intercommunal violence in December 1963.

In the seven years since that time, the government of Cyprus has become a monopoly of the Greek Cypriots while the Turkish community has constituted itself as a separate governing body called the Turkish Cypriot Provisional Council, which is supported by an annual subsidy from Turkey. In view of the amazingly prosperous economy, the Greek Cypriot elite in power has swung to openly favoring independence over *enosis* and has maintained its position in spite of terrorist attacks by some die-hard pro-*enosis* groups who see their dream of union with Greece slowly slipping away. After the crisis of 1967, when Greece lost much of its influence in the island, representatives of the two communities opened talks in search of a formula whereby the two ethnic groups could live in peace together. It has become clear that the majority of Cypriot people want to shape their destiny by themselves and never again be victims of a settlement imposed by the great powers in the fashion of the nineteenth century.

Regardless of the desire of the majority of Cypriots, the future of Cyprus is of direct concern not only to Greece and Turkey, but to the United Kingdom and other countries as well. It could be that by now the pro-independence elements in the Greek Cypriot community are in firm command. Hence, even if a rapprochement by the mainland powers were reached. it might ironically take combined military force by Greece and Turkey to impose an unwanted solution on the government of Archbishop Makarios. Ankara has consistently refused to consider the very mention of *enosis* for Cyprus, yet it could turn out that some modified form of "double" union (a "commonwealth-type" where much of the internal control is left to the Cypriot people while the mainland powers share in defense of the island) could be more appealing to Turkey than the present, free-wheeling coalition of rightists and leftists under the leadership of Makarios. Still, such a solution would be a strained compromise between the former extreme positions of *enosis* and *taksim,* and it would take a massive selling job to convince the majority of the islanders to live with another such "paper solution."

Independence, in the last analysis, appears to be the most acceptable course for the future of the island of Cyprus. As long as the two communities are talking—as they were at the end of 1969—hope does exist for a successful outcome to the deliberations. Idealistically, the emergence of shared values or superordinate goals, with which both communities could identify, would be the necessary precursor to a common Cypriot nationality and in the end the vehicle for resolution of the conflict. It would indeed take time for such a development to come about full-blown, but this may also be the only means by which tranquility can once again return to the fabled island of love.

4: AKEL's Conflict and Integration with the National Environment

Past Strategies

Violence. Neither AKEL nor its predecessor KKK has ever employed the technique of open revolution to gain its objectives. The anti-British riots of 1931 were primarily the inspiration and work of the nationalists and were simply joined in at an opportune time by the island's communists. The quasi-revolutionary tone of the KKK ran against the complacent nature of the Cypriots, who have been traditionally non-violent. During the period of the most intense indigenous revolutionary activity, the EOKA Emergency of 1955–59, AKEL was openly opposed to this method and its members were conspicuously absent from the fighting. The intercommunal violence which began in 1963 also could not be considered in any way a purposeful tactic of AKEL's nor one which they could exploit effectively. In many ways the communists were most chagrined by the last outbreak of violence between the island's Greeks and Turks, since the Turkish minority had always been a target of their infiltration attempts. Even though it may not be historically accurate in every detail, AKEL insists that it is a peace-loving political party that "has never killed, never threatened, and never hurt anyone's ideology."[1]

The closest AKEL and its supporters have come to open revolt was in the late 1940's, during the communist insurgency in Greece. This was in conjunction with a series of strikes carried out through their labor front, PEO. Bombings, arson, and murder were some of the devices employed to intimidate certain large industries, particularly the American-owned Cyprus Mines Corporation. But these attempts did not even achieve their limited goal of gaining recognition from the mining company's management. Later, strikes and obstruction techniques were used against the island's building industry, but these gained little for AKEL. In 1960 there were some abortive protest strikes and picketing demanding a solution to unemployment, but these too were of limited impact. (Paradoxically, most of the recent strikes have been called by the right-wing union, SEK.)

Moreover, AKEL has not carried out any prolonged campaign of terrorism or sabotage. Whatever sporadic violent campaigns they may have employed in the past were probably planned, but they lasted only until the party's leaders realized that they were not achieving the desired objectives. In the eyes of the nationalists, AKEL's only period of prolonged obstructionism occurred during the EOKA period, even though AKEL did not intend its inaction to be taken as an anti-nationalistic protest.

The Cypriot communists currently do not see the opportunity or reason to initiate any other forms of violent activity. If they are ever given directions by the Kremlin to pattern themselves after their Greek comrades on the mainland, there could conceivably be an attempt at a coup d'etat. The party certainly possesses three vital prerequisites for such an extreme venture: a tightly knit conspiratorial organization, the overt and covert support of a sizeable segment of the population, and possibly aid from the Soviet bloc. But aid could come only if the Kremlin should see some clear advantages to a communist-controlled Cyprus, as it may not at present; and AKEL's traditionally pacific nature would surely work against a coup attempt, even if it were directed from without.

Thus far, AKEL has had very little success from its forays into the realm of violent action. The party thrives on its peaceful image and would hardly want to engage in any activities which might jeopardize its legal status. The idea of taking up arms is undoubtedly repugnant to the vast majority of AKEL members. This is true not only because AKEL has pushed the line of "parliamentary socialism," but also because the party members know well that violence would engender a strong counteraction and sure defeat at the hands of the well-armed nationalist forces. Even an unlikely fusion of the Turkish minority with the communist ranks would probably not be able to take over the government by force. Of course, Turkey as well as Greece would probably forcibly resist any communist-inspired coup in Cyprus.

Popular Causes. AKEL's association with the popular nationalist cause of "self-determination" has been a hallmark of the party since the establishment of the Republic in 1960. While AKEL publicly espouses the cause of "self-determination and demilitarization," it has not made its position unequivocally clear on *enosis,* and it is on this issue that the greatest strain has developed between the party and the Greek Cypriot community. PEO and AKEL leader Andreas Ziartides has said: "What we want is national liberation, and in Cyprus this means *enosis*—but we want genuine *enosis,* not the kind proposed by the imperialists as in the recommendations of Dean Acheson."* Apparently AKEL feels safe in straddling the fence on this issue, optimistically sensing that the possibility of union with Greece is becoming more and more remote. In fact, the communists now seem to ignore the *enosis* issue entirely.

In accordance with communist ideology, AKEL leaders repeatedly state that Cyprus "is today in the national-liberation, anti-imperialist stage" of political development, and that the mass movement should be controlled by the "dictatorship of the united front." Therefore Cypriots, Greeks, and obviously Turks must cooperate in order to achieve what AKEL calls "fulfillment of Cypriot independence." The cooperation, in the AKEL view, consists of a "united anti-imperialist democratic front," under the "valuable leadership" of AKEL. In this united front tactic, AKEL may even be willing to share power with the bourgeoisie, though never to give it up completely. AKEL leaders hence refer to imperialism as the "common enemy" of the Cypriots and every opportunity is taken to propagandize the bogey of colonialism. Thus, one of the biggest of AKEL's propaganda guns is aimed at American communication stations and British bases on the island.[2]

From below, through its vast network of trusted cadres in the cities and villages, AKEL keeps its eyes and ears on its "mother, the people." In the past, AKEL has criticized the government for its failure to solve the problems of the people

---

*Personal interview with Ziartides, August 1965. The Acheson Plan of September 1964 proposed that in exchange for *enosis,* a military base on Cyprus would be ceded to Turkey, along with a small Greek island, and that the Turkish community would be given two cantons under its own administration.

because of the lack of a concrete program and coordination between elements in the Republic's bureaucracy. By means of a persistent program in the countryside, AKEL tries to show the "correctness" of its line to the lowliest Cypriot peasant, and in turn picks up the sentiments of the proletariat. When and how to exploit existing issues among Cypriot peasants and other grass-roots elements are still matters to be decided by the top leadership of the party.

Social changes and political developments have also brought into existence right-wing sponsored organizations, such as OHEN and OEKA,[3] and these groups have been a target for penetration by the communists regardless of under whose leadership they might have been established. Cultural events, such as music festivals, dances, and theatrical performances—the OTHAK theater group is supposedly infiltrated—are other ways the communists seek to get their message across. Athletic events and competitions are becoming increasingly popular with the visits of teams from the Soviet bloc. Admittedly, AKEL has its problems in the field by not meeting its "targets" in various undertakings and some leaders have complained that "there were and still are organizations which do not function properly, and in some cases their work is very inadequate."[4]

Behavior of AKEL in Ruling Bodies

National. An aspect of AKEL's strategy can be seen in the behavior of its five Greek members of the national parliament, who consistently travel through villages and towns to familiarize themselves with the myriad problems and demands of the citizenry. In addition to discussion of the desires of various unions and cooperative organizations, the deputies give attention to such problems as: road building, flood control projects, telephone communications, visits by doctors in the rural areas, electrification, farm debts, forest grazing for animals, farm support prices, anti-tuberculosis measures, drought compensation, school construction, and claims of villagers near the base areas of British attempts to take their land. This pattern was explained by Chrysis Dimetriades, the AKEL deputy from Paphos, in an address on the "activities of the leftist deputies in the House of Representatives." He insisted that the conduct of the communists was based upon the "desire for unity among the people," the support of every government measure "serving the interests of the people," and "constructive criticism in matters which do not serve the people." Dimetriades also referred to "disadvantages" under which the deputies are working and to "shortcomings" in the Cypriot Constitution whereby the House has no "power to control the government."[5] Besides Dimetriades, the other four AKEL members of the House are: Papaioannou, Ziartides, Hambis Michaelides (EKA President), and Giangos Potamitis (LOEL advocate and President of the Cyprus Peace Council).

AKEL membership on the standing committees of the House of Representatives may reveal areas of direct concern or expertise of the individual communist members. Presumably by intention, the nationalists who control the Selection Committee have seen that no communists sit on that important arm and that no more than one AKEL member is on any of the other eleven standing committees and no one of them is a chairman. Thus, Papaioannou is on three committees: Foreign Affairs, Commerce and Industry, and Communications and Public Works. Ziartides is on two: Budget, and Labor and Social Insurance. Potamitis is on two: Finance, and Health. Michaelides is a member of Defense and of Agriculture and National Resources. Dimetriades is on the Legal and Interior Committees. While committee voting records are not readily available, it can be assumed that the AKEL members nearly always vote as a unit on all legislation that passes the House. (See Postscript, p. 205.)

Local. AKEL was given three seats in the constitutionally established 21-member Greek Communal Chamber as part of the 1960 election deal made with the Makarios forces. These seats were held by Constantia Varda (Nicosia), Nicos Mavronicolas (Paphos), and Georgios Savvides (Limassol). The Greek Communal Chamber never did work as anticipated and has been in limbo since the 1963 crisis; it was officially disbanded in 1965 and local affairs for the Greek community are now handled by the 35 Greek Cypriot members of the House of Representatives. (In 1967 the Turkish Communal Chamber was replaced by the Turkish Cypriot Provisional Administration as the governing authority of that minority community.) Nevertheless, while the Greek Communal Chamber was in operation, AKEL was most active in it.

Commenting on demands in 1961 that the Greek Communal Chamber be abolished, an AKEL statement indicated that "whatever the weakness or shortcomings [of the Chamber], we are duty-bound to study and evaluate the constructive work which has been done by this body in the 14 months of its existence." Moreover, the statement pointed out that "under present conditions the Greek Communal Chamber is a body of great importance to the life of the island and the future of our people. . . . Therefore, our party believes that negative and sterile polemics against it can cause grave damage to our island." This was followed by a summary of what AKEL considered to have been constructive accomplishments of the Chamber, particularly in the field of education and school construction.[6] AKEL has since urged that some sort of local governing bodies be reinstituted as soon as possible.

AKEL was undoubtedly disappointed when the Greek Communal Chamber and the municipal councils were deactivated in 1965. The mayors of the municipalities were then appointed by Makarios and the communists retained only one of the three town leaders whom they had previously supported, Mayor Pouyouros in Famagusta. AKEL has since looked forward to a future change which would allow local elections.

President Makarios' announcement in early 1969 that there is to be no further extension of the House of Representatives and that elections will be called later has become an issue among people holding or seeking public posts in Cyprus. In response, the leader of the five AKEL members in the Parliament, Ezekias Papaioannou, said that AKEL favored not only parliamentary elections but also elections for municipal and village authorities, even town school committees. He pointed out that Cyprus had been without municipal elections for 15 years and without elections for village authorities for some 40 years. He then cautioned that since elections did not concern only the Greeks but also the Turks, "we must come to an understanding with them, otherwise we would be unwillingly encouraging administrative partition." The AKEL chief reiterated his party's call for a change in the electoral system "to enable the fair representation of all political parties."[7] AKEL wants the electoral system reformed before the next

129

elections because with the present large multi-member districts it could be beaten in every race. AKEL's winding up with no seats at all in the House of Representatives, however, is a highly unlikely prospect in any event.

Promotion of National Interests

In order for AKEL to support its political followers, its leaders are forced to set an essentially nationalist political line for the party and adhere to it. Without the use of nationalist slogans (whatever these may mean to the leaders) AKEL would probably be abandoned by many of its present-day following, exclusive of the hard-core members. This fact is fully appreciated by the AKEL leadership and is the fundamental reason for AKEL's collaboration with Archbishop Makarios today on a minimum program for achieving the nationalist goal of completing Cyprus' independence.

In the economic realm, AKEL was the first party on record to present proposals to the fledgling Republic. A document prepared by the Central Committee was submitted to the President and Vice President-elect on February 11, 1960, containing suggestions for meeting what was described as "the present economic crisis on the island." The party document stated that Cyprus should not turn only to Western nations for assistance but "must look as well to the Eastern countries, which are willing to help in many ways the small and underdeveloped countries to stand on their feet economically, without any political or other obligations." The memorandum to the two Cypriot leaders goes on to say, "We must take a lesson from the example of our neighbor Egypt [in order to] be able to secure loans under the most favorable terms."

Concerning development generally, the Central Committee recommended as follows:

> National expenditure on non-productive purposes should be cut to the minimum. Considerable amounts could be spent on starting such projects as water development, irrigation, construction of houses, afforestation, port improvements and communications, expansion of hospitals.
>
> Such works could solve the unemployment problems satisfactorily, which would lead to the enlivening of business in the

Island. Farmers and stock-breeders should be protected and helped. Local industries should also be protected.

Cyprus capital should be forbidden to leave the Island, thus forcing it to be invested in various industries and projects.

With regard to the need for outside assistance the AKEL memorandum says: "Now is the time for the Greek and Turkish Governments to make their promised grants-in-aid to the Cyprus Republic. An appeal should also be made to the United Nations for finance assistance." Naturally, no mention is made of the United States as a source for aid. The memorandum concluded:

> All these measures should be taken immediately and without any delay. The situation is such that it does not permit any postponement. AKEL is of the opinion that the taking of all these measures could contribute to the complete employment of all the unemployed, to the improvement of the life of our farmers and of all the workers in general and would provide the necessary prerequisites for a step-by-step development of the national economy and conditions of the working class.[8]

The astonishing economic boom Cyprus has had, despite its unsteady political situation, has obviated much of the AKEL criticism in this area. Nevertheless, AKEL knows it must continually attempt to appeal on the economic level by stressing a better distribution of wealth. It made this statement early in 1969:

> The fifth plenum of the Central Committee and Central Control Committee of the party attests to the fact that there is a continuing upward trend and development in the economy of Cyprus. This is resulting in an increase in national income. AKEL at the same time attests to the fact that the national income in general and the increased national wealth is being distributed in the interest of the rich, who are constantly growing richer, and not in the interest of the working class, which is the creator of the national wealth.
>
> Although there are no concrete figures, it is obvious that other enterprises are making corresponding profits. Under such circumstances, fairer distribution and redistribution of the national income becomes an immediate and urgent duty. Fairer distribution and redistribution of the national income means that the workers, all those who are producing the national income through manual and intellectual work, should get a larger share of the national wealth.

The national income may be distributed and redistributed more fairly, in favor of the overwhelming majority of the people, not only by increasing salaries and wages, but also by increasing benefits in general, and by readjusting taxation so that direct taxation on large incomes would increase, while indirect taxation— particularly on widely distributed goods—would be perceptibly reduced or abolished.[9]

Apparently, AKEL does not have a great deal to complain about in the economic status quo.

Promotion of Communist Interests

AKEL, a highly disciplined apparatus, uses every opening to further the interests of the international communist system. From 1960 to 1965 statements like this one were common:

> Communism—that of the Soviet Union and other socialist countries—is that which always voted in the United Nations for self-determination of the Cypriot people and supported by all means this just claim, whereas the United States and the NATO countries always voted against us and proved to be the most fanatic foes of the Cypriot demand for self-determination.
>
> Since the founding of the Republic of Cyprus, it has not been the Soviet Union that has intervened in our domestic affairs and maintained military bases and radio-stations, but Britain and America.[10]

Soviet interests in promoting a "nuclear free zone" in the Mediterranean, explained in a diplomatic note given to the Cypriot President in 1963, were given full support by AKEL.[11] The island's communist press faithfully follows the Soviet-inspired line on both foreign and domestic matters. Much of the *Haravghi* "news" is composed of reprints from *Pravda, Izvestiya, Krasnaya Zvezda,* and other Soviet or satellite periodicals. As early as 1962 the conservative *Cyprus Mail* carried a front-page story claiming that General Secretary Papaioannou had admitted that AKEL was under the complete control of Moscow. In a speech in Prague, he was quoted as saying: "No communist is worthy of his name if he follows a policy not approved by Moscow."[12] *Haravghi* was rather piqued by the story, countering that Papaioannou was incorrectly quoted and that he really said: "A good communist cannot get involved in activities turned against the Soviet Union."[13]

In 1965, after a pro-Turkish statement by Soviet Foreign Minister Gromyko to the effect that federation between the two communities could be a solution to the island's problems, AKEL took strong exception. This was the first time in the party's history that it disagreed with Soviet policy. The issue was further exacerbated later in the year by the abstention of the Soviet Union in voting on the U.N. resolution regarding the territorial integrity of the Republic of Cyprus. Here again, AKEL claimed to be "disappointed" by the Soviet action.[14] That major cleavage with the Soviet Union was soon papered over and AKEL went back to its normal practice of supporting the Moscow line. As late as February 1969 AKEL's Central Committee passed a resolution condemning Makarios' neutrality between the Arabs and Israel after the June 1967 war. It parroted the Soviet line by declaring that "the Israeli government's policy is a provocation against peace-loving mankind."[15]

The success of AKEL's past strategies must be looked upon in the light of the limited objectives they were realistically designed to achieve. There is no reason to believe that AKEL has lost any of its substantial membership or sympathizers by following the Soviet line in those areas in which it does not conflict with nationalist interests, but there is also no reason to believe that AKEL has increased its following since 1965. Electoral results would naturally be the best indicator of communist strength. It may be assumed that in an election held under today's circumstances—if AKEL were competing alone without any coalition, and on the basis of a clear communist platform and slogans—it would probably be able to deliver only the votes of its 14,000 members and perhaps most of the rest of its front group following of approximately 70,000 Greek Cypriots, or approximately 20 per cent of the electorate. If AKEL's current strategy is merely to be satisfied with a share of the power in Cyprus, its cumulative past efforts appear to have been successful. If it still harbors the idea of replacing the government with a communist regime, then AKEL's past strategies have been dismal failures.

Peripheral Organizations (Front Groups)

Trade Unions. The trade-union movement began in the early 1920's in Cyprus and the KKK saw here a ripe area for infiltration. Ultimately, under the able leadership of Andreas Ziartides, the Pan-Cyprian Labor Federation (PEO) and its affiliated unions (also referred to as the Old Trade Unions) have since far outstripped in numbers and influence the other five major union organizations of Cyprus: the SEK (Confederation of Cypriot Workers), the nationalist labor federation which is referred to as the New Trade Unions; the Turkish Trade Unions; POAS (Pan-Cyprian Federation of Independent Trade Unions); the DEOK (Democratic Labor Federation); and the others, including the civil service unions, which are not federated. The total membership of trade unions in 1968 was 67,000, which broke down as follows: PEO 35,500, SEK 17,000, Turkish 3,500, POAS 1,000, DEOK 1,000, and the others 9,000.[16] The accompanying table shows the growth of the trade-union movement in Cyprus from 1932 to 1968.

PEO has been cooperating to some extent with POAS and SEK and calling for a Pan-Cyprian Trade Unions Congress to set up a united labor movement, since only 50 per cent of the Cypriot working force is organized. Even though PEO would like to see the congress come about to enhance its power, the concept has not reached fruition. Through direct control over its own membership and its association with the other unions, PEO has virtual command over the major portion of the island's labor force. The PEO is therefore used as a powerful lever by AKEL in furthering its political aims, and the federation thrives because of the services and welfare provisions it provides its members. It is indeed the best-run labor union in the island.

The PEO has some seventeen affiliated unions and is a member of the World Federation of Trade Unions (WFTU), a communist front.[17] Of these, some are organized on an island-wide basis, while others are on a district-wide basis. The island-wide, or pan-Cyprian, unions have branches in each city, and local organizations in the suburbs of the cities as well as in the villages. Guidance and authority flow from the PEO Administrative Council down to the local councils on the village level via the district administrative councils. With very

THE GROWTH OF TRADE UNION MOVEMENT IN CYPRUS 1932—1968

YEAR	OLD TRADE UNIONS (PEO)		NEW TRADE UNIONS (SEK)		TURKISH TRADE UNIONS		FEDERATION OF INDEPENDENT TRADE UNIONS		DEMOCRATIC LABOUR FEDERATION (DEOK)		OTHER (INCLUDING CIVIL SERVICE UNIONS)		TOTAL	
	Unions	Members	Unions	Members	Unions	Members	Unions	Members	Unions	Members	Unions	Members	Unions	Members
1932	1	84											1	84
1933	1	84											1	84
1934	1	84											1	84
1935	2	99											2	99
1936	5	285											5	285
1937	6	367											6	367
1938	14	772											14	772
1939	46	2544											46	2544
1940	62	3389											62	3389
1941	68	3854											68	3854
1942	73	9991											73	9991
1943	82	9507			1	43					1	78	84	9628
1944	89	10596	25	758	7	436					1	75	122	11865
1945	91	12961	31	1032	13	843					8	644	143	15480
1946	87	11101	30	991	19	681					8	641	144	13414
1947	51	11259	31	1145	15	640					10	792	107	13836
1948	33	9604	36	2641	9	190					11	695	89	13130
1949	31	9447	61	3599	7	160					9	1368	108	14574
1950	32	8924	52	2625	5	131					9	1886	98	13566
1951	39	10281	54	2270	6	130					10	2027	89	14708
1952	42	12540	56	2702	8	444					12	2368	118	18054
1953	47	14427	54	2123	8	477					16	4253	126	21280
1954	47	18085	56	2832	10	740					15	5009	129	26666
1955	43	22925	67	5374	16	2214					31	8502	156	39015
1956	45	27143	69	5129	16	1813	12	2954			25	5889	167	42928
1957	40	30375	130	9767	15	1268	13	2506			30	8549	228	52465
1958	38	31723	190	12852	8	1137	12	2036			36	8794	284	56542
1959	34	33770	236	16867	36	4829	15	2591			21	7324	342	65381
1960	30	35544	246	15587	38	4381	16	2416			24	7452	354	65380
1961	25	36442	232	13321	37	4288	14	2211			26	7919	334	64181
1962	24	37849	57	12158	38	4069	13	1740	19	1189	28	7765	179	64770
1963	18	37378	47	14285	39	4000	11	1436	17	1507	28	7500	160	66106
1964	18	36190	48	13179	48	3733	10	1360	19	1606	18	5895	161	61963
1965	19	36055	46	13179	48	2784	9	1277	25	1666	19	6500	166	61461
1966	19	35847	42	15388	36	3702	6	1233	23	1674	26	8558	152	66402
1967	18	35325	44	16901	22	3771	7	1030	15	1181	24	8942	130	67150
1968	17	35500	40	17000	20	3500	7	1000	13	1000	26	9000	123	67000

Source: Republic of Cyprus, *Annual Report of the Ministry of Labour and Social Insurance for the Year 1968* (Nicosia: 1969), p. 108.

135

few exceptions, principally in local general unions, the unions have been organized on an industrial and trades basis. The mining unions are controlled by the Central Mining Office of the PEO in Nicosia. Each union is assigned a specific sum which is to be collected from its membership and turned over to the PEO as affiliation dues. The membership and finances of PEO allow AKEL the opportunity to continue its working-class approach in the effort to build up an eventual electoral majority.

Trade Associations. POVEK is an organization of middle-class farmers and shopkeepers which was originally founded under the colonial regime to protect the interests of its members against the excesses of the trade-union movement. Gradually the leadership of the association became communist and the conservative members withdrew from it. POVEK's membership today is not known, but most of the shop-owners in the famous Ledra Street shopping district of Nicosia are thought to belong to this communist front group. In all probability POVEK is quantitatively the largest association of businessmen in Cyprus and can exercise a good deal of influence. The real importance of the association is that it represents the point of the clash between small and big business in the island. AKEL can generally look to these sympathizers as a ready source of contributions when the annual fund-raising drive is launched.

Peasant League. The EKA (Union of Cypriot Farmers) was preceded on the Cyprus farm scene by the EAK (Farmers' Union of Cyprus), which was included in the communist proscription imposed by the British colonial government in December 1955. The EKA is the open agricultural arm of AKEL. EKA is intended for the recruitment of farm owners or tenants, whereas the Pan-Cyprian Union of Farm Workers, a PEO affiliate, generally recruits among farm laborers. Membership in EKA is open to all men and women over 16 years of age and dues are two shillings per year.

A number of factors serve to underscore the EKA's connection and relationship with its predecessor, the EAK. Hambis Michaelides, the General Secretary of the EKA, formerly held the same post in the EAK. Prior to his election to the position in 1950, he had been active during the 1946–49 period as the EAK secretary for the Larnaca District. He is credited with organizing the EKA in 1959 and is one of the five AKEL deputies in the Cypriot House of Representatives.

EKA representatives spend a considerable amount of time touring the Cypriot countryside explaining the EKA program, discussing agricultural problems, promoting membership and dues drives, and setting up local organizations. Its policies on farm problems, government aid, land expropriation, British bases, and demilitarization of Cyprus began developing in 1952, following the Fifth Pan-Cyprian Congress of its predecessor, the EAK.[18] The resolutions passed during that congress included (1) one addressed to the Synod of the Cyprus Archdiocese seeking consultation on the matter of the expropriation of church and monastery lands, and (2) another protesting the seizure of lands for British military purposes and asking that Cyprus be demilitarized. Additional aims were promulgated in the EKA program at the founding congress of August 1959. These include land redistribution, farm machinery pools, farm support prices based on production costs, reciprocal trade agreements with other countries, abolition of laws preventing the development of the stock-farming industry, government aid to the development of cooperatives, a social security system, and compensation and medical plans. AKEL has adopted en masse all these provisions in its various party programs.

Student Organizations. The children of AKEL members and sympathizers are often given free university training behind the Iron Curtain; the best are sent to the Soviet Union and others go to the other bloc countries. A total of 600 students in 1968 were reportedly studying in bloc countries: 200 in the U.S.S.R., 85 in Czechoslovakia, 110 in East Germany, 60 in Bulgaria, and the rest in Poland and Hungary.[19] More than 50 Cypriots had obtained scholarships in 1968 alone and gone to the Soviet Union for "higher studies."[20] It may be assumed that these students keep up informal "alumni" associations after returning, since they are thoroughly indoctrinated with communist ideology during their higher educational process. Many students are members of the EDON youth front or become regular party members when they have reached maturity.

AKEL leaders might have mixed feelings about the advisability of sending the children of their working-class members to universities. It is a safe guess that when these students return, they have their own ideas about rejuvenating society and these may not be the same as those espoused by the party bureaucracy. AKEL could be faced with an internal revolt against its authoritarian discipline and inefficiency one day because it sent too many Cypriots off to universities. This was exactly what happened to the Turkish Cypriot students who returned to Cyprus in 1968 and 1969. Many of these Turks were imbued with leftist political ideas and may prove to be a fertile field for cultivating communist sympathy in Cyprus.

PEO too has formed a Youth Department. This has obviously been planned by communist leadership in order to complement the work of EDON and to assist in countering the influence of the nationalists over Cypriot youth, which is exerted primarily through the government-sponsored association OHEN. It is reported that the plans of the Youth Department stress indoctrination of the youth in PEO's labor goals as well as capturing their interest by the provision of social, cultural, and sporting facilities.

It is known that AKEL has even penetrated the youth with the Pan-Cyprian Organization of Secondary School Students (PEOM). This AKEL initiative is a subject of concern to the Greek Cypriot Education Office and once resulted in the transfer of a number of high school teachers in an effort by the government to lessen AKEL influence in the schools. There are an estimated 2,000 members in PEOM.

Women's Associations. During July 1959, the Pan-Cyprian Women's Congress founded the Pan-Cyprian Federation of Women's Organizations (POGO). The women passed resolutions calling for equal social, political, and job rights; equal wages; legal protection of mothers and children; and social insurance. The delegates represented 200 villages and towns.[21]

Many wives of leading AKEL members were named to the secretariat of the congress; they include Kioula Ziartidou, Evgenoula Katsouridou, Evgenia Michaelidou, Maroula Peta, and Froso Partasidou. Most of these women had been active in the Pan-Cyprian Federation of Democratic Women (PODY), the former communist women's organization which was proscribed in 1955.

The 38-member Executive Council which runs POGO is elected annually and most often unanimously. Its principal officers are Olga Papapetrou, president; Sofoula Tsimilli, secretary; and Androula Christoforou, organizational secretary. POGO carries out its duties mainly through the vehicles of cultural and social events. It has an estimated six to seven thousand members and has ties with the international communist front, the Women's International Democratic Federation (WIDF).

Youth Clubs. EDON (United Democratic Youth Organization) was founded on April 12, 1959. It is the youth arm of AKEL and the descendant of AON (Restorative Organization of Youth), the communist Cypriot youth organization which was proscribed by the British colonial government in December 1955. It caters to youths 14 years and over, many of whom are also members of the PEOM student front.[22]

Because of its political orientation EDON maintains close ties with the WFDY, the international union of students, and the various youth and student organizations of the communist world. It sends delegations and representatives to the congresses and meetings of these groups, as well as on visits to the various bloc countries. The First Regular EDON Congress of October 1959 (attended by over 1,000 Cypriot young people) and the First Pan-Cyprian Youth Festival of July 1960 set the pattern for EDON's annual events. Soon after, EDON's weekly newspaper, *Neolaia* (Youth), began publication.

A number of AON veterans are now serving on EDON's Central Committee and its festival committee. AKEL's parliament member Chrysis Dimetriades has been president and Bulgarian-trained Panikos Paionidis, a *Haravghi* reporter, is currently the leader. A considerable amount of recruiting work had been done before the official founding of EDON, despite the proscription of its predecessor group. EDON leaders claimed a highly remarkable membership of 19,000 in 1959, six months after EDON's official founding.[23]

EDON held its fifth congress in Nicosia in May of 1969; it discussed a report on the activities of the Central Council, the problems of youth and EDON, and elected a new governing body. EDON also announced a campaign to enroll new members.[24] The fifth congress coincided with the tenth anniversary of the formation of EDON, which was also celebrated by the Pan-Cypriot Youth Festival later in July.

Specific-Issue Societies. A rather ineffective front group is the Pan-Cyprian Peace Committee (PEE, Pankrypriaki Epitropi Eirinis). At a time when the average Cypriot feels threatened, when a National Guard has to be maintained for the defense of Cyprus, when there has been a Soviet invasion of Czechoslovakia, this group cannot talk too loudly for peace. AKEL's parliament member Giangos Potamitis has been president of PEE since 1955 and is also a member of the World Peace Council.

One front group that finds it particularly hard to carry out its program both inside and outside the AKEL family is the Cypriot-Soviet Friendship Society (SFKS, Syndesmos Filias Kyprou ton Soviet), whose president is the socialist mayor of Famagusta, Andreas Pouyouros. Through this group the Soviet Embassy attempts to promote good will, but its influence has suffered by the various changes of policy toward Cyprus which Moscow has come out with since January of 1965, when it favored a "federation" in Cyprus between the Greek and Turkish communities. There are analogous, though smaller, friendship societies for most of the other Eastern bloc countries even though there may not be official diplomatic representation, as is the case with East Germany.

Another "peace" group in Cyprus is the Afro-Asian Peoples' Solidarity Organization (AAPSO) under the leadership of Dr. Vassos Lyssarides. While this organization is considered to be a communist front group in many of the countries which will allow it to operate, its role in Cyprus is not that clear. Lyssarides is a Marxist who has serious disagreements with AKEL and this may prevent AAPSO in Cyprus from being the typical communist front group. Makarios in fact uses the organization to help keep up his contacts with non-aligned countries.

Summary of Front Groups. While all of the communist front groups suggest a decentralization of leftist activity, AKEL maintains a strict centralization of authority over all of its peripheral organizations. One problem AKEL does have comes from this same centralization of authority, which generates an inertia in the sense that the party is not open to new ideas at home and abroad. This problem was analyzed in an article by Giannis Sophocles, once the Paphos district secretary. He also pointed out that the emphasis on recruiting members, young and old, has blurred the party's identity, and that it is difficult to retain members and keep them active. He claimed that many of AKEL's front groups or cells "lack initiative and accomplish nothing."[25] In actuality, AKEL probably has less control over the members of its various fronts than it would care to admit. In summary, AKEL has eight major front organizations; it should be remembered that the claimed membership figures, available for five of them, are not exclusive because most members belong to several of the organizations at once. The organizations are as follows:

EDON, United Democratic Youth Organization 26,000
PEO, Pan-Cyprian Federation of Labor 35,500
EKA, Union of Cypriot Farmers 12,000
POGO, Pan-Cyprian Federation of Women's
    Organizations 2,500
PEOM, Pan-Cyprian Organization of Secondary
    School Students 2,000
POVEK, Pan-Cyprian Association of Shop-
    keepers n.a.
PEE, Pan-Cyprian Peace Committee n.a.
SFKS, Cypriot-Soviet Friendship Society n.a.

The Ex-Communists

AKEL has very little competition from the island's few admitted Marxists who are no longer members of the party. Again, the matter of personalities looms large in the inability of this splinter group to join in with AKEL. The self-appointed leader of the splinter group—which may not even be so formal as to be called a "group"—is AKEL's former General Secretary, Ploutis Servas. It cannot be known for sure just how many ex-AKEL members or sympathizers fall into this category, but the estimate could not possibly exceed several hundred at the outside. According to his own account, Servas was purged from the party in 1952 along with some other intellectuals, among them Christos Savvides, a tailor, Christos Economides, an automobile importer in business for himself, and George Cacoyannis, a lawyer. Later the journalists Alecos Constantinides, Diomides Galanos, and Christos Katsambas, the builder's supplier Lazaros Christophides, and the former youth leader Vassos Mavratsas met the same fate. These people, together with former General Secretary Fifis Ioannou, are what might loosely be called "revisionists," particularly in the eyes of "orthodox" AKEL members.

Servas himself claims that there are no real communists in Cyprus today, and that the AKEL leadership has "succumbed to the temptation to preserve its present-day status, power, and prosperity." Moreover, since independence the proletariat of Cyprus, which forms the backbone of AKEL, has decidedly drifted away from the communist ideology because of the rising wages and improved living conditions. In short, Servas claims the Cypriot proletariat has lost its class consciousness and its fighting spirit. He criticized AKEL for not joining in the EOKA struggle, claiming that the leadership did not understand what Lenin meant when he said there was no nationalist struggle with reactionary tendencies. He also criticizes AKEL for encouraging Makarios to sign the Zurich-London Agreements and then failing to back him up during the 1959 election. A fervent believer in *enosis*, Servas insists that Greece is bound to become socialist one day and the road to Cypriot socialism is nearer via Greece. He also feels that direct revolution is now antiquated because of "past Soviet mistakes," and communism must be introduced by parliamentary means, although "the road to socialism is longer now than it was 30 years ago." Servas visited Peking with Mavratsas and Christophides in 1966 and in an unpublished article described the "experiment of China" as one "of worldwide importance, the second in our century after the Soviet one." While it may be that Servas is a traditional, old-line Marxist, he cannot be said to be the leader of a non-existent Peking wing in Cyprus.[26] Christophides is thought to be pro-Chinese personally, but he has no following.

So far as promoting their views or indoctrinating, Servas and other ex-AKEL members can use some of the many newspapers and magazines of the island to put their case against the party in writing. Their purpose is probably not to convert anyone to traditional communist ways of thinking, but rather to expose AKEL as a party of contradictions. For his many articles, the AKEL Central Committee has labeled Servas and other "enemies of the party" as "leftist revolutionaries, resurrected Trotskyites, and party outcasts." The committee denounces Servas' articles as constituting a "slanderous and perverted attack against the line and policies of the party and its leadership." AKEL feels Servas has been prompted by the fear of the "imperialists" over the "growing membership, power, and monolithic unity of AKEL."[27] AKEL also includes in its list of deviants such "enemies of the party as the Trotskyites," led by their "representative Georgios Ioannides, this old party enemy who has written anti-party articles since 1939 under the pseudonym of G. Varosiotis."[28]

After AKEL had cooperated with the Democratic Union (DE) party in the 1959 presidential elections, the newspaper of the DE, *Ethniki* (National), began to print some of Servas' critical articles. AKEL Deputy General Secretary Andreas Fantis wrote soon after that he could not understand why a newspaper such as *Ethniki,* whose "mission as an organ of the Democratic Union Party was to unite all the democratic, liberal elements of the urban classes, intellectuals, and petit bourgeoisie" for "cooperation with the AKEL," could become the organ and official rostrum for all the enemies of AKEL, in violation of Democratic Union Party principles.[29] The inability of the DE to explain its anti-AKEL position adequately was perhaps another rationale for AKEL to switch to the side of the pro-Makarios forces in the parliamentary elections which were then close at hand.

There is no adequate measure of the size, cohesiveness, or influence of the anti-AKEL communist force in Cyprus. Most of the opposition leaders are getting along in years and have lost a great deal of their revolutionary *élan.* Hence, it is probably safe to say that AKEL has to endure occasional harassment from its communist "enemies," but that it certainly does not have to be concerned about a movement that would in any way be competitive in trying to win over the sympathies of Cypriots with leftist proclivities.

Competitors on the Periphery: The Socialists

The strongest, and perhaps only, socialist force in Cyprus is under the leadership of Dr. Vassos Lyssarides, a 48-year-old ex-EOKA fighter and nationalist member of Parliament from Nicosia. Lyssarides was never an organic member of AKEL, but was considered a strong fellow traveler until 1952, when he too fell from communist favor along with Servas and the others. Always active in peace movements, Lyssarides founded the Cypriot Branch of the Afro-Asian Peoples' Solidarity Organization in 1962. He has made Cyprus a very active participant in that world-wide movement, and has arranged for Cyprus to be the host country for two international meetings. (The last one, in 1968, drew representatives from both Russia and Red China.)[30]

Lyssarides calls himself a "democratic socialist" who would like to see the Republic of Cyprus follow the lead of certain Scandinavian countries. He admits that he has close connections with Nasser; he agrees with many of Nasser's criticisms of "imperialist" policies in the Arab countries and Africa, and shares some of Nasser's Arab-Socialist beliefs. Lyssarides also claims that there are "many roads to socialism" and that possibly some of his ideas on certain issues "are the same as those of the communists." He fancies himself the "spiritual father of Cypriot non-alignment" and stressed this to Archbishop Makarios when the Republic was formed. As personal physician to President Makarios, Lyssarides undoubtedly can have the "ear" of the nationalist leader virtually anytime he wants it. He said recently that he backs Makarios in the present struggle, but that the Archbishop should be the "above-party leader" and not active directly in the political process.[31]

Dr. Lyssarides has been to the Soviet Union and the bloc countries a number of times and believes that "peaceful co-existence between the East and West is possible when the two economic systems eventually converge to the left." He asserts that he is a friend of the expatriated Greek leftist, Andreas Papandreou; both of them agree on socialist ends and a non-aligned orientation for Greece and Cyprus alike, and both favor *enosis.* In fact the secretary of the Cypriot branch of the Committee for the Restoration of Democracy in Greece, Takis Hadjidemetriou, is a supporter of the Lyssarides movement.

An articulate and persuasive individual, the Cypriot social-ist leader writes prolifically in left-wing journals such as the Yugoslav *Review of International Affairs,* and his press releases appear in the local newspapers *Machi, Phileleftheros,* and *Ky-pros.* In many ways Lyssarides, a talented artist as well as a man with definite political aspirations, is a mystery, and his actual influence in Cypriot affairs is difficult to quantify. He is married to an American from Detroit, Barbara Cornwall, who is also a writer and student of Afro-Asian politics.

When announcements were made in early 1969 that a nationalist party was being formed with the blessing of Makarios, Lyssarides immediately got on the bandwagon and set forth his plans to launch a socialist party in the island. Through the years he had gathered around him a sizeable group of followers who maintained complete personal loyalty to him. In fact, during the 1963 outbreak it was well known that he led a private "Peoples' Army" that was aiding the Greek Cypriot cause against the Turks in the way Lyssarides thought best. Archbishop Makarios considered the battle of Pentadaktalos, which this "army" won in 1964, to be deci-sive. Among Lyssarides' list of friends and supporters is the former head of the right-wing trade union SEK, one Petros Stylianou, who is now a member of Parliament. It was sup-posedly the influence of Lyssarides which caused Stylianou to take on some overt leftist ways and resulted in his defeat for re-election as the head of SEK in 1962. This is the kind of suasion Lyssarides has over key figures in Cyprus and it would be difficult to estimate the size of his ideological and volunteer entourage. By most standards, he is admitted to be a formidable consideration in the minds of nationalist as well as communist politicians.

In a ten-page statement issued in February 1969, Dr. Lys-sarides outlined policies on various issues for his proposed Democratic Union of the Center Party (EDEK):

> Foreign policy. The party supports the non-aligned policy of "positive neutrality" and friendship with the peoples, away from any power blocs.
>
> Cyprus problem. EDEK will strive for the right of self-determination for the Cypriot people: only a solution deriving from this would be a genuine democratic solution, but in the present conditions, the party adopts the policy of President

Makarios for a "feasible solution," for a unitary, independent, demilitarized Cyprus without foreign bases, and with safeguards for reasonable rights of Turkish Cypriots. The party will strive against any foreign-inspired solution.

Home affairs. Equal opportunities for all, law and order, and fair treatment of all citizens. The state should rid itself of all remnants of maltreatment and favoritism.

Farming policy. The land should belong to the farmers, whose per capita income should become one of the highest. Land belonging to churches and the government should be given to farmers. Land consolidation and reforms are essential. The co-operative movement should be strengthened.

Trade. The party favors a readjustment of the country's trade policy so that nations exporting goods to the island should be asked to take certain quotas of the island's farm products.

Labor. Workers must have a share of profits "if we want to increase productivity, and we do not want to make the rich richer and the poor poorer."

Health. EDEK advocates implementation of a general national health scheme.

Education. Free secondary school education, and establishment of a state theatre.

Industry. Nationalization of foreign-owned mines, and state control of the banking establishments.[32]

Dr. Lyssarides feels that EDEK is the only political party in Cyprus that is not affected by foreign pressures. Through small contributions he has raised over 4,000 pounds sterling to finance his newspaper *Nea* (News), founded in 1969, and to pay for the countless trips he makes into the villages in search of support. He says that he will run any campaign for political office on his voting record in the House of Representatives and he is prepared to defend his often independent stands on key issues. If ever forced into the position of looking abroad for either moral or material help, he thinks the left wing of the British Labour Party would be his first choice of a strong force with a similar philosophy. But money is not his most immediate problem—even though he has all but forsaken the practice of medicine—since Cyprus is small and the cost of a political campaign in any phase is not exorbitant. As a result, he does not see the faintest possibility of ever needing to "sell out" to a vested interest, as he accuses certain of his opposition nationalists of doing. So far as a coalition of either the left or the right is concerned, Lyssarides is willing to consider those options when the time comes to form a government with him at the helm. The EDEK appears to want to gain ascendancy through parliamentary socialism and does not loom as a militantly revolutionary party on the left.

Right-Wing Militants

On the right-wing side there are no revolutionary parties per se in Cyprus, even though at least three pro-*enosis* terrorist groups were operating clandestinely during 1969. The EOKA campaign of 1955–59 was the only manifestation of such a large-scale right-wing movement, and withered away with the formation of the Republic. Certain militants (ex-EOKA men) still exist in nationalist ranks; prominent among them are Minister of Labor Tassos Papadoupoulos, ex-Defense Minister Polykarpos Georghadjis, the editor of *Agon*, Nicos Kossis, and the editor of *Machi,* Nicos Samson. These men, along with Vassos Lyssarides, may have directed the fighting of the Greek Cypriots during the early stages of the 1963 violence before General Grivas returned to the island to take command of the National Guard.

Probably the only time that violence would be resorted to again by such individuals would be if Cyprus were either taken over or in imminent danger of being taken over by unwanted foreign elements, or in the case of a political upheaval following the retirement of Makarios. There is no evidence to connect any of these nationalist militants with the activities of the illegal—and possibly Athens-inspired—terrorist groups, known variously as the National Front (*Ethnikon Metapon*), Phoenix, or Akritas. These groups embarrassed Makarios on many occasions during 1969 and have been denounced by the government as criminal elements.

The New Political Parties in Cyprus

Other political groups in Cyprus are now in the process of formation. The Patriotic Front of Archbishop Makarios is apparently splintering up between at least four right-wing groups: the Unified Democratic Party, the Progressive Party, the Progressive Front, and the Democratic Center Party. The desire of one of the leaders of the pro-nationalist Unified Democratic Party, Georghadjis, was expressed this way:

It is common knowledge that the current problems of the various classes cannot be tackled effectively and satisfactorily without organized political life. Even if satisfactory solutions were to be given to the claims of the farmers, the employees, the workers, teachers, and policemen, there would still be a psychological vacuum of doubt which already exists because of the absence of a continuous link between the people and the government, and especially because of the non-participation actively of the people in the formulation of government policies and decisions.
    . . . the absence of political organization led to the languishing of the nationalist forces and cut them off from their leadership.
    . . . They might even become tools in the hands of persons and groups of people who exploited them for personal aims. This sad phenomenon should not be allowed to continue because it might prove disastrous to the nationalist front.[33]

Allied with Georghadjis is Glafkos Clerides, President of the House and a likely successor to Makarios, and about half of the SEK labor union.

The Socialist Party head, Dr. Lyssarides, made a veiled attack against the Clerides-Georghadjis movement when he said: "We, as true democrats and patriots, could never accept a covered parliamentary dictatorship that would lead to the end of freedom and the enslavement of the people." This was the reason why, he added, he had decided to issue his call to "all democrats" to form a front to make the people masters of their destiny under true popular democracy.[34] The leader of the Progressive Party, Mr. Nicos Samson, also attacked the United Democratic Party from the foreign involvement angle when he claimed that the British originally supported the idea for the movement in hopes that the nationalists would form only one party rather than separating as they did.[35]

The establishment of the Progressive Party was announced in February 1969, after consultations between agricultural and labor leaders, scientists, intellectuals, and many old EOKA fighters. The new party's primary aims are to be the preservation and strengthening of the island's Greek character, the evolution of the Cypriot people to higher levels of economic development and social progress, and the full democratization of public life through the application of the principle of rule on merit.[36] The movement is the personal creation of Samson and has little power or appeal to the populace.

The third pro-nationalist group is the Progressive Front, led by the right-wing farmers movement, PEK. This group has actively sought the support of the Orthodox Church as well as the anti-communist trade union and probably holds the allegiance of the other 50 per cent of SEK's membership. The Progressive Front released a statement from "senior officials of SEK" who said that following the decision for members to act on their own they had decided to collaborate with the Progressive Front, which they considered "the only one in line with the professional and national aims of the free labor movement."[37] The ostensible leader is Nicosia's mayor Ioannides, but the PEK leader Azzizas is the power behind the throne. Leading the pro-*enosis* right-wing opposition to Makarios is Dr. Takis Evdhokas, who won 4 per cent of the vote in the 1968 presidential contest. His group is called the Democratic Center Party and is quite small. Their main issue is "instant *enosis*," and this platform has less and less appeal to Greek Cypriots.

"Organized political life" has not yet come to Cyprus, so it is impossible to say what success any of the factions, right or left, will have. The date for the next parliamentary elections has not yet officially been set, but it is rumored that elections will be held in July 1970. Whenever they do occur in Cyprus, the nationalists under Clerides and Georghadjis should command a plurality. There always is the possibility of coalitions being made among any of the numerous right and left factions which appear to be forming, but the pro-Makarios forces should be able to withstand any opposition regardless of how it is constituted.

AKEL's Peaceful Strategy

AKEL has consistently emphasized its peaceful and parliamentary nature. When the party was still legally, though not completely, proscribed under the British in 1959, General Secretary

Papaioannou held an interview after the secret Ninth Party Congress. At that time, the AKEL leader outlined the party's strategy by explaining that "AKEL does not intend to ever impose socialism" but that it would "fight democratically and legally" to obtain a plurality and to convince Greeks and Turks that "socialism alone can secure a happy life for the people." He also stated that the AKEL program took into account the "freedom and independence of all Cypriot parties" (obviously referring to the Turks as well).[38]

Less than a year later Deputy General Secretary Fantis, commenting on why AKEL took no part in the EOKA struggle, claimed "AKEL is not a party which has been accustomed to adventurous action, but a party which sees everything in the light of the people's interests."[39] Then in 1962, the General Secretary found an occasion to describe his movement this way:

AKEL is a serious political party of the working people of Cyprus and criticizes whenever necessary, but it has the courage and the strength to support every good action from wherever it comes. AKEL never attempted to monopolize a struggle. It is always ready to cooperate on any matter concerning the people and its cause. AKEL is not distinguished for its arrogance, but for its modesty. It does not boast that it has known everything, and its brains are not inflated. It always learns from its mother, the people; it improves daily while in the service of the people from which it comes and for which it lives, struggles and sacrifices.[40]

While some of these sources may appear dated, there is very little difference between what AKEL stated six years ago and what the leadership says today. Though some new issues may have arisen, such as the current intercommunal talks between the island's Greeks and Turks, the underlying problems of Cyprus still remain. Thus, the General Secretary speaks in much the same way today as he has spoken since the creation of the Republic.[41]

Thus from the time of Cypriot independence to the present, AKEL has sought to project the image of a peace-loving political party, dedicated to legal means to achieve its ends. But the communists in Cyprus have not always been accepted in that manner by everyone, nor are they fully accepted in Cypriot political life. In 1962, Makarios told a British correspondent that regardless of what approach AKEL might use, should the communists ever "dominate Cyprus" they would be "dealt with" in a physical way by former EOKA activists and other nationalist militants.[42] From that time on, AKEL has lived in fear of losing its legal status and has worried for the well-being of its members. Since the outbreak of the troubles in 1963, AKEL has been reluctant to take any anti-nationalist positions, apparently valuing legality and safety more than pure communist ideology. In October 1967, when the Turkish community was apparently quiet, there were rumors that the then Minister of Interior Georghadjis was prepared to embark on a "red witch hunt." The clandestine radio station, the Voice of Cyprus, presumably communist-run, played up this alleged plot in an effort to incriminate AKEL's right-wing archenemy. More than once the following report was broadcast to listeners of the Voice of Cyprus:

> A plan similar to the one used against the Turkish Cypriot community in December 1963 will soon be used to annihilate Greek Cypriot communists. Under the slogan "the Greek Cypriot communists rebelled against the state" all AKEL members, leftwingers, and their sympathizers will be wiped off the face of this island.
>
> If Georghadjis gets the opportunity to implement his devilish plans, Cyprus will find itself in the midst of yet another unprecedented tragedy. As long as Georghadjis remains in office as interior minister, the danger remains and he has been sounding out U.S. Embassy officials on the likely American stand in the event of a communist rebellion in Cyprus. We understand that he has been discouraged by the American attitude.
>
> The signs are that his sick mind is bent on seeing his plans through to the end—plans which he considers to be for the achievement of the so-called national ideal. Whatever the case, we have some advice for Greek Cypriot communists and their sympathizers: The signal XC-67-19, whether broadcast by the Cyprus Broadcasting Corporation or published in any daily or weekly paper, will spell the beginning of the massacre of communists in Cyprus. This is the code they have agreed on.[43]

Later, the same clandestine radio announced that a "Blue Guard" had been formed among ex-EOKA terrorists pledged to eliminate every communist and sympathizer in a slow but sure way. Though there were a rash of bombings at the AKEL and PEO headquarters during the year, no concerted drive was ever initiated to rid the island of communists. When the mainland Turks threatened another invasion in November of 1967, the matter of Cypriot communism was pushed into the background once again. With a wry smile, that did not appear to be the epitome of innocence, Georghadjis later denied the whole plan.[44]

Summary of AKEL's Conflict with the Environment

Historically, communism in Cyprus has been tolerated because there was always some problem of greater concern to the majority of the islanders. Anti-British activity, supported by the outlawed KKK, was the major interest in the 1930's. After AKEL was formed in 1941, the Second World War demanded full attention, and the communists displayed their patriotism by joining in the effort on the side of the Allies. In the absence of any organized political following, AKEL did produce surprising election victories in 1943 and 1946, but again the war overshadowed these advances. The postwar strikes and the abortive attempts at violence during the Greek Civil War in the late 1940's was a complete miscalculation by the communists, causing the formation of a right-wing union and drawing stern opposition from the Orthodox Church. The early 1950's marked the beginning of the militant *enosis* drive, the leadership of which the communists could never manage to wrest away from the Church.

In 1955, when the Emergency Period was declared, communist organizations were again proscribed by the British, and ostensibly pushed far back into an ineffective limbo. After 1960, the trials and tribulations of a fledgling new state with a most unusual constitution took immediate precedence over any worries about a legal communist party that professed allegiance to the national hero, Archbishop Makarios. In what seemed to be a period of relative stability in 1962–63, some attention was focused on AKEL and its possible plans. But intercommunal trouble again broke out in 1963, and the threat of communism once more receded. The 1967 period of heated right-wing interest in AKEL was soon to be superceded by an external threat from Turkey, and preoccupation with this exists today, for good reason, within the Greek Cypriot government. In short, AKEL has usually been forced by over riding national conditions to back off from any strategy of its own and to give tactical support to the nationalist forces.

Consequently, as long as AKEL continues this modus operandi, it will probably remain legal but will hardly constitute a danger to the bourgeois regime of the nationalists. Makarios also appreciates this reality and, knowing how AKEL is impelled to support his policies, can consciously use the party as an ally to offset opposition of the *enosis* extremists and terrorists, as well as the disaffected elements among the pacific nationalists. The obvious question is whether AKEL will suffer a crisis of identity or simply stagnate while it waits for the opportune time to employ its long-range strategy for making Cyprus a socialist state.

The Soviet Union finds itself in a somewhat perplexing situation with regard to its loyal communist party in Cyprus. By trying to support the Greek Cypriot communists' self-determination goal, while concurrently searching for ways to patch up an age-old feud with the mainland Turks, the Soviet leaders have experienced the embarrassment, as has the United States, of having to "sit on the fence."[45] There were anti-Soviet demonstrations in Cyprus in the winter of 1966 after Chairman Kosygin made what was interpreted as an anti-*enosis* remark. Also a Russian cultural attache was declared persona non grata early in 1967 for being involved in a spy ring within the NATO countries. To add insult the Government of Cyprus even rejected the Soviet protest note after the demonstrations.

The Soviet desire to effect a solid rapprochement with Turkey—which along with Iran controls the Russian land route to the Arab countries—cannot give much comfort to AKEL. Simultaneously, this interest does not put the Kremlin leaders in much of a position to make open demands on Cypriot communists. Russia has allowed quiet neutrality to hide its true attitude and is apparently using much the same approach when it comes to any conflict situation between Greeks and Turks. For example, Soviet Ambassador Tolubeyev, to the gathering marking the 51st anniversary of the October Revolution held in Nicosia, made this safe statement: "The Soviet Union continually and always supports the independence and territorial integrity of the Cyprus Republic—the peaceful solution of the differences between the Greeks and Turks of Cyprus without any interference from outside."[46]

Of course, the Soviet Union is fully prepared to sacrifice any non-ruling communist party if the interests of the two happen to clash. Compared to the Russian stake in Turkey, Cyprus is small; and size has always been a determinant in Soviet policy-making despite some mistakes on this score in the past. It cannot be known if AKEL members understand this simple reality and if so whether it affects their behavior.

Despite past adversities and present dilemmas, the communists in Cyprus seem to persist with noteworthy patience and resilience. As of the winter of 1969, AKEL had not moved too far from its "united front from below" tactic, which characterized the immediate post-independence period. As a critical nationalist editorial described the AKEL position: the Cypriot communists were careful to put forth a "political resolution" which called for "national cooperation" with the other parties based on a "minimum program" designed to reach a "realistic" political solution. The editorial then concluded:

> If AKEL is satisfied with a "minimum" political program, the Cypriot nationalists by contrast would like to see everything coming under a maximum national program, to use the peculiar communist phraseology. Honest, clear, and permanent cooperation can be achieved only if in agreeing over the present we do not disagree over the future, and if in uniting on superficial matters we do not divide over innermost orientations.[47]

Despite the derisive tone of the editorial, it would seem that AKEL could have been having a problem explaining its program to the people. It is often true that the contorted language of certain of AKEL's public documents is used intentionally to confuse the reader. At other times pleasant words are used to show concern for the island's fate and genuine uneasiness over the future, so that AKEL can appear statesman-like and far above the political thicket. But more often than not, it is most important to look for what is not said in AKEL policy statements. Through this sort of analysis AKEL can be shown in recent history to have been against the *enosis* cause and far from an outspoken opponent of the Turkish Cypriots. (See Appendix C for a typical AKEL resolution.)

5: AKEL's Conflict and Integration with the International Environment

History of the Soviet Union's Relations with Cypriot Communists

The influence of the Soviet Union on the choice of leadership, policies, activities, and behavior of both the KKK and AKEL has been substantial. The Communist Party of Cyprus received official recognition by the Comintern in 1931 and in the same year was given its first punishment for its poor performance in the anti-British riots with the rightists. While there was a change in the KKK leadership at that time, there is no clear connection between that event and a directive from Moscow. Because of the Soviet Union's friendship with Kemal Ataturk in the early 1930's, there may have been pressure on the KKK to pay attention to the Turkish minority; in any case, such a policy position was reflected in the slogans of the time. After the KKK was proscribed by the British in 1933, the party did not amount to much politically for the rest of the decade. Thus, there is little reason to believe that the Communist Party of the Soviet Union (CPSU) was then particularly concerned with Cypriot affairs. Throughout the 1930's the island's communists were ostensibly against *enosis* and in favor of an independent Cyprus, a policy probably in accord with the classical Leninist line for "self-determination" of territories under colonial domination.

When it became apparent that the British government had no intention of legalizing the KKK and the underground party was not attracting adherents, it could have been—while there is no evidence to support this—on a signal from Moscow that a new organization was formed in 1941. Also, the clever decision to make the new party a respectable liberal-thinking group, following the communist line without initially admitting a direct connection with the movement, does not sound as if it were made by a defunct group of indigenous communists. The move was similar to the now familiar communist tactic of

156

creating a crypto-communist organization which could form a "national front" with respected members of society whenever expedient. AKEL's decision to join the war effort could have been spontaneous, but there was little choice after Russia allied itself with the West. The covert nature of AKEL was maintained until after the Second World War when it seemed that the Soviet Union would gain prestige by showing, despite the abolition of the Comintern, that its movement was worldwide and flourishing even in Mediterranean islands.

The censure of Servas in 1945 and the purge of General Secretary Ioannou in 1949 have the Stalinist trademark, but there does not seem to be any strong reason why the Soviet Union might have been dissatisfied with either of these long-time followers. Papaioannou was ambitious, and having ingratiated himself with the Kremlin, could have convinced them in an unusually forward thinking manner that a "cult of personality" was developing in Cyprus and should be nipped in the bud. In the case of Servas' downfall, it was later explained by saying he had "held the party back for many years, denounced anyone who did not agree with him," and had developed the "cult of personality" in the party along with the theory of his "indispensability."[1]

Papaioannou's elevation to AKEL's seat of power in 1949 was accepted by the Soviet Union without noticeable fanfare. His continuation in the job ever since is an apparent concession by the CPSU that he is successful and is fitted to the conditions of the host country. There is no record of AKEL ever having anything but support for Moscow before 1965 and no evidence of revisionists in the party. Allegedly, Papaioannou has used his support within the Soviet Union to beat down any opposition which might ever surface within the party's inner circles.

The decision by AKEL not to engage in or support the EOKA movement in 1955 is difficult to analyze. One strong Marxist and ex-AKEL member, George Cacoyannis, wrote his long critique in which his main thesis was that by turning down the chance to join EOKA, "the opportunistic leaders of AKEL had the audacity to distort Marxism and endeavor to twist it to their aid."[2] His interpretation of dogma was immediately challenged by AKEL with selected passages from communist writings that justified their position, but the apologia never had much impact on the public. The stand of the Soviet Union at this time was not enunciated with precision, even though the Kremlin line in 1958 became one of vocal support for the "liberation of the Cypriots from their foreign oppressors."[3] There is little doubt that Moscow saw scant advantage in having Cyprus joined to Greece, and AKEL may have taken its orders from the Soviet Union to be in opposition to this popular nationalistic cause, even though the mistake was ultimately recognized after the Republic of Cyprus was formed.

Soviet Policy Toward Cyprus
Since World War II

In general, while the Soviet Union attempted to exploit the unrest on Cyprus throughout the postwar era, it simultaneously had to consider the impact of its position on the Cypriot communists, the Greek majority on the island, and the Turkish minority, as well as its effects on Greece, Turkey, the United Kingdom, and the United States. Under these circumstances, Soviet policy toward Cyprus since the formation of NATO in 1949 has sometimes appeared ambivalent and contradictory.[4] Today Moscow simply says it "supports Cyprus' independence, sovereignty, and territorial integrity."[5] In reality, however, the fundamental Soviet strategic objectives vis-à-vis Cyprus have remained constant, despite continual shifts in tactics. These are (1) to exploit the dissension connected with the Cyprus issue in order to supplement other moves in a long-range campaign to intensify divisions within the NATO alliance; (2) to insure the removal of all vestiges of British influence on the island, including the abrogation of British military bases and overflight rights; and (3) to keep alive the unrest and political instability in Cyprus, thereby at least partially diverting the attention of the leaders of the U.S., the U.K., Greece, and Turkey from other problems.

Soviet tactics have deviated frequently in the last two decades. Notwithstanding certain overlaps and ambiguities, six distinct tactical phases of Soviet policy between 1949 and 1969 can be identified:

First Phase.—Overt cooperation by the U.S.S.R. From 1949 until Cyprus won its independence from the United Kingdom in August 1960, the U.S.S.R. worked closely with the indigenous Communist Party—overtly when circumstances permitted, and covertly and less actively during the five years when AKEL was outlawed. As soon as AKEL had regained its status as a legal political party when the Republic emerged, it enjoyed Moscow's vigorous and open support in its efforts to recoup its obvious losses and to strengthen its revolutionary potential, both as a political party and as the controlling element in its front organizations on Cyprus.

Second Phase.—Double tactics: support for AKEL, overtures to Makarios. Soviet tactics between August 1960 to June 1964 involved continuing support for AKEL, on the one hand, and initiating cautious overtures to the Makarios government on the other. Both AKEL and Moscow relied primarily on parliamentary tactics—supplemented by Soviet economic assistance to Makarios—to enhance the possibilities for achieving their mutually shared, long-term revolutionary goal. During this period the Cyprus question expanded into the international political arena and ceased to be an issue only among the guarantors of the Zurich-London Agreements: when Turkey threatened invasion, the matter was referred to the United Nations. Soviet decision-makers were thus compelled to deal with additional international political elements in their tactical approaches to the problem. The crisis after December 1963 afforded opportunities to attack the principal Western powers for interfering in what the Kremlin termed "Cypriot domestic affairs," which could enhance Russia's position with President Makarios. To this effect Khrushchev sent letters to the major powers warning against a planned NATO intervention. The Soviet ploy here was probably "to put pressure on Makarios," with the aid of AKEL, "to force the evacuation of the British military bases."[6]

Third Phase.—Khrushchev buys time. During the tactical phase, which lasted from late June to the end of August in 1964, the Soviet Union was faced with intense intercommunal military hostilities and Turkey's threat to invade the island. The U.S. made clear that it would support the U.N. peace-keeping force and work for a cease-fire. Greece intensified its support for President Makarios. Khrushchev undoubtedly decided that if he went too far he might risk provoking even more vigorous U.S. countermeasures and reduce rather than increase dissensions among the principal NATO powers. While he was not ready to abandon AKEL or antagonize Makarios, he did not want to send Soviet troops to assist the Archbishop and provoke an East-West confrontation. Moscow's tactics during this period were somewhat contradictory and cautious. Khrushchev was, in classical Leninist fashion, "buying time" in anticipation of a high-level Kremlin reassessment of the issue.

Fourth Phase.—The Kremlin courts Makarios. Between September 1964 and the end of the year, the Kremlin courted Makarios and his followers with offers of arms and expanded economic assistance. Further, to placate the Archbishop for Moscow's earlier equivocation, official Soviet pronouncements voiced loud opposition to the presence of the U.N. peace-keeping force on Cyprus. During this period, AKEL was virtually ignored and left to solve its own local problems. Apparently, the Soviet leaders had decided that these new tactics would not provoke a more vigorous U.S. series of countermeasures. The U.S.S.R. was repeating a policy it had applied to other newly emergent nations—fulfillment of its doctrinal commitment to support "national liberation movements" through offers of military and economic assistance to the indigenous charismatic leader. The short duration of this phase of the Kremlin's tactics and the fact that the agreements negotiated were not fully implemented suggests that an element of deception was involved. The ouster of Khrushchev after the agreements were negotiated undoubtedly prompted the new Soviet regime to modify its tactics as soon as it had an opportunity to reconsider the Cyprus problem. The abstention of the Soviet Union on a pro-Makarios U.N. General Assembly resolution in December 1965 was a decided slap in the face of AKEL.

Fifth Phase.—The U.S.S.R. seeks rapprochement with Turkey. The period from January 1965 to late April 1967 was characterized by a gradual abandonment of political and military support for Cypriot President Makarios, and by concerted efforts to establish a rapprochement with Turkey. An obvious corollary to the Kremlin's overtures to the Turkish leaders was a shift from endorsement of *enosis* to advocacy of the "two communities" solution to the Cyprus problem, which had long been espoused by the Turkish government. This, in turn, led to an increasingly strained relationship between Moscow and AKEL; the Communist Party of Cyprus still found it advantageous to continue—at least ostensibly—to endorse Makarios' pro-*enosis* arguments. However, AKEL did not see fit to break its ties with the U.S.S.R. completely. Ultimately, the U.S.S.R. responded to Turkish pressures and not only stopped its own arms shipments to Makarios but even condemned subsequent military assistance from Czechoslovakia. These changes in Soviet tactics not only embarrassed AKEL and antagonized President Makarios but also introduced new strains in Soviet relations with Greece.

Sixth Phase.—From 1967 to the present, continued loyalty of the AKEL to the U.S.S.R. The Soviets in July 1967 adopted an official stance of watchful waiting, although they undoubtedly have tried to influence the Turkish government through diplomatic channels not to agree to any Cypriot settlement which would threaten the continued legal existence of AKEL and its front groups. Nor do they want to do anything that might help strengthen NATO's southeastern flank. The Soviet leaders have committed themselves to a vigorous endorsement of independence and the cessation of all "foreign" interference in the internal affairs of the Republic of Cyprus. This may be interpreted as an attitude favorable toward Turkey's line on Cyprus, but still not in total disregard of AKEL's position. To preserve its flexibility of action, the Kremlin now makes most of its interim moves through private diplomacy instead of through official public pronouncements.

After the Turkish invasion threat of November 1967, the Soviet leaders could not effectively decide on a new detailed plan of action. Given the U.S.S.R.'s current interests in the Eastern Mediterranean, Soviet policy toward Cyprus could again be in a state of transition. The current tactical phase which began as a consequence of the April 1967 coup in Greece seems to be primarily a holding operation. As long as the Cyprus problem remains "a bone of contention between two NATO members," it will continue to provide "a possible additional point of entry for Soviet influence in the Eastern Mediterranean."[7]

AKEL's support of Russia's Czech invasion of 1968 reinforces the solid Cypriot communist alignment with the U.S.S.R. AKEL has been so consistent in its loyalty to the Soviet leaders that Moscow may feel it can give the Cypriot communists a great deal of apparent autonomy without actually ever losing control. If in the process AKEL must suffer from the contortions of Soviet policy, it will simply have to accept its fate. It seems obvious that the Soviets have no intention of damaging their recently improved relations with Turkey in order to appear more sympathetic to the cause of AKEL or the Greek Cypriot nationalists.

Inputs from Ruling Communist Parties

AKEL's contacts with ruling communist parties are generally handled by the members of its General Secretariat, all of whom, particularly Papaioannou, are inveterate travelers. Visits to the bloc countries are regular, and often publicly justified as being for "health treatments"—Papaioannou has chronic gall bladder problems and Ziartides is afflicted with sinusitus, which apparently "require" them to take a number of trips to Moscow every year.[8] Usually strategy meetings take place when communist leaders appear together in Cyprus or elsewhere on the pretext of some innocuous function. There is little evidence of specific couriers going back and forth between the bloc capitals and Nicosia, but Papaioannou does spend a good deal of time in Bulgaria, which is the nearest pro-Soviet country to Cyprus. Such meetings are reportedly to enable an exchange of views on party matters and international developments, but they may also be assumed to be the vehicle for giving guidance to AKEL on the Soviet line.

Instructions for AKEL from the CPSU are also probably derived from the series of decisions taken at the various conventions of communist parties meeting in Moscow or in other capitals. In October 1960, Papaioannou attended the 43rd anniversary of the Soviet Revolution in Moscow and stayed over for the meeting of 81 communist parties the next month. Upon his return, an editorial praised the conference and hailed the CPSU as the "vanguard of the Communist movement." The "Moscow declaration" from the conference, continued the editorial, "constitutes a sermon and a motive of brotherly struggle for peace all over the world."[9]

On crucial policy matters which confront AKEL, it is believed that the Soviet Union advises the General Secretary of AKEL directly. The rank and file of the party, as well as the Central Committee at times, are not aware that a policy question is being deliberated until a decision is made and then circulated to the lower echelons by the General Secretary. On less sensitive issues, the Soviet line can be transmitted openly through press wire services and via the bloc radio, which transmits programs daily in Greek to listeners in Cyprus. In addition to travel contacts and propaganda campaigns, the U.S.S.R. also makes inroads in the cultural fields. For example, the Cypriot-Soviet League of Cultural Relations, organized in March 1961, sponsors regular exhibits of Soviet scientific achievements, literary works, books for children, and recordings of Russian folk and classical music. Orders and subscriptions are always accepted during such exhibits at very low prices.

The Soviet Union, in spite of its conflicting strategic interests, still tries to demonstrate its concern for AKEL and the Cypriots. The U.S.S.R. maintains the largest embassy in Nicosia with over seventy members, some of whom can speak either Greek or Turkish. All the other pro-Soviet bloc countries also have sizeable delegations in Cyprus and the total complement of foreign communists far exceeds the analogous bodies from the West. All of these individuals make a practice of traveling over the island at an indefatigable pace, picking up sentiments and spreading as much good will as they can. Furthermore, Cyprus is an unusual example of a country in which the legal communist party is so well organized and trustworthy that members of AKEL are hired by communist embassies to fill jobs which in other countries are reserved for an embassy's own nationals.

Since independence, the communist bloc has become active in all fields—political, military, economic, and cultural. For example, the Soviet Union purchased the island's surplus stocks of raisins, a heavy burden on the economy, in exchange for Soviet fuel oil, cement, and lumber in both 1963 and 1968. Moreover, other communist countries have concluded bilateral trade agreements with Cyprus providing for import and export of a variety of commodities which at the end of 1968

163

amounted to 9 per cent of Cyprus' trade. Poland was previously awarded an engineering contract to expand the port facilities at Famagusta for a price equal to only half of the estimated cost. These agreements were well received by a sizeable portion of the population and improved the position of AKEL. In the summer of 1964, when anti-Western feeling was at its peak, the Soviets responded to a request from the Greek Cypriots and sent sizeable arms shipments to Cyprus, which were gratefully received; the Czechs did the same thing in 1967.

The offer of training and official-visitor grants by the U.S.S.R. and its satellites to government officials and other Cypriots connected with the island's political, economic, and industrial life also contributes to the enhancement of AKEL's prestige. Even in the last few years, returning grantees say they have been impressed and pleased with Soviet hospitality and the implicit and explicit support given by the Soviets concerning the Cyprus problem. In March 1969, a Soviet agricultural delegation put the following coloration on the Kremlin's policy toward Cyprus: "The Soviet delegates assured the participants in the talks of the support of the Soviet organizations and the Soviet people to the Cyprus people's struggle for a unified and independent Cyprus."[10]

The Soviet Union must see the value of Cyprus as an independent, neutralist bastion in a politically sensitive region. It also probably finds the utility of Cyprus and AKEL in psychological and symbolic measures which redound to the prestige of the Soviet Union as the leader of a Marxist movement which is considered legitimate even in patently hostile states.

AKEL's Perceived Position in the World Communist System

By any conceivable criteria, AKEL must surely be considered one of the most disciplined and docile communist parties in the world. One might justifiably ask why a country so small has so large a communist party. The obvious answer seems to be that there are substantial material rewards for being a party member in Cyprus. This vested interest has kept the leadership intact and the followers in tow, both forever beholden to the Soviet Union. There are no philosophical minds of any stature which have survived the rigid authoritarianism of the Papaio-annou regime, and consequently there are never any sustained hints of deviating from the stated Moscow line. What minor deviations AKEL must express to secure its domestic position are accepted as expedient and temporary.

The Soviet Union, therefore, takes AKEL for granted and with statements such as the following ever ready to fall from the lips of AKEL members, the Russian attitude is indeed understandable:

> We [AKEL] do not stand alone in our struggle. The people of Cyprus enjoy the sympathy and support of the mighty and invincible socialist camp, the first country building communism—the Soviet Union—many countries, which have cast off the yoke of imperialism, and all nations fighting for the triumph of freedom and peace on earth.[11]

Two years later, the General Secretary wrote: "The great socialist camp, headed by the Soviet Union, came forth in defense of the just cause of the nation [sic] of Cyprus."[12]

Admittedly, these statements came before the obvious Soviet overtures to Turkey in 1965, so in 1968 AKEL tried to place the Russians in a good light by emphasizing benefits to the Cypriots not in the political arena but in the economic realm of trade:

> It is the Soviet Union which solved our acute problem of disposing of our vine products, thanks to its willingness to buy all our raisin stocks. Thanks to the Soviet market, thousands of vine growers have been freed from the nightmare which tortured them for years, of uncertainty regarding the disposal of their products which sometimes rotted.[13]

By the fall of 1969, however, AKEL had fallen back into its traditional mode of unwavering allegiance to Moscow, as this editorial illustrates:

> The Soviet Union supports Cyprus' independence, sovereignty, and territorial integrity. The Soviet Union has always consistently and steadily supported this position, which is also in keeping with the officially proclaimed Cyprus Government line. As the Cypriot people well know, this support has had its vigorous expression not only in the political sector, with the well-known Soviet statements

on Cyprus during every crucial phase of our problem, and in the diplomatic field, with the important speeches of Soviet delegates at the United Nations and other international organizations—this support has also been manifested in the most practical, and we would say saving manner, in the form of military and financial aid the Soviet Union granted Cyprus in the most difficult moments of its modern history.

The Cypriot people are of course grateful for this support, which constituted one of the decisive factors contributing to small Cyprus' ability to foil the imperialist plans for its enslavement.[14]

Considering such current statements it is difficult, if not impossible, to foresee AKEL ever forsaking Moscow. Even if AKEL action takes the form of future collaboration with the nationalist forces of the right or left so as to adapt to the electoral conditions of Cyprus, it would hardly be done without regard to the effect such a move might have on the Soviet Union. This is another of AKEL's serious limitations. (See Appendix C.)

AKEL's Attempts to Influence the CPSU

After the U.S.S.R. sent massive arms shipments to Makarios in support of the AKEL and Greek Cypriot aspirations, it later found that not all elements in the complex Cyprus situation were subject to external control. The very intensity of the intercommunal bitterness and fighting on the island, along with new developments in Soviet relations with Ankara, caused Moscow to make some tactical adjustments in 1965. Following its reputation as a docile communist party, AKEL had no record of ever trying to influence any of the ruling communist parties up to then. But the change of policy on the part of the Soviet Union, which could have threatened AKEL's domestic position had it been accepted without some dissent, forced the Cypriot communists to take an atypical stand in 1965.

When AKEL had belatedly and reluctantly swung over to a position, however vague, in support of Greek Cypriot nationalist aims and *enosis*, Soviet Foreign Minister Gromyko declared in a radio interview in January 1965 that the "internal organization of the Cypriot state is a matter for the Cypriots themselves" to determine. And he went on to suggest that, among other alternatives, "they may choose the federal form."[15] This suggestion of a federation as a possible solution of the Cyprus problem was acutely distressing to AKEL. In order to satisfy the Greek Cypriots, the party had to say something critical of the Soviet suggestion, but at the same time it could not afford to alienate the Soviet leaders.

Accordingly, its response was a conscious attempt to meet both of these conflicting pressures. On January 26—immediately after General Secretary Papaioannou and two other AKEL officials returned from an "enlightenment mission" to the Soviet-bloc countries—the party's Central Committee met and issued a statement declaring that it rejected the federal system for Cyprus "for reasons of principle and because it is an erroneous and impractical idea [which would help] the divide-and-rule policies of the imperialists." The AKEL statement, however, was careful to approve other parts of the Gromyko interview—such as his expression of Soviet opposition to foreign intervention and his call for the removal of foreign bases and the maintenance of the island's independence, sovereignty, and territorial integrity—as a "most positive and immense contribution." In conclusion, the statement insisted—somewhat optimistically—that "the Soviet Union continues to stand by Cyprus and will defend the Cyprus case along with Greece in the United Nations."[16]

A short while later, on February 7, 1965, General Secretary Papaioannou again referred to the Gromyko interview in noticeably cautious terms. Addressing an extraordinary party meeting, he stated that "our party disagrees with Mr. Gromyko's reference to federation," but he noted that the Soviet Foreign Minister had also said that "it was up to the people of Cyprus to decide this question." Papaioannou went on to reject charges of a Soviet "betrayal" of Cyprus and asserted that the Russians were and always had been friendly to the Greek Cypriot cause.[17]

The rapprochement between the Soviet Union and Turkey was confirmed in August 1965 by Prime Minister Urguplu's state visit to Moscow; he was the first Turkish leader to make such a visit in 30 years. This placed AKEL in a situation similar to that of the Greek Communist Party during the Greek Civil War, when it had to adapt itself to a painful Soviet decision on the delicate issue of Macedonian independence. In the

Cyprus situation, while recent Soviet policy may be said to have helped avert a Turkish invasion of the island, it certainly has not satisfied anyone involved, and it has made the Greek Cypriot community aware of Soviet duplicity. As former AKEL General Secretary Ploutis Servas caustically remarked, "When it comes to making Russian policy on Cyprus, AKEL is not part of Moscow's planning process."[18]

The Soviet antipathy to *enosis,* to which AKEL then paid lip service, was shown at a meeting of the U.N. Security Council in August 1965. The Russian delegate, Morozoff, inferred that his government supported a federal solution to the problem. When it was suggested in Cyprus that Moscow's opposition to *enosis* was due to the fact that this would link Cyprus with a NATO-member country, AKEL countered by claiming that the Soviet line was based on the principles of the national integrity of Cyprus and non-intervention in its internal affairs.[19]

Whatever the misgivings of AKEL leaders over the anti-*enosis* position mirrored in the Soviet-Turkish rapprochement, they did not voice them until December 18, 1965. A day earlier, the U.N. General Assembly's Political and Security Committee had debated a pro-Greek Cypriot resolution calling on all member nations to "respect the sovereignty, unity, independence, and territorial integrity of Cyprus and to refrain from any foreign intervention or interference." On the final vote in the committee, the Soviet Union and the other communist countries (with the exception of Cuba and Yugoslavia) abstained, even though the Political Committee had before it a Soviet-sponsored draft resolution condemning any interference in the internal affairs of other states. This communist action triggered an immediate and unprecedentedly sharp reaction from the AKEL leadership. The following statement appeared on the front page of *Haravghi* the morning after the vote:

This position of the Soviet Union and of the other socialist countries is wholly disappointing to the Politburo of the Central Committee of AKEL and to the Cypriot people. . . . The Politburo of the Central Committee of AKEL maintains its belief that the Soviet Union and the other socialist countries, which in the past gave significant and fruitful spiritual and material aid to the struggle of Cyprus, a fact which is esteemed by the Cypriot people, will finally vote for the resolution of the 32 non-committed countries in the General Assembly of the United

Nations, thereby furnishing the additional strength to secure the necessary two-thirds majority for a pro-Cyprus resolution.[20]

Despite this plea, the Soviet bloc again abstained the next day when the resolution was put to a vote in the General Assembly. It cannot be said with certainty what the Soviets hoped to gain by this maneuver, but it was one that provided no satisfaction to the Turks, the Greeks, or the Communist Party of Cyprus. All that AKEL could do was try to forget the matter and hope that the U.S.S.R. would see fit to modify its position in the future along lines more palatable to the Greek Cypriots.

Presumably with that end in mind, AKEL General Secretary Papaioannou and his deputy, Andreas Fantis, flew to Moscow in January 1966 for talks with CPSU Central Committee members Suslov and Ponomarev. After lengthy discussions, a joint communique was issued affirming, among other things, the Soviet belief "that the Cyprus problem can be solved through peaceful means, and that this necessitates the safeguarding of the rights and interests of the two ethnic communities." This part of the communique was apparently calculated to please the Turks rather than the Greek Cypriots, but the AKEL leaders did not leave Moscow entirely empty-handed: they could at least find some satisfaction in the communique's further statement that the Soviet Union "supports the abrogation of the restrictive ties imposed on the Cypriot people under the Zurich and London Agreements."[21] Still, they must surely have gone home with the feeling that the U.S.S.R. was not firmly behind their own position, and that of Archbishop Makarios, on the future of Cyprus.

The visit of the AKEL leaders to Moscow was followed up with an article by Andreas Fantis in which he spelled out AKEL's opposition to a federal solution—though he attacked as "imperialist complications" the "invented theory of two separate national communities" and federation. But the article was surely an implicit reminder to the Soviet Union that further references to federation would be unacceptable to AKEL.[22] This point was pressed home by Papaioannou in his report to the 11th Party Congress in Nicosia at the beginning of March. After thanking the Soviet Union for its "most important aid . . . its arms and its strong voice," he said that

AKEL "could not but criticize" references to federation in statements made by Gromyko.[23] Replying to this rebuke, the leader of the Soviet delegation, A. M. Rumyantsev, reiterated the terms of the joint Soviet-AKEL statement of January, and spoke of the Soviet Union's "consistent support" for the independence, sovereignty, and territorial integrity of Cyprus.[24]

AKEL Attitudes Toward Important Issues in the Communist World

The Cypriot communists have explicitly aligned themselves with the Soviet Union in the Sino-Soviet split. On September 29, 1963, following a plenary session, the party Central Committee issued a 5,000-word statement which included a passage denouncing the Chinese communists and their "civil war methodology." The statement declared that AKEL's aim was to bring about a communist Cyprus, but that the "proper" way to achieve this was through "absolutely democratic and peaceful methods."[25] General Secretary Papaioannou reconfirmed the party's position three years later in stating that "our party condemns all splitting activities and fully supports the striving of the CPSU and other fraternal parties for the firm unity [sic] of the international communist and workers' movement."[26]

Despite the fact that the leaders of AKEL have friendly relations with and a high regard for the Italian communists, they look upon "polycentricism" as another "splitting activity" and consequently refuse to consider the ramifications or potentialities this concept could offer. While AKEL leaders must surely see the slow but irresistible change of world communist parties into the natural political styles of their host countries, AKEL still follows the Soviet model. This is so because the CPSU obviously continues to maintain undue influence in the affairs of communists in Cyprus, regardless of minor tactical disagreements with AKEL.

This predilection was surely reconfirmed in August 1968 when AKEL unequivocally backed the Soviet Union in the Czech invasion. In a more reflective mood in London a few weeks later, Papaioannou put the AKEL position this way:

170

The Cypriot working people regretted the course taken by events in Czechoslovakia, because they were hoping that the Czechoslovak leadership would take all the measures which, jointly with the other Warsaw Pact countries, had been decided on to effectively confront those who were undermining socialism, both internally and externally. The fact that the five Warsaw Pact countries were compelled to give even military assistance to Czechoslovakia shows that very serious dangers were threatening the socialist achievements and peace. The Cypriot people are confident that the people of Czechoslovakia, under the leadership of the Communist Party and with the resolute help of the five socialist countries of the Warsaw Pact, will successfully solve all the problems created by the subversive antisocialist forces, with the assistance of the imperialists-revanchists, and will firmly move forward to translation into practice of a program of development of the socialist economy and socialist democracy.[27]

In June of 1969, AKEL once again traveled the well-worn road to Moscow to occupy its seat in the often-postponed conference of 75 communist parties from around the world. AKEL had attended the previous communist world congress in 1960 and loyally followed the Soviet Union's lead each time it proposed such a conference in the intervening years. AKEL was one of the 68 parties which met in Budapest in February 1969 to plan for the Moscow meeting, and was at many of the other preparatory meetings which had failed to reach agreement. The AKEL delegation at Moscow consisted of General Secretary Papaioannou, Central Committee member Savvides, and Politburo member Pombouris. At a press conference, the delegation explained why they were at the Moscow meeting:

We believe that the conference has particular significance for the Cypriot people who, under present conditions, are in great need of international solidarity and help to achieve the successful outcome of their hard struggle. In this respect, AKEL's participation in the conference constitutes a direct contribution to the Cypriot people's struggle for a fully independent, unified, territorially intact, and demilitarized Cyprus.[28]

Dutifully, AKEL signed the final conference document and managed to skirt the issue of the "Brezhnev Doctrine" of limited sovereignty before, during, and after the meeting.

AKEL's Relations with Other Non-ruling
Communist Parties

Prior to independence for Cyprus, AKEL was thought to receive its policy guidance from the British communist party. AKEL has always maintained a contact man in London and through this person could keep abreast of developments in the British capital. Before independence, this person was Georgios Pefkos and the last known individual was Giannis Sophocles. While AKEL is now considered autonomous and no longer depends on the British communist party, it is important that an AKEL man be stationed in England. There are over 100,000 Cypriots in London alone and not an insignificant percentage of these are overt communists or fellow travelers. Moreover, London is one of the few places in the free world where a Turkish Cypriot could openly admit to being a communist and feel safe. It may be assumed that much of the work directed toward the Turks in Cyprus—and possibly even to those in Turkey—is planned in London by AKEL members living there.

The adjunct of AKEL in London has existed under a number of different names since it was founded as the "Cypriot Communist Party of Great Britain" in 1931. It later became the "Cypriot Branch of the Communist Party of Great Britain" until it was pressured by the British communist party to end what appeared to be a faction. The present British General Secretary, John Gollan, insists that there is only one communist party in Great Britain and that the ex-Greek Cypriot communists who are British citizens must join it and follow its line.[29] Nevertheless, there is a communist-front group called the "Union of Cypriots in England" which has about 1,250 members. This organization operates mainly in the Camdentown section of London, where it maintains a social center mainly for Greek Cypriot immigrants.

The Greek Cypriot communists living in London thus tend to follow the AKEL line but keep up close relations with the British party, even though some are ineligible to join because of the passports they carry. The London-based Greek Cypriot communists put out a weekly paper in Greek, *Vema* (Life), which has a circulation of some 6,000, and they generally support Labour candidates when no communists are running in elections.[30] The British communist party insists that it does not interfere with AKEL, but it does express its solidarity and fraternity with the Cypriot communists. The British party tries to keep close ties with all the nations now under or formerly under British colonialism, but there has not been recently a "British Commonwealth Communist Parties" meeting such as those which were held in 1947 and 1954.

Before 1960 relations with the Italian Communist Party were substantial in the field of labor; PEO leaders were known to spend much time in Rome. This is less the case now that Ziartides and others are free to travel behind the Iron Curtain. But AKEL still thinks enough of the Italian communists to have sent a delegation to their 1969 Congress in March. In some ways AKEL must envy the creative thinking that emanates from the Italian Communist Party, especially in its dealings with the Church and the socialists. Nonetheless, AKEL is reluctant to introduce any of this Italian-bred revisionism into its own circles.

There do not seem to be very many contacts with the illegal parties in the Arab countries, and AKEL relations with the badly split Israeli communists are not overly intimate. Notwithstanding the Soviet stand on the Arab-Israeli issue, AKEL and the Israeli communists have a geographical if not fraternal bond, as is indicated in this statement by one of the latter:

> We know the imperialist powers. They create conflicts because of their own narrow interests. This is the way it happened between the Israelis and Arabs, and this is the way we see it on Cyprus today, where the imperialists have planted discord between Greeks and Turks, who have lived peacefully side by side through centuries [sic]. Israel's communists have pointed to the dangers connected with the Cyprus struggle. We maintain that the aim of the U.S. and England on Cyprus is to transform the island into a military base directed against the national social liberation movement in the Middle East. We do not believe they will succeed, for the popular resistance to the English-American policy is very strong.[31]

AKEL seems to have better relations with the pro-Arab RAQAH (a faction which split from the original Israeli communist party, MAQI, in 1965) than with the nationalist group (still called MAQI), as indicated by the meeting in Nicosia of the RAQAH leaders in December 1968. (See Appendix F for the list of delegates to AKEL's Twelfth Party Congress, 1970.)

AKEL does meet with other non-ruling communist parties in formal settings such as the Conference of the Communist Parties of the Capitalist Countries of Europe, held in June of 1965. This was a particularly interesting meeting since it came on the heels of Gromyko's controversial endorsement of the federation solution for the Cyprus problem. While this particular issue was not raised specifically in the final communique, the conference did pass a resolution supporting the "Cypriot people's right to self-determination."[32] This was markedly different than the Soviet position, which carefully tried to show for the sake of the mainland Turks that Cyprus had two communities, one larger and one smaller, but both with the implied right of "self-determination." AKEL apparently was successful in selling the same position both at the 1966 Tricontinental Conference in Havana and at the April 1968 meeting of Mediterranean leftist groups held in Rome.

AKEL's Relations with the Greek Communist Party

Relations with the illegal KKE party in Greece exist but are not considered to be close. After the original Communist Party of Cyprus was ordered by the Comintern to report to the British communist party in 1931, the ties between Cypriot and Greek communists became tenuous. Some Cypriot students went to Greece to fight in the Greek Civil War (1947–49), but AKEL gave no more than verbal support to the communist cause, though it assumed some degree of militant activities at the same time in Cyprus. By and large the Greek Civil War was the determining factor in formulating the present attitude which AKEL holds for the KKE—it is a party of extremist revolutionaries who want AKEL to become more aggressive than conditions will allow in Cyprus. While the two parties were fraternal in the 1950's, such demands today are in direct conflict with the AKEL policy of close cooperation with the Makarios government and therefore are a cause of tension. In the early days of the EOKA struggle—especially before Zachariades was deposed in 1956 as General Secretary of the KKE—the communist slogan, faithfully echoed by EDA (the crypto-communist legal party in Greece), was: "a free Cyprus

united with a free Greece," the word "free" meaning a communist-dominated state. Since most mainland and Cypriot
Greeks were passionately committed to *enosis,* "the communist agitation, unhindered by any consideration of allied
Western unity, and prudently clothed in purely patriotic
phraseology, was of wide appeal."[33]

AKEL—as the Soviet Union—has taken no stand on the
current deep split in the KKE between the forces of Koli-
yannis (pro-Moscow) and Partsalidis (revisionist), since such
a move would further rupture the Greek communists. One of
the chief explanations why a rivalry exists between Greek
and Cypriot communists could be that while the Soviet Union
might consider the KKE a more important party in the world-
wide movement, AKEL feels it is domestically much the
stronger and more influential of the two. Also both parties
are proud, considering themselves autonomous and capable;
thus, they resist attempts at mutual support for fear it may
appear undignified or degrading. Moreover, AKEL knows it
has developed some respectability in Cyprus and this is even
more prized now that the right-wing junta is governing Greece.
In general, Cypriots have little confidence in mainland Greeks,
who are facetiously called *"calamaras"* to indicate their pomp-
ousness. Getting away from nationalist fervor, mainland and
Cypriot Greeks are realistically opposed to one another because of psychologically deep-seated hostilities; this may even
carry over to the communists of the two states.

Irrespective of what rivalries or jealousies may exist below
the surface between AKEL and KKE leaders, the following
message was sent by the AKEL Central Committee on the
occasion of the KKE's 50th anniversary in 1968:

Dear Comrades: On the occasion of the KKE's 50th anniversary,
the AKEL Central Committee addresses a most cordial salute to
the brotherly KKE. We greet the party of Greece's working class,
which has been struggling for 50 years to raise the Greek working
people's standard of living, and for democratic liberties, justice,
and socialism.

In the course of this 50-year-period and of the struggle for a
new, joyful, and happy Greece, the KKE and the Greek working
people have suffered many trials. Today Greece is suffering under
a fascist dictatorship while its best children are either in prison
and concentration camps or being persecuted. In this situation

the KKE, as the Greek working people's party, shoulders new and more serious duties. In order to respond to these duties, all the Greek communists, all the progressive forces, all the Greek democrats must rally. This will enable the waging of decisive struggle for the overthrow of the fascist dictatorship and the opening of the road toward a new, democratic, and progressive Greece.

On the occasion of the KKE's 50th anniversary, we whole-heartedly hope for unity of the Greek communists and democrats and complete success in their struggles.

Long live the KKE. Long live the unenslaved Greek people. Long live the Greek people's democratic forces.[34]

The off-handed "hope for unity of the Greek communists" is the boldest statement AKEL has made on the KKE schism, which is growing more and more irreconcilable.

The actual extent to which mainland Greek communists are operating in Cyprus is not altogether clear. It may be assumed that expatriated KKE members can come to Cyprus from Iron Curtain countries with impunity and that many do. (There was no evidence, on the other hand, that any KKE member was at AKEL's Twelfth Party Congress in March 1970, even though sixteen countries sent representatives.) Whether the KKE is working at a program different from AKEL's when they are in the island is a difficult question to answer. The time communists from the Greek mainland were supposedly found to be functioning independently in Cyprus had to do with the "*Aspida* affair." *Aspida* (shield) was a leftist group of Greek Army officers whose stated purpose was to "democ-ratize" the armed forces, whereas in truth they hoped to cause it to disintegrate in a gradual manner. The plot was first made public in 1966 and gradually unfolded to show that many people in high places were involved, particularly Andreas Papandreou, the son of the former Prime Minister.

An official investigation soon established the presence of conspirators of center-leftist convictions within the Greek Army ranks. After rumors that political guidance for the organization was being provided by Andreas Papandreou and that several other Cabinet ministers were involved, Prime Minister George Papandreou would only place responsibility for the conspiracy on unnamed "dark forces," which he felt were trying to bring his government down. Throughout 1966 and early 1967 the leftists continued their pressure tactics, attempting to secure through Parliament a dispensation of immunity from prosecution for Andreas Papandreou, who had reason to fear the disclosures which would come to light about his connection with *Aspida* if he had to face a court of law. Furthermore, the younger Papandreou refused to help relax political tensions and persisted in making forceful statements about his eventual rise to power.

At the same time, General Grivas in Cyprus was carrying out his own investigation of the National Guard and felt he had produced conclusive evidence that the conspiracy did exist in the island. In cooperation with the Greek intelligence service (KYP), he began to weed out suspected Greek Army officers and have them sent back to Athens to stand trial. Again it is not clear if the KKE were in any way connected with *Aspida,* but the situation was settled on April 21, 1967, when the right-wing colonels of the Greek Army carried out their successful coup d'état and proceeded to incarcerate Greek leftists whether they might be communists or not.

AKEL's Relations with Other International Organizations

The one non-communist grouping in which AKEL may have a covert role to play, as determined by the Soviet Union, is the British Commonwealth. The Indian communist party might be considered the strongest in the Commonwealth because its numerical size is fully ten times as large as AKEL's. But the Indian communists are hampered from taking a leading role in furthering Soviet interests in the Commonwealth for three overriding reasons: (1) there is already a big enough job for them to do within their own country; (2) there is the anthropological barrier which makes the Indian a second-class citizen in certain of the Commonwealth nations; and (3) there is a deep split in India between followers of Peking and Moscow. Even though the British communist party, including that of Northern Ireland, is larger than AKEL, the communists in Cyprus are far more active and close to Moscow than the parties in the British Isles. The legal communist parties in Australia, Canada, Ceylon, and New Zealand are very small and far from capable of exercising any power. The other Commonwealth states in Asia and Africa which have communist movements have outlawed them and consequently these parties (not the countries) are insignificant. It is not clear what the Soviet designs for the British Commonwealth may include, but whatever they may be AKEL is perforce the pivotal point in whatever long-range communist strategy exists for that particular international organization of the Free World.

Since AKEL has been supporting the Makarios government it has not taken independent action in any of the international organizations of which Cyprus is a member—the U.N., the Council of Europe, or the Commonwealth, for example. AKEL has consistently clamored about the dangers that would face Cyprus if it should join Western-oriented associations such as NATO or the European Common Market, and this follows the Soviet line of attempting to reduce Cypriot ties with the West.* AKEL has, on the other hand, encouraged Makarios' participation in all conferences of non-aligned nations. This deliberate courting of the Afro-Asian and neutralist countries paid off with a favorable U.N. General Assembly resolution passed in December 1965. The vote was 47 in favor, 54 abstentions, and only 5 opposed (the United States, Turkey, Iran, Pakistan, and Albania); but the resolution has turned out to be of little help to the Makarios government. The President's positions with the neutralists on occasion have chagrined the Cypriot communists. This was particularly true at the Belgrade Conference in 1961, when Makarios called for a U.N. plebiscite in which both the East and West Germans could decide whether the country should remain divided. The communist press was most critical, but this did not cause Makarios to back off from his stand.

*Papaioannou warned of "the inexorable consequences" for Cyprus should the island decide to join the European Common Market. He pointed out that Cyprus could become a new colonial state for foreign monopolies, market for their products, source of inexpensive material, and, moreover, as a result of subsequent permanent unemployment, a source of inexpensive labor force for the countries of the Common Market. He concluded that, consequently, "our position—regardless of whether Britain joins the Common Market or not—is that Cyprus should neither join nor associate with this imperialist, monopolist organization." *Haravghi,* September 11, 1962.

Certain pro-Greek junta diplomatic observers have noticed a communist attempt to infiltrate and direct the proceedings of the Consultative Assembly of the Council of Europe on one recent issue. "Using the socialists as tools, [they are] attempting to gain acceptance of a proposal to the Ministerial Committee calling for the immediate expulsion of Greece from the Council."[35] AKEL's hand in this was not visible, but the Cypriot communists indeed must have been overjoyed when the junta government withdrew from the Council under pressure in December 1969.

The one obvious international organization where AKEL should logically have a strong role is the left-wing Afro-Asian Peoples' Solidarity Organization (AAPSO), but in reality the Cypriot communists have effectively been pre-empted from exploiting this leftist front group. AAPSO is the private domaine of Dr. Vassos Lyssarides, and his bitter resentment of AKEL does not allow them any opportunity whatsoever to engage in the activities of the Cypriot branch of this worldwide group.[36]

In the various world communist front groups for labor, youth, and women, AKEL keeps up its membership but does not exercise a great deal of influence in the various policy-making bodies. AKEL members continually attend the world congresses of such groups, where they can obviously interact with other communist party members for social as well as for policy reasons. Because of AKEL's consistent adherence to the Moscow line, it can be assumed that most international communist organizations must take the Cypriot communists almost for granted. While it is the opinion of R. Palme Dutt—a venerable communist theoretician who is neither Greek nor Cypriot—that "AKEL is not a gramophone of Moscow," such an optimistic appraisal is surely belied by the party's actual behavior, especially outside the confines of its little island.[37]

6: The Principal Determinants of AKEL's Behavior

National Determinants

There are possibly five key determinants from the national scene which motivate AKEL leaders and inspire their current pattern of behavior: (1) the fear of being outlawed; (2) the fear of *enosis* and what might happen as a result; (3) the desire to remain respectable by backing Makarios and the nationalists; (4) the desire to function in a peaceful manner through legal means; and (5) the desire to maintain professionalism and salaried status within the party hierarchy.

AKEL's tactics in the years since the creation of the Republic of Cyprus have been carefully tailored to give the impression of dissatisfaction with the bourgeois Makarios government. But their tactics have never been allowed to go so far as to be interpreted as work designed to undermine the state. While some government officials would jump at such an excuse for proscribing the party, such a case has not yet been made. Obviously, AKEL takes pride in being one of only two legal communist parties in the entire Middle East, and it apparently thrives in open operation. In the two periods of history in which the communists were outlawed, they were comparatively ineffective as underground movements. Moreover, AKEL leaders have learned to enjoy the benefits of urban life, and the island of Cyprus has but six urban areas, all of which are small enough to be effectively policed; if the communists were proscribed, they would probably opt to leave the island rather than take to the hills to continue their struggle as fugitives. In this the Cypriot communists differ markedly from their mainland Greek counterparts. The advantages of being free, the ability to come and go as they wish, and the continuation of the joys of the good life in Cyprus are values to which AKEL members have become accustomed. Apparently, the island's communists would be most reluctant to engage in any revolutionary or otherwise subversive activities which could result in their facing deprivation, hardship, or proscription.

Throughout the long and tortuous record of Cypriot communism vis-à-vis the issue of *enosis,* the underlying strategy of opposition to the nationalists' goal is apparent. Despite the variety and forms of government which have emerged in Greece since the end of the First World War, the mainland has consistently been looked upon by Cypriot communists as suffering under "monarcho-fascism." None of the various Greek governments has taken kindly to leftist movements, be they parliamentary or revolutionary in nature. The 1947–49 Civil War with the militant forces of the KKE will not soon be erased from the memories of those who fought in it— or from the memories of their children, who were raised to hate the very mention of communism. AKEL, in a Cyprus controlled by Athens, would have a very short legal lifespan. Therefore, *enosis* coupled with the seeming inability of the party to function in a clandestine manner would probably spell the end of the communist movement in the island.

The respectability that communists have in Cyprus (i.e., they interact with ease on all levels of society) is tolerated for two logical reasons: (1) they follow the policies of Makarios; and (2) they are part of the Greek community, which must stay united in face of the Turkish threat. Articles reporting the activities and statements of AKEL leaders leave the impression that they are trying to create, in the minds of Cypriot noncommunists and anti-communists, an image of being the "loyal opposition." AKEL continuously emphasizes its "willingness to cooperate with representatives of the people and the government to overcome the adversities" which the party sees in all aspects of the current political situation in Cyprus. Moreover, AKEL is driven by the need to overcome by all possible means its egregious blunder of not backing EOKA in the waning days of the British occupation. This is also a paramount concern in the party's short-range planning. AKEL's careful work in that regard has had some payoff inasmuch as the EOKA issue seems to be raised less frequently with each passing year, except among small bands of right-wing militants. In short, most everyone in Cyprus seems to be rallying support for the "feasible," not the "desirable," solution. With this AKEL is definitely at ease, since the "feasible" solution is continued independence, not *enosis*.

The aversion AKEL has shown in recent years to militancy or outright violence appears to be a strong factor in the behavior of party members. The party leaders have accepted the revisionist thesis that communism does not have to be introduced by revolution and that there is little or no chance of seizing political power in Cyprus in the classical Marxist-Leninist sense. Even in the labor field, PEO has not taken the lead in calling any of the major strikes which have occurred recently in the island, such as the one against the government's tele-communications agency in the fall of 1968, or the one against Cyprus Airways in the spring of 1969. The right-wing union, SEK, has taken that aggressive role away from PEO, and as a consequence has increased its membership and enhanced its prestige. Perhaps PEO leaders have become somewhat atrophied from being at the pinnacle too long and now take their following too much for granted. AKEL spokesmen may be able to deceive their followers by repeating empty slogans in endless speeches at home and abroad, but labor unions are measured by the benefits they are able to win for their members. In an effort to regain the membership which PEO has been losing of late, there may be demands by the communist leadership to increase pressure on certain large employers, but it is most unlikely that these activities will ever reach the proportions or extremes manifested in the immediate postwar years. AKEL as well as its labor union front have learned to adapt to the local environment in Cyprus, and this means peaceful pursuit of their objectives, whatever they may be.

AKEL has developed a structured bureaucracy of salaried professionals who depend on their position in the party's hierarchy for all visible means of support. Decision-making and policy formulation is consequently a function of the wishes of party leaders to survive and perpetuate themselves in their present capacities. This means not only that the party must remain legal to do this, but also that its members must pay due deference to the institutions which supply the leadership with operating funds. The various commercial businesses which AKEL controls must continue to show a profit and the demands of the international forces which also supply a good measure of assistance must be met. The party leadership, therefore, is made up of cautious men who are not prone to embark on adventurous or untried courses of action, unless directed to do so by higher authority—viz., the Soviet Union. With the Soviet Union seemingly content with the role of AKEL in the affairs of Cyprus, it is doubtful if the call to arms will ever be sounded for the island's communist party.

International Determinants

The chief international determinant of AKEL behavior is the earnest desire to please the Communist Party of the Soviet Union and to further the Kremlin's foreign policy objectives. By so doing, AKEL hopes to develop the respect which goes along with being a vital, autonomous communist party in a politically sensitive region. This sense of importance in the eyes of the Soviet Union is something AKEL leaders treasure highly and they are undoubtedly grieved when it is not acknowledged.

For instance, the fact that Cyprus was pointedly omitted from the Soviet slogans on the 1965 anniversary of the October Revolution and again from the 1966 May Day slogans, could not have been ignored in Cyprus, particularly by AKEL. Cyprus was first included in the greetings to non-communist countries in the 1964 May Day slogans, and in 1965 the Soviet Union sent "warm greetings to the people of Cyprus . . . selflessly defending their independence against imperialist encroachment." But in 1966 Cyprus was, apart from Switzerland, the only West European country to be overlooked in the Soviet slogans, while Turkey retained its place. This was the punishment AKEL apparently received for its disagreeable behavior over the Soviet position favoring the Turks in 1965. Because of subsequent stabilization in AKEL-Soviet relations, Cyprus regained its place in 1967, in 1968, and again in 1969. These rewards are part of the psychic income AKEL members surely enjoy, and Cypriot communists know they must remain faithful to the CPSU for such credits to continue.

In addition to the verbal plaudits which come on ceremonial occasions, AKEL doubtless derives more material benefits from its close relationship with the Soviet Union. Financial support for the salaries and the extensive travel of higher echelon party members obviously cannot be met through dues collections or annual fund drives. While Papaioannou vigorously denies receiving any monetary contributions from Moscow, his continual traveling expenses alone, not to mention his salary and other personal expenses, could be enough to make a sizeable dent in the coffers of AKEL. When these expenses are added to those for travel of other party members, as well as the subsidies for publications, the funding of cultural events, and other operating costs, AKEL's annual budget is quite substantial. There are no public revelations of AKEL's balance sheet, but it is highly questionable that the party is able to subsist on its own ability to raise money. Therefore, in order to keep the funds flowing, AKEL must yield its place in policy-making to its financial and political patron, the Soviet Union.

One alleged use the communist bloc countries make of AKEL members is that of observers of and couriers to other Middle Eastern countries. If such jobs are done they are probably done quite well, for it is an innate trait of a Cypriot to love intrigue and activities with hidden meanings. Such pursuits are surely profitable and would be another motivation for AKEL to avoid doing anything which would provoke the Cypriot government into banning the party. Hence, there are more advantages than mere respectability accruing to AKEL for keeping intact its legal status in the Republic of Cyprus.

The close affinity of AKEL leaders to the Soviet Union may also explain why there is no mention of dissension, revisionism, or deviationism within party ranks. While there is strong evidence of a pro-Peking faction within the Communist Party of Greece, for instance, nothing of that sort has ever surfaced within AKEL. AKEL's incessant propaganda barrage against NATO and the British bases in Cyprus must certainly follow a cue from the Soviets. Obviously AKEL knows it can contribute little itself to rid the island of the British Sovereign Base Areas and would be defeating one of its own indigenous causes if this ever were to happen. The British bases are one of the largest employers on the island and a good share of the several thousand Cypriots working there are members of the communist-dominated trade union, PEO. It would be in AKEL's self-interest to keep the bases as a target for propaganda and as an employer of many of their sympathizers, but hardly to realize the Soviet aim of actually dismantling them. Even though the British bases are likely to remain for the foreseeable future, the neutralist foreign policy of the Makarios government is apparently an adequate enough trade-off for the time being so far as AKEL and the Soviets are concerned.

AKEL's one minor altercation with Moscow in 1965 over the federation endorsement represents the limit to which the Soviet Union will allow its Cypriot followers to go in order to defend their credibility. AKEL understands that any further disagreement, particularly over substantive policy issues, could likely result in the CPSU taking strong punitive action. Soviet countermeasures could be a withdrawal of financial support, or the formation of a rival party, or the launching of a vendetta which would discredit or purge the incumbent leadership of AKEL. The loose rein which the Soviet Union apparently uses to control AKEL's behavior could be tightened quite easily, and the party's leadership sees scant benefit in doing anything rash enough to cause the Soviets to exercise any of the sanctions open to them.

Other Determinants

AKEL is in many ways a captive of its standard propaganda lines. To back off now from the positions which have been traditional with the party since 1960 would probably cause a crisis of conscience among AKEL's following. Thus AKEL is expected to play a specified role in the debate over national issues in Cyprus and the party generally abides by these pre-ordained norms of behavior. In addition to urging the removal of the British bases and the continuation of Cyprus' neutralist foreign policy, AKEL also promotes the normalization of Greek Cypriot relations with the Turks on both the island and mainland, as well as the continued unfettered independence of the Republic. It is a pleasant coincidence for AKEL that the Makarios government has gradually moved away from *enosis* as a national goal and now appears to favor sovereign status through the maintenance of the Republic. This démarche affords AKEL the opportunity to give the impression of solid support for the nationalist forces of President Makarios while simultaneously advancing its own position.

Though some of AKEL's propaganda lines—due to circumstances beyond their making or control—have become policy for the Greek Cypriot government, AKEL is still not able to depart entirely from its established positions in order to demonstrate complete allegiance to Makarios. The Cypriot communists have shown in the past that they can accommodate to the government in power without losing their identity. Therefore, as opportunities arise AKEL can be expected to make other "deals" with the nationalists for a relatively small share of political power without essentially compromising their basic tenets.

The effect on AKEL's behavior of its natural, ethnic bond with the communists of the Greek mainland is a difficult phenomenon to unravel. Perhaps there is a morbid love-hate relationship which has developed between AKEL and the KKE. The two parties are probably more than fraternal, but despite similarities each has had separate patterns of growth and vastly different experiences. A rivalry could have generated from disparate efforts to seek an individual identity as autonomous communist parties, each exercising independent lines to the CPSU. Surely the language and cultural bonds between the two are never to be denied and a substantial interaction must therefore be carried on. Yet how this relationship is demonstrated in the behavior of AKEL is not clear. The current main split in the KKE between a revisionist faction and a pro-Moscow wing has been further confused with the emergence of a pro-Peking group, as well as abortive attempts by the crypto-communist party, EDA, to become an independent socialist force. AKEL may feel that the modern Greek drama being acted out among the elements of the left on the junta-controlled stage of Greece is enough of a justification to forget about their kinsmen temporarily and proceed as if there were no Greek communists other than themselves.

Competition from leftist forces on the periphery does not seem to be much of a concern for AKEL at present. The disgruntled ex-communists are not organized and the socialist forces of Dr. Lyssarides have yet to prove their vote-getting ability in an election. AKEL shows no desire to unite the forces of the left at this time, but that attitude could change as needs arise.

Reconciling communist ideology with the dogma of the Greek Orthodox Church does not loom as an immediate problem for AKEL. Most Greek Cypriots are habitual churchgoers; many because they are devout, but many because it is a socializing process which is capped off by a visit to the *cafeneo* for a round of gossip. AKEL members are known to attend church, especially in the villages, for its use as another vehicle for indoctrinating the populace, especially afterwards during the coffee-drinking sessions. The Church and the Greek Cypriot communists cannot afford the luxury of an open confrontation while the intercommunal troubles continue to demand a united front against the Turks. In more normal times, however, AKEL may have to reach some accommodation with the Greek Orthodox Church if it is to prevent an anti-communist campaign mounted from the many pulpits in the island. Makarios has reportedly said he can keep the communists in line by using the power of the Church against AKEL; as yet he has not found it necessary to do that.

The traditional communist obsession with exploiting the unrest of minority groups in any country has its manifestation in Cyprus, too, and possibly affects AKEL's behaviorial pattern. AKEL has never completely written off the Turkish Cypriot community and has sympathized with their plight since 1963—at least as far as they can without alienating the Makarios government. AKEL claims that it is the only true representative of "the working class in a very small country," and this mandate necessarily forces the communists into the logical role of defender of the Turkish Cypriot proletariat. AKEL envisions the possibility of the day when the class struggle will replace the ethnic struggle in Cyprus. Such a development would naturally cut across communal lines and could even catapult communism into the common cause around which all the workers could unite against their "oppressors."

Such an occurrence might not be entirely out of the realm of plausibility. For example, the young Turkish Cypriot students who are returning from studies in the universities on the mainland are often imbued with leftist ideas about the need for their community to "share the wealth" equally among all its citizens, particularly the $16 million subsidy that comes annually from Ankara. Such suggestions are obviously resisted by the established power structure and civil servants, who instead make their case for salary increases or more perquisites for themselves. In fact, the current Turkish Cypriot leadership sees a growing threat in a body of educated student activists in its midst and has allegedly issued an official communication urging new graduates to seek jobs on the Turkish mainland.[1] It is not unlikely that these young Turkish intellectuals, if sufficiently frustrated in their goals, could turn for succor to leftists in the Greek community, who would undoubtedly receive them warmly. Such individuals, carefully cultivated by AKEL, could serve as infiltrators in the Turkish community to spread the communist line among the "impoverished masses," which unfortunately do exist there. Any substantial number of Turks who could be convinced to support AKEL, be it in an election or merely as fellow travelers, would help meet a long-standing yet unattained communist objective in Cyprus.

A final reality which exists in Cyprus and may also prove to be a key determinant of AKEL's modus operandi concerns the competition from the right-wing labor movement. In many social and economic areas, the Confederation of Cypriot Workers (SEK) has adopted the positions normally held by AKEL, and in some ways has far exceeded these demands or promises for their own workers. This right-wing initiative was demonstrated in late 1969 in the area of scholarships for Cypriot students. SEK's General Secretary, Michael Pissas, sent a memorandum to President Makarios and the cabinet ministers in which he tied the need for scholarships to the fight against communism. The SEK memorandum illustrates how the right-wing union uses some of AKEL's principles, such as free education, to fight its archenemy. Among other things, the memorandum states:

> All of us realize international communism and its branch in Cyprus are following a long-term plan to weaken our national convictions, adulterate our racial ideals, and replace them with unilateral adherence to Soviet socio-economic and political theory to prepare the masses for a social revolution and impose the dictatorship of the proletariat.
>
> It is our duty to point out in writing the terrifying danger Cypriot society is called upon to face and respectfully submit

several of the many measures that it is imperative to adopt as soon as possible:

(1) Free education in all secondary schools—classical and technical—and in the higher technological institute.

(2) The Cyprus Government to set up a scholarships council and grant sufficient scholarships in all branches indicated by the Government Planning Department. The countries to which those on scholarship will be sent should be Greece first and then— particularly for post-graduate studies and specialization—West European countries and the United States.

(3) The governments of Cyprus and Greece to conclude an agreement to abolish competitions for scholarships organized by the Greek State Scholarships Foundation (IKI). Arrangements should be made for Greece to grant a steady large number of scholarships to Cypriots directly through the government scholarships council.

(4) To abolish once and for all the government decision recognizing the diplomas of communist universities. It must be made clear that the propaganda university agencies of international communism—whose nationally corroding and harmful purpose is well known—will no longer be recognized.

(5) The embassies of Western countries—such as the United States, Great Britain, France, West Germany, Italy, Canada, and so forth—should be called on to undertake part of the burden of the anti-communist struggle by granting a large number of scholarships to rightist Cypriots, as well as facilities to scientists doing postgraduate study.

(6) A decision should be reached quickly to purge the government machinery and semi-official enterprises of communists who hold key posts and through which they exercise internal control. Rightist civil servants should be given the opportunity to occupy posts which are the basis and guarantee for the smooth functioning of the state machinery.

We believe these are matters that should be studied as soon as possible. It is the responsibility of the government to adopt measures to stem the imminent danger because the 1,300 new Cypriot scientists who are being schooled in Marxism will return with written instructions in their briefcases for corrosive activity.[2]

The SEK leadership undoubtedly had the guiding hand of the enlightened Ministry of Labor and Social Insurance behind it, but the impact on AKEL is in no way diminished. The fact that AKEL is seeing its "bread and butter" issues slowly slip away because of progressive proposals and legislation by the government must give its leaders reason for pause. Such measures are obviously building up a strong Cypriot middle class, especially in the Greek community, and consequently are narrowing down the once-fertile field of the exploited Cypriot peasant and worker. AKEL is witnessing much of its past program being implemented, but ironically without receiving credit for it in the process. The Cypriot communists will probably be forced to seek newer issues by which they might hope to extend their appeal and provide social and economic benefits to their followers. Such demands on the leadership, which have not existed of late, could produce potentially crippling anxieties within the party.

7: Summary and Conclusions

The Communist Party of Cyprus has been enjoying political freedom since Cyprus became an independent Republic in 1960. Despite the dominance and resistance of the anti-communist nationalist forces under Archbishop Makarios, the local communists may yet have the opportunity to play a crucial role for the Soviet Union in an area of the world that is vulnerable to power politics. AKEL's chances for success will surely increase if the nationalist government is unable to safeguard the territorial integrity of the island or fails to maintain its present socially progressive leadership. For the time being the nationalists, while witnessing some internal stresses within their ranks, still appear to be unified in the face of the crisis over their relations with the Turkish community in the island.

The communists, however, are politically less effective in Cyprus than their organization, experience, and resources may otherwise indicate. Regardless of their deliberate pro-government campaign, they have yet to overcome their anti-*enosis* position taken during the EOKA uprising against the British in the late nineteen fifties. Since independence, however, AKEL has followed a course of token opposition to the nationalists. The party has been cautious not to challenge the leadership of Makarios or to do anything which could be interpreted as outright subversion. AKEL thus behaves legally and peacefully to prevent its being outlawed once again. In fact, the communists have shown greater cooperation at times with Makarios than some of his own ministers have. This "soft," pro-nationalist position of AKEL is a radical change from its outspoken opposition to EOKA and is clear evidence of the party's ability to change tactics as circumstances demand.

The Communist Party of Cyprus has resorted in the course of its history to a variety of tactics—strikes, violence, non-violence, electoral coalitions, and now patriotism. Two major factors seem to have played a formative role in the evolution of the Cypriot communist party: (1) the fundamental conspiratorial and ideological concepts which form the foundation of any communist party beholden to Moscow; and (2) the Cypriot stage on which AKEL has been obliged to perform.

Since its formal establishment in 1941, AKEL has been handicapped by its traditional line of advocating "self-determination" but never fully embracing *enosis*. The communists cannot reconcile the promotion of *enosis* with the strategic, political, and diplomatic interests of the Soviet Union, which is against the union of Cyprus with Greece, a NATO member. The Soviet interest in Cyprus lies essentially in using the issue to undermine the eastern flank of NATO by embittering relations between members of the Western alliance and forcing withdrawal of American communication facilities, as well as the British bases, from the island. Another feature of the communist campaign inside Cyprus has been the attempt to turn Cypriot public opinion against Great Britain and the United States by suggesting that both nations side with the Turks against the Greeks.

Realizing the stage on which it must act, AKEL's platform during its 10th Congress, held in March 1966, is instructive. It called for unfettered independence, complete sovereignty, territorial integrity, and application of the principle of self-determination to obtain *enosis* without concessions, bases, or foreign intervention. The communists also demanded closer relations between Cyprus and what they describe as the island's natural and unselfish allies—the socialist and non-aligned countries. AKEL believes in demilitarizing Cyprus, and at least in keeping the government in the neutralist bloc of nations if it cannot impose a pro-Soviet orientation on it. Furthermore, the party reiterated its "support" of the Makarios administration. They also demanded that the majority exercise control over governmental affairs despite the restrictions of the Zurich-London Agreements, but that the Turkish community be given fundamental guarantees of free action. Finally, the party expressed the desire that close cooperation between "people and government" should continue and even be strengthened as long as the internal problems in the island remain unresolved.

Objectives Compared to Achievements

Initially, the objectives of the communist movement in Cyprus could have been those of any liberal party in the West. The first resolutions of the KKK showed only the most superficial overtones of Leninism and reflected the well-intended, idealistic nature of its founding fathers. Ridding Cyprus of foreign exploitation, as well as of its social and economic ills, was a goal endorsed by many intellectuals of the time. In addition, the communist slogan of removing the British colonial yoke from the Cypriot people was certainly a shared value of the vast majority of the populace. Other than the creation of the "Soviet state of Cyprus," the early communist objectives for the island have largely been met in time through the winning of independence, extensive unionization, enlightened social legislation, and a growing prosperous economy. Had the original communists of Cyprus lived to see it, they might have considered themselves highly successful. But the early nature of communism in Cyprus was not characteristic of what was to evolve in the years that followed. Through crisis, proscription, intrigue, purges, and perfidy, the movement that the early idealists founded gradually became AKEL, the Progressive Party of the Working People.

AKEL is a far cry from the unpopular little movement spawned by its predecessor, the KKK. It is now one of Moscow's best and most faithful communist parties in its part of the world. Its present membership—whatever the actual count may be—is highly organized at all levels. Through the party's apparatus and fronts, communism has infiltrated into the urban workshops, village cooperatives, foreign-owned mines, and the farms of Cyprus. There is no real way of determining over how much of the population the Party exercises its leadership and control, but it is probably far more than the founders of the KKK ever dreamed possible. In this respect, AKEL has achieved a degree of strength and legitimacy which eluded those who first brought communism to Cyprus.

To enhance its prestige and power, and following the dictates of its ideology, AKEL has methodically catered to certain economic levels, social groups, and occupations in Cyprus. These are: labor, intellectuals, farmers, minorities, Makarios and his nationalists, and specific industries. Speaking of the party's future program soon after the creation of the Republic, one high official stated that even in the most highly industrialized countries, one rarely finds such a "high percentage of workers in party ranks." To overcome this it was submitted that AKEL must expand its efforts in the direction of recruiting more farmers, women, middle-class persons, and intellectuals.[1]

This points up the essential fact that AKEL has derived much of its strength and influence over the last 30 years from its ability to control the island's largest labor union (PEO), "the vanguard of the workers." This is probably the only field in which AKEL has achieved the goals it set up for itself. Although showing signs of a decline in membership, PEO still remains the most effective trade union in Cyprus. Its right-wing competitor, SEK, has so far not matched PEO's bargaining skill and services to workers, even though SEK has taken the lead in recent large strikes, as well as in making progressive legislative proposals. With the support of the Ministry of Labor and Social Insurance, the material and technical assistance from the International Confederation of Free Trade Unions, and American encouragement in general, SEK may eventually grow into a strong counterforce which will challenge communist domination of labor. If this happens can AKEL's labor front continue to maintain the prestige and sympathetic following it has traditionally enjoyed among workers? This is a matter which the communists cannot afford to take lightly.

In appealing to intellectuals, AKEL has been less successful. The leadership of the party, while clever and articulate, certainly includes no great original thinkers. (It would be difficult to determine, for instance, who AKEL's "Suslov" is today, if indeed there actually exists such a philosopher or theoretician in the party. Possibly Andreas Fantis does that job, for what it is worth.) Many Cypriot intellectuals—Greek and Turk alike—are concerned about most of the same socio-economic problems which AKEL attempts to exploit. The government, too, recognizes the problems, listens to advice, and has consequently made significant strides in improving the economic infrastructure, including the lot of the farmer and the worker. There is, hence, little reason for the highly educated Greek Cypriot to join AKEL in order to gain a forum for the expression of opinion. The same rationale, however, may not obtain for the educated Turkish Cypriot. Even though it is apparently recognized that intellectuals, once in the party, tend to become stultified and lose much of their innate creativity with the passage of time, a frustrated Turk may have no other outlet now or in the foreseeable future.

Farmers present a particularly challenging group with whom AKEL could build up its power and prestige. The vast majority are reasonably content with their simple way of life. Through its farmer front group, EKA, the communists make a diligent effort to attend every meeting of local or regional farm associations, irrespective of sponsorship. The communists have marginal success with this tactic and often conclude such meetings by joining in praise of Makarios. Although AKEL had pushed for land reform and legislation which would forbid ownership of land to noncultivators, this has not engendered any great amount of political activism among the deprived.

There are two reasons which may explain the modest success the communists have had among farmers. First, Cypriot peasants tend to resist change, are very loyal to the Church, and are most parochial in their outlook. Second, the Orthodox Church is the largest landowner in the island and many farmers work as tenants on vast holdings belonging to the Archbishopric and to certain monastaries. To push for land reform— particularly to the extreme of expropriation, which was advocated in the detailed program of the Ninth Party Congress of 1959—would incur the wrath of President Makarios, and hence the government in the bargain. That the AKEL cannot afford to do. Makarios, in his role of Archbishop, has made serious efforts to sell off Church-owned land and could easily eliminate a favorite communist issue if he continues the practice. It could be added that the independent cooperative movement is a free and strong mass organization among Cypriot farmers. This collectivist style of marketing farm produce is difficult for AKEL to attack or change.

AKEL one day must also make some sort of reconciliation with the Orthodox Church. The Church now tolerates the atheistic communist movement because it is part of the Greek Cypriot community, which Archbishop Makarios now wants to keep unified at almost any cost. The obvious trend toward adaptation of communism in Cyprus may have to include a recognizable accommodation of AKEL and the Church. From the beginning of the ethnarchy idea under the Ottomans the key to success in Cypriot politics has been the backing of the Church, but it is difficult to see how the communists will ever become respectable enough in the eyes of the Orthodoxy to receive its endorsement. Without that seal of approval, AKEL's parliamentary drive for power does not stand much of a chance.

The AKEL position on Makarios and his nationalist-dominated government is an expedient forced on the communists by circumstances. Since 1960 AKEL's political strategy has been to avoid open conflict with the President. The party's official line toward him was clearly stated soon after independence: "We support the Archbishop and President of the Republic of Cyprus on every particular issue against the colonialists and on behalf of the defense of the people's interest. We criticize him on every particular issue where his position clashes with the popular national interests."[2]

The communists have supported the President on such major issues as constitutional revision and a non-aligned foreign policy. They also have encouraged his cordial relations with Tito and Nasser and have successfully urged him to support the communist-dominated Afro-Asian Peoples' Solidarity Organization, whose 1968 Executive Committee meeting took place in Nicosia. It was at this meeting that Makarios reaffirmed his intention to reject all military alliances. AKEL supports Makarios' desire to prohibit the use of the Sovereign Base Areas as airfields for British bombers carrying nuclear weapons or as a refueling port for Polaris submarines. But this policy has been passively enforced and has hardly deterred the United Kingdom's deployment of troops and facilities on its "sovereign chunks of England on the littoral of Cyprus."

The communists must also face the problem they have with the minority Turkish Cypriot population. AKEL had traditionally been "anti-chauvinistic" in its policy toward the Turks: it did not favor a partition of that community from the Greeks. The need to back the nationalists over the current unsettled ethnic problem in the island has forced AKEL to postpone—but certainly not to eliminate—attempts to gain influence among the Turks. Papaioannou, speaking at the 40th anniversary celebration, claimed that the "bloodshed between the Greek and Turkish Cypriots was to the great satisfaction of imperialism and its tools." He went on nostalgically to say that "the party's work for the Turkish masses [the inroads made by PEO under British rule] has not been in vain . . . and they [the nationalists] will never wipe out the spirit of friendship and cooperation which we have nurtured with thousands of Turkish workers."[3]

There is deep distrust of communism among the Turkish Cypriots because they associate the movement with the Greeks. In fact, the Vice-President of the Republic, Dr. Fazil Küçük, expresses his attitude and that of his followers very simply: "If a Turk becomes a communist in Cyprus, then he also becomes a Greek."[4] It was not accidental that two Turkish communists were murdered in 1958, two more in 1962, and the last overt Turkish communist was also dispatched in a similar manner in 1966. Though there is a small Cypriot Turkish communist group in London headed by Abdullah Tahir and Ahmed Sadi, there has been notably little success in introducing the ideology into the Turkish community in Cyprus. The same may be said about the Cypriot Armenians, although AKEL has much more contact in that community. Most of those Armenians who were declared communist have since left Cyprus for the Soviet Armenian Republic, however.

A resolution adopted by the party's Central Committee in February 1969 specifically stated that any Cyprus settlement must be on the basis of a fully independent Republic "in which the rights of the Turkish Cypriots are clearly defined and adequately safeguarded." In short, AKEL knows that continued independence and stability in Cyprus can only come about after provisions are made to meet the Cypriot Turkish demands, which are backed up by the Ankara government. To look out for the Turks in the island thus serves a dual purpose for AKEL: it will help keep the island independent and thus prevent *enosis* from happening; and it bolsters Soviet policy regarding its present rapprochement with Turkey. By the same stroke, it puts AKEL on a razor's edge respecting its tactical support of the nationalists. The Turks in Cyprus always have been, and are likely to remain, a tempting group for the communists to defend in a campaign to develop sympathizers. Infiltration among the Turks has not been at all profitable in the past, and efforts in the future could likely have the same fate— except perhaps among the socialist-minded young Turkish university graduates who now spout Marxist demands to their ruling establishment. Despite previous attempts and present lip service, AKEL must necessarily chalk up its previous ventures into the Cypriot Turkish community as complete failures. Whether the future will hold better fortune for AKEL among the Turks can only be a matter of speculation.

On the industries issue, AKEL has consistently urged increased taxation on the profits of foreign companies operating in Cyprus, as well as government control of production and prices. AKEL favors nationalization of the island's mines. In 1962 Papaioannou declared that the American-owned Cyprus Mines Corporation "alone has an annual net profit of 66 million pounds ... estimated to come to approximately 120 million pounds if capitalization and amortization are taken into account." He cited an earlier address in the House of Representatives in which he had stated that the projected Cyprus Five-Year Plan could be financed "with the income obtained from the mines." He then suggested that the government "should study the entire problem, beginning with a substantial increase in taxes on mine profits."[5]

Formerly owned by mainland Greeks, the Hellenic Mines Corporation has lately come under Church trusteeship and consequently is not receiving the full brunt of AKEL's broadsides. However, this firm, too, must have been included in a more recent statement by the General Secretary: "According to their own figures, these mining companies made a clear profit of 22,410,337 pounds in 5 years, from 1963 to 1967. A total of 20,240,682 of this belongs to the American Cyprus Mines Corporation. During the same period, the per capita income of the miners was 400 pounds."[6]

Another favorite industrial target of the communists is the Fasouri Plantation near Limassol, which has a substantial private Israeli investment. This is one of the largest citrus producing developments of its kind in the Middle East. Many of the workers are Turks and this company has yielded in only a limited way to PEO attempts to organize its personnel.

AKEL has enjoyed much more success in organizing than in carrying out substantive programs. It is apparently still not satisfied with the hold it has over a significant proportion of the Greek community and has set about to increase its influence. The job AKEL has defined for itself is still great: it must expand efforts in broadening its base in the direction of re-cruiting more farmers, women, middle-class persons, and intellectuals. But is AKEL, as presently constituted, up to the task? Can its dogmatic leadership develop the alternatives to the nationalists in face of the modern challenges in Cyprus? Is Ezekias Papaioannou, born in 1908 and in control of the party since 1949, able to inspire and appeal to the youth of Cyprus to join the ranks of AKEL? Can the 49-year-old General Secretary of the farmers' front group (EKA), Hambis Michaelides, whose son is being educated in the Soviet bloc outside the Greek environment, appeal to the Cypriot peasant who owns and cultivates his own land? Can the General Secretary of AKEL's labor arm (PEO), Andreas A. Ziartides, 50, provide the Cypriot worker with adequate rewards and a sense of mission for a free and independent Cyprus? These, undoubtedly, are questions the top Cypriot communists wish they did not have to ask themselves. In sum, the leadership of AKEL is not dynamic, to say the least, and the record of com-munist results contrasted with aspirations in the island is not particularly impressive. Yet AKEL continues to work for a so-cialist state in Cyprus with undaunted and optimistic diligence.

Conclusions

The communists in Cyprus cannot afford to deny the existence of immutable traditions nor are they able to avoid the hard realities of change which characterize the environment in which they must perform. AKEL should have conceded long ago that it must act on the political rather than the revolutionary level. The communists have no chance to bring about a Soviet-type socialist state in Cyprus through force. AKEL may now wish to expand its small share of political power in the government through bargaining and collaboration with forces of the right or left; but if this is their strategic choice, what does this do to their classical communist identity? Must AKEL also revise its doctrines and relationship with the Soviet Union in order to adapt to the demands of its local environment? If the party does demand more autonomy to deal with the social and political exigencies on the Cypriot stage, it could risk losing the financial and ideological anchorage in Moscow which has thus far been its ultimate solace. If AKEL should yield to the framework of its host country merely to become an eccentric party of the left, it will no longer be able to insist on the purity of its past propaganda line. Still, AKEL appreciates that it can keep its options open and defer making an agonizing reappraisal of its situation until the intercommunal problems in the island are solved. This fortunate contingency could give AKEL a few years more to search for workable alternatives which would perpetuate its life in Cyprus.

The use the Soviet Union has for the communists in Cyprus must be a factor that weighs heavily in the thinking of the AKEL leadership. The relative strategic importance of such a group as AKEL to the Soviets is not readily discernable. There is certainly some prestige to be derived by the Soviet party (CPSU) from having a legal political party parroting its given line in a critical area of the world. Also there are benefits simply from the standpoint of international representation. AKEL's existence helps prove that communism is a world-wide movement which thrives even on Eastern Mediterranean islands; and the simple numerical count of communist parties has always been of value to the CPSU. It is thus symbolic and salving to have AKEL in its fold despite the fact that the party has very little actual power. AKEL may thus be of minimal political use to the Soviet Union—which probably would prefer to see a Cyprus Republic having a communist-supported regime rather than one actually ruled by communists. If AKEL were ever to gain power in Cyprus, it would probably generate some immediate reaction from NATO, and the Soviet Union would undoubtedly rather not risk an East-West confrontation over defense of so small a communist government. For the time being, the neutralist policy of the Makarios government is apparently quite acceptable to the Soviets, and AKEL must learn to live with this.

In the overall Soviet strategy for the Middle East, AKEL may yet serve some useful purpose. The main Soviet targets in the area, Turkey and Iran, have been largely neutralized; but fears of the aggressive tendencies of the age-old Russian adversary have not totally vanished, and emerged again with the appearance of the Soviet fleet in the Mediterranean and the Warsaw Pact intervention in Czechoslovakia in 1968. With a growing flotilla in the Mediterranean, the Soviet Union has the opportunity to make its presence directly felt by showing the "hammer and sickle" in what was once an "American lake" and in ports that formerly knew little more than the U.S. Sixth Fleet. The Soviets now realize that a naval force can support national interests anywhere on the high seas and can do so without commitment or encroachment on foreign territory or territorial waters. Thus, Soviet prestige has been enhanced and has compelled all Mediterranean and Middle East states to acknowledge the sizeable Soviet strength in the area. Simultaneously, the risks are obvious: in the event of a local conflict, particularly a conflict involving one of its client states, Soviet decision-makers must face the dilemma of either ignominiously withdrawing support or of pushing such a conflict into a much wider encounter with the West. The part AKEL is assigned to play in the regional Soviet strategy for the Eastern Mediterranean, whatever it is, could prove to be significant.

Prospects

Any uses the Soviet Union can make of the communists in Cyprus are possibly gratifying to the AKEL leadership, but they are by the same token something of a brake on AKEL's drive to achieve its stated objectives. If there is neither reason nor encouragement for the communists to make a bid for power in Cyprus, the party could have a much easier and secure future as an opposition party of the left. It is conceivable that AKEL already fits into a current Soviet design for the region and has therefore been directed to keep on its steady keel until further notice. This would not displease the AKEL careerists, who seemingly enjoy the euphoria which results from the ex officio status accorded them by the CPSU. AKEL has had its share of adversities in the past and, in contrast, present conditions in Cyprus may well represent some of the best times the communists in the island have ever experienced. This does lend credence to the overriding necessity for AKEL to avoid doing anything which could threaten its legal existence. It may follow that the communists have an implicit understanding of the tolerable limits of their behavior in the nationalist-run government of Cyprus. In like manner, the nationalists may also acknowledge this tacit agreement and accept the communists as long as their bounds are not transgressed. The result could well be a non-competitive stand-off in Cyprus which works out in the interests of all concerned.

According to recent observations, the police and security forces of the Ministry of Interior have set up an elaborate system of surveillance over the members of AKEL. The leaders are certainly well known and most of the cadres have also been identified. Supposedly the membership of AKEL is interlaced at all levels with spies in the employ of various domestic and external interests. The clandestine and conspiratorial nature of the party's operation is for all intents and purposes uncovered, and security forces of the island have declared that they have the communist situation in Cyprus "well in hand."[7] In an island the size of Cyprus, where the communists have concentrated themselves in the urban areas and towns, it is quite possible that most of the active communists can be watched systematically. If this revelation, on the other hand, serves to reinforce the obvious Cypriot nonchalance towards communism, it could have an effect opposite to the one intended by the security forces.

A thoughtful portion of the population has become increasingly worried over the resurgence of communism in Cyprus. There is a growing urge among anti-communists to organize themselves to expose the danger and counter the external threat, but these private groups are largely ineffective. The fervent anti-communists try to show that the current declared position of AKEL—that of supporting the national government of President Makarios—is a tactic which can quickly and easily switch into opposition. And, they say, if the interests of international communism should call for it AKEL could initiate a program of strikes, riots, arson, and intimidation, as in 1948, a program calculated to damage the economy and undermine the government's position. But those overly concerned with communism are still in the minority and are even regarded with suspicion by some liberal-thinking Cypriots.

The anti-communists who do not believe that the communist threat has reached a dangerous point remain inert and complacent. They accept the Makarios government's policy that as long as the Cyprus problem remains unsolved, all Greek Cypriots should remain united. Their justification is that the internal political problems of the Greek community should be tackled after the intercommunal struggle is settled, and that attitude appears to prevail in Cyprus.

Many of the social and political conditions which may have paved the way for communist gains in Cyprus in the past have been changed since the island won its independence in 1960. Staunch anti-communists in the island insist that the way to beat communism in Cyprus is not by simply outlawing its political party, but by getting an enlightened and farsighted Ministry of Labor and Social Insurance to carry out the very sort of socio-economic reforms that were traditionally advocated by AKEL. Cyprus is one of the first countries in the Middle East to have established a research institute, run on contract by an American institution, the State University of New York, to study the various problems of its development. The forward-thinking recommendations which could emerge from such studies are likely to be fed into the economic planning of the Republic, in order to endure a stable rate of progress for the Cypriot people. It is the firm belief of the nationalists now in power that a steadily improving living standard for the people is the best defense against the ideological attacks of Marxism-Leninism, and Cypriot living standards have been improving steadily.

In view of the surprising prosperity in Cyprus, and despite the unsolved communal troubles, the communists may have already begun to reassess their position; the members of AKEL have proved to be patient individuals who have faced setbacks and successes with equanimity in the past. The party is likely to continue to accommodate itself to local political conditions in hopes of preserving its legal existence. The new leaders who will have to assume control of the party in the next few years will be university-trained, broadminded, and perhaps more confident of their own abilities. AKEL could quite possibly drift away from the domineering influence of the Soviet Union and develop a political style of its own, one more relevant to conditions in Cyprus. The Cypriot communists may now be reacting at long last to the gradual transition of the world-wide communist movement into a group of loosely connected individualized parties, each adapted to the national environment in which it must ultimately function.

Possibly the real stimulus for a future change in the structure and function of AKEL will be the realization that the

Greek Cypriot by his very nature is everything that a stereo-typed communist is not. The Greek Cypriot is patriotic, religious, emotional, loyal to friends and fierce with his ene-mies. Above all he has his *philotimo,* for which honor or self-respect are inadequate translations. No matter how poor a peasant may be, he has a strong sense of private property. He is proud that Greece, the land of his ancestors, is called "the cradle of democracy" and to the idea of democracy he is passionately devoted. Communism in Cyprus made its mark on the unlikely Cypriot people during past times of stress and national anxiety, but the cut has not been deep and with en-lightened treatment the scar may not be lasting.

Postscript

(September 1970)

The most significant development in Cyprus since this manuscript was finished in spring of 1970 was the July 5th elections for the House of Representatives. All 50 seats were up, including the 35 Greek Cypriot community members. Surprisingly, the communists almost doubled their representation, from five to nine seats, without running in any coalitions. An immediate analysis would indicate that voter apathy and a low turnout were major reasons for the AKEL increase. The total island-wide vote was 200,141, or 75.8% of the 263,857 registered Greek Cypriot voters, but that figure is some 100,000 less than the estimated number of eligible voters from that community. (See footnote, p. 2.) Total straight party voting for AKEL amounted to 68,229 or 34% of the turnout; adding the split-ticket vote, the 1970 communist electoral strength approached 40% of the actual vote cast. (See p. 133 for pre-election estimates.)

The nine communist victories were spread over the six main districts, and along with the mean average percentage of the overall votes were: Larnaca—Andreas Ziartides, 45.4%; Limassol—Ezekias Papaioannou and Giangos Potamitis, 43.6%; Paphos—Nicos Mavronicolas, 42.1%; Famagusta—Hambis Michaelides and Andreas Fantis, 39.0%; Nicosia—Dinos Constantinou and Georgios Savvides, 37.5%; and Kyrenia—Christos Koutellaris, 32.3%. The four new communist seats as contrasted to the 1960 results were in Limassol, Larnaca, Famagusta, and Kyrenia. For some reason Papaioannou and Ziartides left Nicosia and ran in different districts where both won anew, while AKEL was retaining its two seats in Nicosia with staunch Central Committee members. A new seat was picked up in Kyrenia by an official in the farmers' front, EDK, as the Paphos seat was taken by a lawyer who replaced the incumbent AKEL member, Dimetriades.

Perhaps it is trite to say that eternal vigilance is the price of democracy, but the past elections in the Republic of Cyprus may have demonstrated the point. AKEL undoubtedly had every one of its sympathizers registered and obviously made sure that each turned out to vote. In this situation, at least, indifference and apathy in the majority apparently fertilized communist growth. Judging from the wistful editorial reactions of the non-communist press, the 1970 election results in Cyprus may have shocked the nationalists into realizing the potential of the communists in the island.

Appendixes

Appendix A

Documents from the trial Rex v. Ziartides, et al., Nicosia, Assize Court, 1945

AN INFORMATION FILED BY OR ON BEHALF OF THE ATTORNEY-GENERAL

In the Assize Court of Nicosia.

(I) 1. Andreas Ziartides, of Nicosia.
2. Antonios M. Psathas, of Famagusta.
3. Stelios Iacovides, of Nicosia.
4. George Christophorou, of Limassol.
5. George Christodoulides, of Larnaca.
6. George Tembriotis, of Nicosia.
7. Takis Frangofinos, of Paphos.
8. Chrysanthos Savvides, of Nicosia.
9. Kyriacos Ragouzeos, of Nicosia.

10. Agathangelos Emmanuel, of Paphos.
11. Savvas Ioannou, of Nicosia.
12. Michael Xenophontos, of Nicosia.
13. Pais Photiou, of Famagusta.
14. Hambis Nicola, of Famagusta.
15. George Minas, of Limassol.
16. Cleanthis Silvestros, of Limassol.
17. Nicos Georghiou, of Limassol.
18. Andreas Tsaparillas, of Nicosia.

Accused

Committed for trial on the 10th day of August, 1945, by (2) Mr. G. Theocharides, District Judge.
Depositions taken (3) at Nicosia, on the 7th, 8th, 9th and 10th August, 1945.

Law under which information is laid. (4)	Particulars of offence. (5)
Cyprus Criminal Code, 1928 to 1944, sections 58, 61 (a) (i) and 358.	1. The accused on divers days between the 24th day of September, 1944, and the 11th day of May, 1945, both days inclusive, at Limassol, Nicosia and divers other places in the Colony, did conspire together, and with other persons unknown, to commit a felony, to wit, by writing or otherwise to encourage the doing of an unlawful act, to wit, the overthrow of the constitution of the Colony of Cyprus by revolution.
Cyprus Criminal Code, 1928 to 1944, sections 58, 61 (a) (ii) and 358.	2. The accused at the time and place in count 1 hereof mentioned, did conspire together, and with other persons unknown, to commit a felony, to wit, by writing or otherwise to encourage the doing of an unlawful act, to wit, the overthrow by violence of the established Government of the Colony of Cyprus.
Cyprus Criminal Code, 1928 to 1944, sections 49 (1), 50 (1), 21 and 36.	3. The accused, at the time and place in count 1 hereof mentioned, did conspire together, and with other persons unknown, to do various acts in furtherance of a seditious intention, common to all of them, to wit, an intention to bring into hatred the Government of Cyprus as by law established.
Cyprus Criminal Code, 1928 to 1944, sections 49 (1), 50 (1), 21 and 36.	4. The accused at the time and place in count 1 hereof mentioned, did conspire together, and with other persons unknown, to do various acts in furtherance of a seditious intention, common to all of them, to wit, an intention to excite disaffection against the Government of Cyprus as by law established.
Cyprus Criminal Code, 1928 to 1944, sections 49 (1), 50 (3), 21 and 36.	5. The accused at the time and place in count 1 hereof mentioned, did conspire together, and with other persons unknown, to do various acts in furtherance of a seditious intention, common to all of them, to wit, an intention to excite the inhabitants of Cyprus to attempt to procure the alteration, otherwise than by lawful means, of matters in the Colony of Cyprus as by law established (other than its sovereignty.)
Cyprus Criminal Code, 1928 to 1944, sections 49 (1), 50 (5), 21 and 36.	6. The accused at the time and place in count 1 hereof mentioned, did conspire together, and with other persons unknown, to do various acts in furtherance of a seditious intention, common to all of them, to wit, an intention to raise disaffection amongst the inhabitants of the Colony of Cyprus.
Cyprus Criminal Code, 1928 to 1944, sections 49 (1), 50 (6), 21 and 36.	7. The accused at the time and place in count 1 hereof mentioned, did conspire together, and with other persons unknown, to do various acts in furtherance of a seditious intention, common to all of them, to wit, an intention to promote feelings of ill-will and hostility between different classes of the population of Cyprus.
Cyprus Criminal Code, 1928 to 1944, sections 57 (1), 61 (a) and (b), 21 and 36.	8. The accused between the 1st of October, 1944, and the 11th of May, 1945, both days inclusive, at Nicosia and divers other places in the Colony were members of the Pancyprian Trade Unions Committee (PSE), which is an unlawful association in that, being a body of persons unincorporated, by its propaganda encourages the overthrow of the constitution of Cyprus by revolution, the overthrow by violence of the established Government of Cyprus, the overthrow by violence of organized Government and the doing of acts purporting to have as an object the carrying out of a seditious intention as set out in counts 3 to 7 hereof.

Law under which information is laid. (4)	Particulars of offence. (5)
Cyprus Criminal Code, 1928 to 1944, sections 57 (2), 61 (a) and (b) and 21.	9. The accused 1 to 12 both inclusive at the time and place in count 8 hereof mentioned, did act in an office of the Pancyprian Trade Unions Committee (PSE), an unlawful Association as set out in count 8 hereof.
Cyprus Criminal Code, 1928 to 1944, sections 57 (2), 61 (a) and (b) and 21.	10. The accused 1 to 12 both inclusive at the time and place in count 1 hereof mentioned, did occupy a position in the Pancyprian Trade Unions Committee (PSE), an unlawful Association as set out in count 8 hereof.
Cyprus Criminal Code, 1928 to 1944, sections 58, 61 (a) (i) and 21.	11. The accused on divers days between the 1st of January 1945, and the 31st of March, 1945, both days inclusive, at Nicosia and divers other places in Cyprus, by writing, to wit, by the periodicals entitled "Bulletin of the Pancyprian Trade Unions Committee" and "The Propagandistis," fortnightly organ of the Central Cultural Office of the Pancyprian Trade Unions Committee, translated extracts from which are set out in Schedule "A" attached hereto, did encourage the doing of an unlawful act, to wit, the overthrow of the constitution of Cyprus by revolution.
Cyprus Criminal Code, 1928 to 1944, sections 58, 61 (a) (ii) and 21.	12. The accused at the time and place in count 11 hereof mentioned, by writing, to wit, by the periodicals described in count 11 hereof, translated extracts from which are set out in Schedule "A" attached hereto, did encourage the doing of an unlawful act, to wit, the overthrow by violence of the established Government of Cyprus.
Cyprus Criminal Code, 1928 to 1944, sections 58, 61 (a) (ii) and 21.	13. The accused at the time and place in count 11 hereof mentioned, by writing, to wit, by the periodicals described in count 11 hereof, translated extracts from which are set out in Schedule "A" attached hereto, did encourage the doing of an unlawful act, to wit, the overthrow by violence of organized Government.
Cyprus Criminal Code, 1928 to 1944, sections 60, 50 (1), 21 and 36.	14. The accused in February, 1945, at Nicosia and divers other places in Cyprus did publish a periodical entitled : "Bulletin of the Pancyprian Trade Unions Committee" No. 2, February, 1945, translated extracts from which are set out in Schedule "B" attached hereto, having a seditious intention, to wit, an intention to bring into hatred the Government of Cyprus as by law established.
Cyprus Criminal Code, 1928 to 1944, sections 60, 50 (1), 21 and 36.	15. The accused in March, 1945, at Nicosia and divers other places in Cyprus did publish a periodical entitled "Bulletin of the Pancyprian Trade Unions Committee" No. 3, March, 1945, translated extracts from which are set out in Schedule "C" attached hereto, having a seditious intention, to wit, an intention to bring into hatred the Government of Cyprus as by law established.
Cyprus Criminal Code, 1928 to 1944, sections 60, 60B, 61 (a) (ii), 21 and 36.	16. The accused on or about the 11th May, 1945, at Nicosia and divers other places in Cyprus did have, without lawful authority or excuse, in their possession the documents described in Part 1 of Schedule "D" attached hereto, details and translated extracts from which are given in Part 2 of the same Schedule, which encourage the doing of an unlawful act, to wit, the overthrow by violence of the established Government of Cyprus.
Cyprus Criminal Code, 1928 to 1944, sections 60, 60B, 50 (1), 21 and 36.	17. The accused at the time and place in count 16 hereof mentioned, did have, without lawful authority or excuse, in their possession the documents described in Part 1 of Schedule "E" attached hereto, details and translated extracts from which are given in Part 2 of the same Schedule, having a seditious intention, to wit, an intention to excite disaffection against the Government of Cyprus as by law established.

(Signed)

Attorney-General

N.B.—*The names of the witnesses who appeared before the Magisterial Court or whose affidavits are filed should be endorsed hereon.*

The Officer of the Court should also endorse the date of the trial hereon and subscribe his signature.

208

TRANSLATED EXTRACTS.

EXTRACTS FROM THE " BULLETIN OF THE PANCYPRIAN TRADE UNIONS COMMITTEE ",
No. 1, JANUARY, 1945.

Page 3 :

" FROM THE REPORT ON THE ACTIVITIES OF PSE (Period 1.10.1944–25.12.1944) submitted by the comrade General-Secretary of PSE to the 2nd Ordinary Meeting of all the members of PSE.

*　　　*　　　*　　　*

A.—POLITICAL SITUATION.

1. *External.*—At the 3rd Pancyprian Conference of Trade Unions we have arrived at the following conclusions on the external, military and political situation. . . . . . the war has been transformed into a social revolution. The bourgeoisie is unable to govern, whilst on the other hand, the masses of hungry and miserable people have become active to the highest degree.

To-day, only two months after that historic conference of ours, the situation is so clear to us, that nobody can doubt the correctness of that conclusion."

*　　　*　　　*　　　*

Page 29 :

" Third Lesson. POLITICAL ORGANIZATIONS OF THE LABOUR CLASS.—The demands of the labourer are directed not only towards a certain employer but towards the State, which is nothing else in its substance than the representative of the interests of capitalists."

*　　　*　　　*　　　*

Page 30 :

" The labourer, therefore, cannot confine his efforts for the improvement of his position within the limits of the existing regime. At a particular stage of the struggle of the labour class, it starts to be realized that the real welfare of the whole world can be brought about only by a change of the existing regime. It is then that the labour movement starts to embrace socialism and to direct its efforts for the application of its system. The main weapon in this struggle is the party of the labour class, without which an organized effort with hopes of success cannot be conceived.

The Socialist Labour Party is the highest form of organization of the labour class.

*　　　*　　　*　　　*

It is, therefore, in its basis the organ of the labour class."

*　　　*　　　*　　　*

Page 31 :

" The aim of this party must be to guide all the other organizations of the labour class as, for instance, trade unions, and to lead their efforts in the right socialist way.

*　　　*　　　*　　　*

The struggle, however, on these watchwords strengthens the labour movement, makes labourers class-conscious and experienced of the struggle and prepares them for the struggle for socialism which is the final aim of every real labour party and of every progressive man."

*　　　*　　　*　　　*

Pages 32–33 :

" Fourth Lesson. FORMS OF THE ORGANIZATIONS OF THE LABOUR CLASS. DEMOCRATIC CENTRALIZATION.—Although the various political parties of the Second International in Europe have declared that their aim was the establishment of socialism, yet they have no clear theory of what they mean by socialism and how its establishment is going to be effected. Most of the followers of these Parties believe that it is possible for the capitalistic regime to develop to socialism peacefully by various improvements of the position of the labour class and, generally, society (gradual nationalization of enterprises, gradual rise in daily wages, application of social insurance, etc.). In most cases the only condition imposed on a member of these Parties is that he must not admit the use of means of violence in the struggle for the imposition of socialism. Not only do these Parties not help the struggle of the labour class but they betray it by preventing the development of the formation of class-conscience by teaching the conciliation of classes and preventing the use of favourable conditions for the success of socialism, as for instance during the last war.

A real labour party must have a definite ideology and programme based on Marxism. This ideology must be accepted by every member of the Party. A member of the Party must not be entitled to support ideas and theories which are contrary to the programme and ideology of the Party. It is imperative that the ideology and the programme should be Marxist, because experience from history has proved that only by the imposition of Marxism there is even a remote hope for the success of socialism. It is not sufficient for one to be a good fighter, an efficient organizer or to favour the Party. It must admit unreservedly its ideology. The entry into the Party of persons who have reservations for the one or the other point of its programme weakens the Party and lessens its political maturity."

*　　　*　　　*　　　*

Page 45 :

" It is not therefore the Party of the labour class which breaks up its (the labour class) powers. On the contrary, it concentrates under its monolithic guidance the forces of the proletariat and it directs its struggle with the aim of establishing socialism under which the means of production and exhange constitute a common property, and equal opportunities for work, education and rest are secured to all the working people."

*　　　*　　　*　　　*

Page 46 :

" From the bosom of the Cyprus labour class, when the conditions became ripe, the vanguard was born, the political organization of the labour class, its Party : the AKEL."

[*continued overleaf.*

Pages 46 and 47 :

" Only in this way can the leadership of our Party be understood and that of every proletariat Party. In the organization of the labour class such a leadership was dictated by the 3rd Pancyprian Conference of Trade Unions, which voluntarily approved the suggestion of PSE for the recognition of the political leadership of AKEL ".

*   *   *   *

Page 53 :

" If the transition from the slow quantitative change to the violent and rough qualitative change forms a law of evolution, then it is obvious that the revolutions of the oppressed classes form natural and unavoidable social phaenomena. Thus the passing from capitalism to socialism and the liberation of the labour class from the yoke of capitalism cannot be achieved by quiet changes and reforms but only by the qualitative change of capitalism, by revolution ".

EXTRACTS FROM " THE BULLETIN OF THE PANCYPRIAN TRADE UNIONS COMMITTEE", No. 2, FEBRUARY, 1945.

Page 18 :

" The focus, therefore, of our effort (must be) the struggle ' FOR BREAD AND FREEDOM '. Mobilization, therefore, to the maximum. The forces of our class must be called on a general mobilization. In this struggle for the amelioration of the standard of living of our people we must continuously mobilize more and more historic forces of ours until the time comes when fully armed by the side of the other peoples we will rush into the arena for the liberation of our most tortured island. Our organization must be converted into military camps in which will move fervently the forces of the hopeful morrow."

*   *   *   *

Page 21 :

" Lesson No. 2. The importance of the education of the labourer."

*   *   *   *

Page 23 :

" The labour movement cannot have but only one ideology. Such ideology will be either the socialistic or the capitalistic one which presupposes the possibility of the continuous improvement of the position of labourers under the capitalistic regime. There is no middle way. Anything which weakens the influence of the socialistic ideology automatically strengthens the influence of the capitalistic ideology and renders easier the continuation of the exploitation by the capitalists. Only a continuous culture of activities of the labour organizations, an activity based on Marxism, can maintain the labour movement which will lead to socialism."

*   *   *   *

" THE PROLETARIAT ", SAYS MARX, " DURING ITS STRUGGLE WITH THE BOURGEOISIE, IS COMPELLED BY THE FORCE OF CIRCUMSTANCES, TO ORGANIZE ITSELF AS A CLASS . . . . . WHICH BY THE FORCE OF THE REVOLUTION BECOMES THE RULING CLASS, AND AS SUCH, SWEEPS AWAY THE OLD METHODS OF PRODUCTION."

*   *   *   *

Page 49 :

" THE NEW STRUGGLE AND THE DUTIES OF THE LABOUR MOVEMENT IN OUR DISTRICT. BY STELIOS IACOVIDES.

" PSE has laid the foundations for the commencement of a new struggle.

*   *   *   *

It is the struggle for the survival of the people and at the same time the struggle for making the foreign Government understand once again that our people knows perfectly well that its happiness cannot be secured, its happiness cannot materialize so long as it is enslaved, and that he is ready to suffer every sacrifice for his liberation with which only can the people succeed in all his other rights.

*   *   *   *

Page 50 :

" GREAT STRUGGLES BRING ABOUT GREAT VICTORIES. FORWARD FOR GREAT STRUGGLES."

EXTRACTS FROM " THE PROPAGANDISTIS ", ORGAN OF THE CENTRAL CULTURAL OFFICE OF THE PANCYPRIAN TRADE UNIONS COMMITTEE, No. 3, MARCH, 1945.

Page 14 :

"QUESTIONNAIRE.

Question No. 1 : Is it possible to apply socialism without a revolution ?

Answer : . . . . The violent revolution, short though it may be, is unavoidable. Not because the proletarian class asks for it (on the contrary, it is a class which loathes bloodshed), but because the bourgeoisie with its fascist mentality renders it unavoidable. The bourgeoisie will not give up its privileged position without a hard struggle. The proletarian class simply will respond to the provocation. The same thing will happen in the society as it happens in nature, where the violent change at various intervals of time becomes unavoidable by the refusal of the out-of-time organisms which are created to give place to the better naturally fitted ones. Similarly here, the violent step will open the road to a better-adapted class.

GIVE WAY TO THE PERSONS WHO HAVE A RIGHT TO THE LIFE."

TRANSLATED EXTRACTS FROM THE BULLETIN OF PSE, No. 2, FEBRUARY, 1945.

Page A :

" FOR BREAD AND FREEDOM.—1. In setting out to-day for a new struggle we must regard it as one, the target of which is the imperialistic policy of the Government, that policy which keeps our people in hunger and degradation.

. . . . . Consequently our struggle of to-day must be conducted under the motto ' Forward for Bread and Freedom '. "

Page D :

" The hatred against the imperialistic administration must be kindled and turned into an unextinguishable flame."

Page E :

" We should miss no opportunity for making it quite plain that no happiness can be understood under a colonial regime, no matter how many temporary concessions we may succeed in obtaining. Only thus shall we render acute the struggle against the foreign domination and shall give to our struggle a political and national character. This historical duty is cast on our shoulders, as officers of the movement."

*　　　*　　　*　　　*

" 4. Besides the hatred against the foreign Government, we must develop a deadly hatred against the local reaction, the ally of the foreign Government."

*　　　*　　　*　　　*

The Pancyprian Trade Unions Committee.

211

TRANSLATED EXTRACTS FROM THE " BULLETIN OF THE PANCYPRIAN TRADE UNIONS COMMITTEE ", No. 3, MARCH, 1945.

Page 1 :

" ALL IN THE STRUGGLE FOR BREAD AND FREEDOM.—The poverty and degradation of our people has reached its limit. The indifference of the Government has gone past the limits of abandonment of the people to the mercy of misery to such an extent that the life of our people is becoming intolerable, tragic.

The financial policy opposed to the interests of the people followed up to now by the Government leaves no doubt that our country will never feel the joy of sufficiency and of care-free life as long as it remains enslaved by it (the Government).

The demands submitted now-a-days by the working people to the foreign Government are demands, the solution of which will bring about a somewhat tolerable life. Yet a conquering power is not interested in, nor is it in a position to effect a solution of these elementary problems. The object of conquest is to take away and not to add to the welfare of the conquered. Consequently for a foreign Government to continue to be in charge of our country, means the sucking of the people's blood and the poverty and degradation of the people.

For this reason the maxim " NO ENSLAVED PEOPLE CAN BE HAPPY " is a historic law. And since people cannot live a most miserable life ungrudgingly, the people has to fight with all its might to drive away the conqueror "

Page 5 :

" TOWARDS RADICAL SOLUTIONS.

*　　　　*　　　　*　　　　*

We too must get prepared. Our children will soon be back from the fronts of the antifascist struggle of the whole community. We must all stand by each other in a fighting line, to support them, and their claims. For the prize of victory.

The people along with them and the families of the heroes should no longer be hungry and suffer from privations of all sorts. And in order that the working people of this country should cease to be hungry, it should fight hard, regardless of any sacrifice, which is necessary to drive away the conqueror, who has been sucking our blood for 67 years now."

*　　　　*　　　　*　　　　*

Page 6A :

" LABOURERS, FARMERS AND POOR MIDDLE-CLASS PEOPLE OF THE TOWNS, ...

IF YOU SEARCH FOR THE SOURCE OF YOUR MISERY, YOU WILL COME UPON THE CURSED AND POISONED IMPERIALISTIC SOURCE ; HENCE THE ENEMY IS COMMON TO ALL.

ALL WITH ONE HAND AND ONE HEART, SO THAT THE IMPERIALISTIC MORASS MIGHT DRY.

*　　　　*　　　　*　　　　*

Page 8 :

" THE SOLE ENEMY OF THE WORKING PEOPLE IS THE LOCAL FOREIGN GOVERNMENT. HENCE, LET US ALL TAKE PART IN THE STRUGGLE AGAINST THE COMMON ENEMY."

*　　　　*　　　　*　　　　*

Pages 14–16 :

" VICTORY OR DEATH.—In a shameful, beastly, assassin-like, fascist way did the bullets of the organs of the Executive Authority get into the breasts of our brothers. Without any provocation, without absolutely the least justification whatever, cold-bloodedly, premeditatedly did the Executive Authority, raise a murderous hand. Our brothers, who were proceeding to their club premises in a peaceful manner, with their hands up and proudly holding their banner of Liberty, fell down dead and speechless, on the blood-stained stony road. No power can make our murdered brothers rise again. The breasts, full of hopes for a better life, will breathe no more. The wandering eyes in pursuit of a distant vision, free of the tyranny of a nightmare, have closed never to open again. But the hot blood of labourers shed in the narrow street of a small village of a small island by a Great Government of a great country, has not dried and will never dry. The thousand eyes, the thousand souls, which had turned to tragic Lefkoniko have now dried, the beating of the heart has stopped and have made a vow. They have vowed that the blood, so ruthlessly shed by the black Government of slavery and tyranny, shall not be forgotten. They have vowed that the wound inflicted on the heart of us, labourers, will go on bleeding until the hour, when the punishing hand of the people will put a definite and final end to the blood-stained tyranny.

The motive which made the barbarous and blind hand of two organs of the Government rise at Lefkoniko, lies hidden very deeply in the roots of Government. We claim and we shall succeed in getting the punishment of the hideous assassin, who acting in blind obedience to the Government's directions stained with blood a peaceful and lawful procession. Should Government refuse to proceed to punishment, we shall ourselves undertake the imposition of an exemplary and cruel punishment which will preclude the repetition of such cruel crimes. But this is the least, that we claim, it is the least that we shall achieve. Because this act is not an act of two idiot policemen and of a warped criminal sergeant. This act is the necessary result of the general policy of the Government. This act is the unavoidable result of the course prescribed by the Government. The oppressive laws, the horrible and illiberal decrees, the enchainment of the freedom of the people, the efforts of the Government to stifle by the use of the whip any rising against the financial and political bonds which Government builds up in a manner which gets more horrible every day, these are the motives.

The social current drives at the abolition of the capitalist Governments. The Cyprus current drives at the creation of resistance against its national enslavement. And the Government, faithful to the rules prescribed by Marx, tries to stop by force and fascism, the course of history. For this reason the Government secret publications have become of late more shameless than the most shameless Nazi documents. The orders issued by the Government, which have got into our hands read as follows :—

‘ In case of any public manifestation do anything you like and be sure that you will be in the right. If you keep inactive, then you will always be in the wrong.’

[*continued overleaf.*

212

This and other similar mediaeval orders are sent by our ' liberal ' Government to their uneducated and warped policemen, who, boldened by the attitude of the Government, murder peaceful citizens and try to create an atmosphere of fear and terrorism. And even worse. According to our latest information, the Lefkoniko police authorities were keeping in continuous telephonic contact with Famagusta. That is why Government, with a shameless, immoral, impudent and insolent communique, tries to shield its faithful children, as though they had killed our brothers by somewhat outdoing the zeal of Government. But the time when the people was terrorized and scared off by such manifestations is past. The Government is making a gross mistake if it thinks that these measures are likely to curtail the movement which is growing bigger and bigger and is claiming the political, national and financial liberation of the people. These events only exacerbate the people and make them feel more keenly their position and hasten and sharpen their struggles. It is not with fear that the Lefkoniko events have filled up our soul ; IT IS WITH RESOLVE, INDIGNATION AND REVOLUTIONISM. And we, with dry eyes and stretched out fists, have pressed our soul which was weeping for our unjustly murdered brothers and we have made our terrible vow which none of us will ever forget.

DEAD AND WOUNDED BROTHERS OF LEFKONIKO : Over there at Lefkoniko, in a narrow street, the passer-by will notice two red spots, two small pools of blood. Over there at Lefkoniko, two souls are wandering and hovering over a bloodstained Greek flag with a thousand holes. Over there at Lefkoniko, some heroic souls have perished in a horrible and unequal struggle. Over there at Lefkoniko an eternal anathema has been placed on the disgraceful English colonial policy. Over there at Lefkoniko the passer-by shakes and shudders while passing by the two small pools of blood and hearing the simple peasant narrating their story. Over there at Lefkoniko there has been written the first line of the sepulchral lamentations of the local fascism. But it is not only the lamentations and anathemas that have sprung up in the tragic rural village. Over there at Lefkoniko there has been written the first page, blood-stained, sad, but full of resolve and pride, of our war for national liberation. Over there at Lefkoniko there has been built a grave, imaginary, but full of life, which magnetizes and attracts the eyes of every Cypriot combatant. Now we are no longer bound up with words and promises only. Now we are bound up together by the blood that was murderously shed at Lefkoniko. Now we are ordered by our murdered ones, who seek revenge, who ask for a struggle for the sake of freedom in the cause of which they have given their lives. We, therefore, faithfull to the sacred memory of theirs, with uplifted fists, make the following sacred vow :—

' We shall never forget the unjustly-shed blood of our gallant brothers who gave their lives holding up the banner of freedom. I shall go on fighting until the unjustly-shed blood is paid off and mankind breathes in relief on account of the joyful feeling of revenge.'

I shall never forget that the hand which was murderously raised against our brothers, is rooted in the political tyranny and the national enslavement imposed by the foreign Government. For this reason I shall not cease fighting until the political tyranny dies out and the national integration is effected.

We shall not forget that we shall be considered as traitors or that we shall blur the memory of the Lefkoniko heroes, if even for a moment we let our mind calm down and our body rest, before we are victorious in the struggle the sole watchword of which will be VICTORY OR DEATH.

The war will soon be over and all of us will be called upon to give all we can in the struggle for the liberation of our people.

Brothers, colleagues :

REMEMBER LEFKONIKO AND YOU WILL NEVER LOSE HEART.

VICTORY OR DEATH.

(*Intld.*) V. L."

PART 1.

DESCRIPTION OF DOCUMENTS.

1. The Bulletin of the Pancyprian Trade Unions Committee, No. 1, January, 1945.
2. The Bulletin of the Pancyprian Trade Unions Committee, No. 2, February, 1945.
3. "The Propagandistis," fortnightly organ of the Central Cultural Office of the Pancyprian Trade Unions Committee, No. 3, March, 1945.
4. A document entitled " Appreciation and Thesis on our National Liberation Struggle " (undated).
5. A document entitled " The Voice of the Labourer " dated 16th January, 1945.
6. A document entitled " The Propagandistis " dated 15th January or February, (torn up) 1945.
7. A document entitled " The Voice of the Labourer " dated 7th April, 1945.

PART 2.

DETAILS AND TRANSLATED EXTRACTS ON DOCUMENTS DESCRIBED IN PART 1 HEREOF.

1. For extracts from items 1, 2 and 3 of Part 1 hereof see Schedule " A ".

2. Extracts from item 4 of Part 1 hereof, to wit, a document entitled " Appreciation and Thesis on our National Liberation Struggle " (undated).

Page 14 :

". . . . . But we declare that we shall struggle by the side of the Greek Communist Party and EAM for the domination of the people's rule and the passing into socialism.

On this line we must enlighten and train our members, on this line we must enlighten and train the people.

Paragraph 12 :

The struggle for national liberation for the Cyprus people can be successfully conducted only under the following method of revolutionary action :—

(a) full training of the people on the right proletarian solution of our national question ;
(b) through the organization of the revolutionary, national liberation front of the labourers and the other liberal strata of society under the hegemony of the Proletarian Party. We must use every factor of the realization of the united front, but mainly we must direct ourselves to its realization and hammering from downwards because only thus shall we embrace the masses and their anti-imperialistic feelings and conduct them into the revolutionary channel ;
(c) through the actual struggle of the people for our national question in such a way as to combine the struggle for the financial demands of our people as well as the attack against the illiberal laws and decrees. This struggle can be successfully conducted only through mobilizations under the united front and on the basis of a pre-arranged plan ;
(d) by securing a regular and concrete linking up with the Greek movement—with a view to achieving a cohesion in the objects, the pursuits and the struggle—with the revolutionary movement of Great Britain—with a view to achieving a unified action for the liberation of our people—and with the movements of the neighbouring enslaved countries—with a view to conducting a common anti-imperialistic struggle.

It is an imperative need that our linking up should be done as soon as possible and within a prescribed time limit."

3. Extracts from item 5 of Part 1 hereof, to wit, a document entitled " The Voice of the Labourer " of 16th January, 1945 :—

THE REPOSE OF LULL.

*   *   *   *

" The cause of the people of Greece, same as that of all the other peoples on earth, is a clear, honest and sincere cause. Nevertheless the treacherous reactionary forces succeed in perverting this cause and in taking, from our progressive revolutionary camp, uninformed forces. It is, therefore, our bounden duty to enlighten the broad popular masses so that in the opportune time in the near future to be ready to declare any deeds and in a fighting way our solidarity with the heroically struggling Greek proletariats." ·

" It must become a faith to each one of us. Our indifference is criminal. We are a revolutionary force and our opponents counter-revolutionary. But, unfortunately, till now our opponents were always on the attack and we, almost on the counter-attack, and this because we were unable to gather together our forces. The second and probably final phase of our struggle must not find us indifferent and uninformed ".

" We must start preparatory work from now onwards so as to be fully prepared. Every delay is a blow on our own body and it is not time now to receive blows but to give."

4. Extracts from item 6 of Part 1 hereof, to wit, a document entitled the " Propagandistis ", dated 15th January or February, 1945.

THE UNITY OF OUR PEOPLE.

*   *   *   *

" The socialist parties are united to-day with the communistic ones with the main objective of unifying all revolutionary forces for the uplifting of humanity.

In obedience to this watchword we have been forced to approach the treacherous party of the big capital of our country in order to be able to concentrate the fighting revolutionary forces which, upon training, to throw into the struggle against the enemy."

[continued overleaf.

5. Extracts from item 7 of Part 1 hereof, to wit, a document entitled "**The Voice of the Labourer**" of the 7th April, 1945.

FORWARD FOR GREAT STRUGGLES.

"The situation created owing to the scandalous and moral indifference of the blood-sucking Government towards the problems of the Cypriot working people cannot really be tolerated any longer.

. . . . . One cannot play so easily with the sufferings of the people. Above all, to-day everybody has heard so much about the ' welfare ' of the peoples from the official lips of our gaolers so that the distinction between the promise and naked reality cannot but push the working people to struggles for real solution of the tormenting problems concerning them.

The local Government must very soon confront our bulk in the struggles because, alas if we let Government believe that it can tie us feet and hands together with promises or even with forced threats. A people cannot live always a tortuous and unbearable life (given) by drops. This people must certainly counter-attack with spite, being indifferent about the sacrifices, so that the destructive Government machine should be rendered unable to function unimpededly. It is only in this way that we can hope that we can start our real, historic struggle, a struggle the maximum aim of which should be the expulsion of the tyranny as the only pre-supposition of the radical solution of all the economic, political and social problems of our people.

. . . . . BE READY THEREFORE FOR THE GREAT STRUGGLES THE MAXIMUM AIM OF WHICH SHOULD BE THE LIBERATION OF OUR COUNTRY "

Part 1.

LIST OF DOCUMENTS.

1. Bulletin of Pancyprian Trade Unions Committee, No. 2, February, 1945.
2. Bulletin of Pancyprian Trade Unions Committee, No. 3, March, 1945.
3. A document entitled " The Voice of the Labourer " dated 3rd March, 1945.
4. A document dated 18th of March, 1945 (without any title).

Part 2.

DETAILS AND TRANSLATED EXTRACTS FROM THE DOCUMENTS DESCRIBED IN PART 1 HEREOF.

1. For extracts from item 1 of Part 1 hereof see Schedule " B ".

2. For extracts from item 2 of Part 1 hereof see Schedule " C ".

3. Extracts from item 3 of Part 1 hereof, to wit, " The Voice of the Labourer " dated 3rd March, 1945.
" 3rd of March, 1945.

THE GREAT DAY.

*   *   *   *

. . . . . The suggestions of our representatives on the various committees met with the absolute indifference of the satiated Englishmen who were going round the villages fishing for fodder for imperialistic guns.

All these and many other things forced PSE to knock resolutely at the door of the Government. But our friends turned a deaf ear. Cold-blooded, indifferent and scornful as always they stated : ' After a most careful consideration we find that the labour wages are most satisfactory.'

This reply of the people-strangler Government could not but fill up the labour cup of bitterness. And there followed the historic struggle of the 1st of March. Those unforgettable days held up our labour movement high, so high that even the last Cypriot of the remotest corner of our island could see and applaud it.

We struck down to the ground like an octopus not only the foreign foul (base) Government but also the local traitors and exploiters who could not fight openly the struggling Cyprus people.

*   *   *   *

The struggle of the 1st of March definitely unmasked the shameless Government before the eyes of even the last man in our island. With this Government we shall meet soon again, this Government we shall meet regularly until we get rid of its filthy and destructive presence. Already thousands of labourers nowadays have not the means of living. The old wages of 4/6 made to them a present of hunger. Those who still continue to work find it very difficult to make both ends meet. The few money, that had circulated in our country, has been absorbed by the Government through a thousand foul means and sent to the London safe. Life in our country appears to be incomparably more tragic than it was on the eve of the historic struggle of the 1st of March. It is time that we should meet again with the Government who is hated by the people. It is time we should strike some blows against it by using its inefficiency and its inconsistencies as well as our due demands which shall not be anything else but our hunger, its shameless policy and our liberation.

It is high time the proletarians took the way towards the military camp. We must mobilize again for greater and more decisive struggles. The people are body and soul on our side ; by our present struggles we are going to isolate the pro-Government plutocrats of our country and advance as PEOPLE united in our great struggle : OUR NATIONAL LIBERATION STRUGGLE. And then we shall really get in the way of achieving our integrate aim by struggling FOR BREAD AND FREEDOM."

4. Extracts from item 4 of Part 1 hereof, to wit, a document dated 18th March, 1945 (without title).

" When a slave slaves for whole 67 years under a cruel and criminal master who keeps him hungry, without a roof and in rags and he (the slave) does not rise and does not rouse up to break his bonds and become a man then this slave does not deserve to live and to be called a man.

*   *   *   *

The Cyprus people, who for 67 years now is tortured in the most inhuman manner by a foreign, cruel and criminal government, has to rise and either live or die. Human mind has offered so many things to man so as not to live in privation, not to be hungry, not to be in rags and not to be without a roof. Nevertheless, a handful of men, because so they want it, hold the man shut up in cages with iron bars and exploit him as much and in the way which they desire.

*   *   *   *

Churchill spoke clearly : ' Our joy and our happiness must be based on the weepings and the pains of the other enslaved world. Your death is my life.' We must think of all this very seriously ; as fas as anything depends from the stranglers of the people, lords of England, we shall be the means for the building up of their happiness.

*   *   *   *

Our demands are very just and must be satisfied. A foreign government which bases its happiness on our own misfortune will not satisfy these demands of ours. If they meant to satisfy them, they should, first of all, set us free. The whole of the Cyprus people, therefore, in mass let us throw ourselves in the big national liberation struggle for the liberation of this place, this being the basic pre-supposition of the demands of our people."

216

Appendix B

These EOKA and AKEL Pamphlets were distributed in Nicosia in 1956 on May 15 and May 21 respectively. The translations were made at the American consulate at the time.

TO THE "LEFTISTS" OF CYPRUS

I have spoken to you also on another occasion when the leadership of AKEL, in betraying the liberation struggle of the people of Cyprus, took up arms against us and insulted us as terrorists, trouble-makers, etc., and even accused us of not struggling against the English but against AKEL!!! You will all remember the speeches of Zachariades who insulted and at the same time betrayed us, and you will remember the proclamation of AKEL on the 1st of April 1955 and the articles in "NEOS DEMOCRATIS" lest anyone should think we are making unjust claims.

The facts have proved to everyone who are the real patriots; who are struggling in arms against the British, and who are wishing, at least so they say, to solve the Cyprus question solely through the bureaucracy. They have proved who those are who risk themselves, sacrifice themselves and everything for the liberation struggle, and who those others are who seek to make capital out of the struggle *in a party spirit* or for their *personal* interest.

We are aware of the fact that all "leftists" do not agree with the attitude of AKEL towards our struggle and that most of them think patriotically as we do and acknowledge the fact that they have been misled by AKEL because of the false promises of its leadership. At this moment we address ourselves to the "honest leftists" *and not to AKEL in general,* and call upon them to sever their responsibilities from the leadership of AKEL which has been proved as not serving the interests of the people of Cyprus. We summon these *honest* leftists to shake off Satan, that is to say AKEL, and to join the ranks of our national liberation movement. We shall gladly accept them as individuals, because our purpose is that everyone who thinks patriotically, as a Greek, and who wishes to strike the conqueror and tyrant should participate in this struggle so that on the morrow, after the liberation, all of us, and above all the labourers and farmers, the two pedestals of our present regime, may meet in understanding and be rewarded for our pains and sacrifices.

We are neither imperialists nor capitalists but poor children of the people who live by their sweat, but who have a National pulse, pure Greek, far from any foreign influence and propaganda.

217

What we seek is included in these words: We are ardent nationalists, with national ideals and a love of freedom, virtues which we have inherited from our fathers who, the same as ourselves, have shed their blood in order to be freed from the foreign yoke; but we love a *just community* as well in which everyone will be rewarded according to his pains and where the individual will not remain undefended and be exploited by the clever.

FANATIC PATRIOTS, BUT FANATICALLY JUST IN THE DISTRIBUTION OF WEALTH. THIS is our "CREED." For this we are now shedding our blood.

Forward the FAITHFUL in order to acquire these things: A FREE COUNTRY, SOCIAL JUSTICE.

E.O.K.A.
THE
LEADER
DIGENIS

REFORM PARTY OF THE WORKING PEOPLE (A.K.E.L.)

TO THE PATRIOTIC PEOPLE OF CYPRUS

A leaflet headed "To the Leftists of Cyprus" and signed "The leader Digenis" was circulated recently. With this, "Digenis" slanders AKEL as betraying the national struggle and summons the "leftists" to follow him.

Leaving aside the demagogy and boastings contained in this leaflet to the effect that only "Digenis" carries out a national struggle, and without stooping to retaliate, which would greatly please the enemies of our national cause, we must stress the following points. If AKEL and its leadership are as "Digenis" presents them, then the imperialists would not have dealt it such a powerful blow; they would not have illegally closed its press publication "Neos Democratis" or arrested its leaders and put the whole party under persecution.

AKEL has a clear policy and an equally clear strategy and tactics. The aim of AKEL is absolute self-determination for all the people of Cyprus. Its strategy is the unification of all the patriotic forces of the people for the effective carrying out of the liberation struggle and its tactic is the all-people's open, democratic struggle.

AKEL believes firmly that in order to advance effectively the national liberation struggle of the people of Cyprus it requires principally *the unification of all our patriotic forces of the people of Cyprus and that the struggle be conducted democratically.* That is why AKEL has never tried to monopolize the national struggle but always tried to form a United Patriotic Liberation Front. The whole history of the national struggles of nations has proved that their success is based upon patriotic unification and democratic action. Unfortunately "the leader Digenis" himself wants to give orders from the side wings and wants everyone else to fulfil his orders without having the fundamental right to discuss whether the one tactic or another is the proper one under the Cyprus conditions. AKEL being a party inspired by democratic ideals cannot accept this because it would not be consistent with its principles and would not serve the national interests of the people.

AKEL continuously criticized in the past the policy of the Greek government towards the Cyprus cause. Some sections of the right-wing then called AKEL a "traitor." We believe now that those same sections acknowledge that AKEL was right and criticize more strongly the tactics of the Greek government.

AKEL does not intend to conceal the fact that it disagrees with the tactic of "Digenis." Not out of fear, but because it believes that Cyprus reality and conditions impose the need for a mass, democratic struggle, which, as experience has proved, gains more allies both between the English people and internationally. We believe that those who now approve the tactics of "Digenis" will in future be convinced by their own experience about the correctness of the aspects of AKEL regarding the right tactic of struggle, in the same way as they have now been convinced of the correctness of the estimates of AKEL regarding the role of the Greek government.

The tactic of the mass, democratic struggle, with the decisive putting forward of the Cyprus question in the U.N.O. by the Greek government, which we must insist has to be done, and having the solidarity and support of all the liberal humanity we shall eventually win self-determination for the people of Cyprus.

What then is "Digenis" seeking with his slanders? Is it perhaps the disruption of the people and a civil rending, that enemies of our national cause would like? For once again, the C.C. of AKEL without fearing the threats and not allowing its mind to be clouded with thoughts of retaliation, and being fully aware of its responsibilities to the people and our national struggle addresses itself to all Cypriot patriots, right-wing, leftists and independents, Greek and Turks, and summons them to maintain a patriotic watch and to unite. To the propaganda and the disruptive slogans of "Digenis," AKEL replies: It is our aim to strengthen the unification of the people. To carry out a mass, all people's open, democratic struggle for self-determination. Unification and not disruption. A democratic struggle by all our people against the colonialists, and not civil war.

THE C.C. [Central Committee] OF AKEL

219

Appendix C

An AKEL Central Committee Resolution, 1969, *Haravghi,* Oct. 23, 1969
(Foreign Broadcast Information Service Translation)

The AKEL Central Committee and the Central Control Committee held a special plenary session in Nicosia on 20 October and discussed in detail the current phase of the Cyprus issue and the Cyprus situation in general, and unanimously passed the following resolution:

The AKEL Central Committee and the Central Control Committee special plenary session was held at a period when the inter-Cypriot talks are going through a critical phase, when the imperialist circles are showing great interest and developing unusual activities, and when the Cyprus home front is being seriously tried because of the criminal activities by fascist and terrorist organizations.

The inter-Cypriot talks are continuing but there are differences on the substantial question of local administration which threaten the future of the talks. According to available reports, the Turkish proposals are such that they would lead to the establishment of three separate administrations—a Turkish Cypriot for the Turks, a Greek Cypriot for the Greeks, and a central mixed administration. Such a system is contrary to the idea of a unitary state.

The AKEL Central Committee believes that the inter-Cypriot talks are the only course for a peaceful Cyprus solution and must be continued. Our party firmly opposes holding a Greek-Turkish dialog or a five-party conference because neither of them would give a solution in the interests of all the Cypriot people. It would serve Anglo-American and NATO interests at the Cypriot people's expense, at the expense of the neighboring countries, and of the progressive anti-imperialist powers working for world peace.

AKEL reaffirms its belief that the interests of Greek and Turkish Cypriots lie with a fully independent, sovereign, territorially and administratively unified, and demilitarized Cyprus where all the citizens' democratic and human rights will be fully respected. The AKEL Central Committee appeals to the Greek and Turkish Cypriots, to the government, and to the Turkish Cypriot leadership and urges them to show sincerity and goodwill for a solution based on the aforesaid lines. The AKEL Central Committee also believes that both the government and the Turkish Cypriot leadership must promote mutual confidence, understanding friendship, and cooperation. This can be done if the government, for example, repairs the houses of Turkish Cypriots for their subsequent return to their villages, and if the Turkish Cypriot leadership reciprocates the government pacification measures. The people can also help remove suspicion and promote confidence and good relations by establishing systematic contacts and cooperation with the Turkish Cypriots. Demagogy and chauvinism are dangerous and make the continuation of the talks difficult.

The AKEL Central Committee and the Central Control Committee firmly believe that the talks can be successful if the Turkish Cypriots sincerely accept a unitary and indivisible Cyprus state. If this is not done the talks might reach a deadlock. In such an event our party proposes that the President of the Republic should call a conference of deputies, party representatives, organizations, and other leading personalities to exchange views and lay down a common line.

The AKEL Central Committee notes the increased undermining of activities by imperialist circles—primarily the Anglo-Americans and their espionage services—and the intensified terrorist activities of the illegal fascist organizations.

Cyprus' enemies are preparing various adventurous plans at a time when normalcy and tranquillity are needed more than ever.

The main aims of the various imperialist conspiratorial plans are: To undermine and finally torpedo the talks; to cause upheaval and tension; to disrupt the people's patriotic unity; to carry out political murders and even provoke civil war; overthrow President Makarios through a coup; and impose on Cyprus a [word illegible] partitionist solution. The champions in these anti-people and treacherous plans are the Anglo-American imperialists—those who prepared the criminal "Rafford" plan for the suppression of the democratic, anti-imperialist movement in Libya, and the 10-1 plan for the extermination of the people of Europe through a thermonuclear, chemical, and bacteriological war. The champions in the new conspiratorial plans against Cyprus are the very same imperialist circles which have prepared the Ball, Acheson, Lemnitzer, and Vance plans for the partitioning of Cyprus and its enslavement to NATO.

Under these conditions the activities recently developed by illegal fascist organizations become particularly dangerous. They serve the diabolical aims of the imperialist enemies of Cyprus.

The AKEL Central Committee fully approves and unreservedly supports President Makarios' statement branding the criminal activities of terrorist elements and organizations as acts of "high treason." By these acts Cyprus is being led straight to partition and enslavement to NATO.

Our party calls on the government to take all the necessary measures to combat these criminal activities, end this situation, and restore the people's sense of security and confidence. The party also calls on the people to intensify their vigilance, strengthen their patriotic unity, and rally around the line approved by the people for a realistic Cyprus solution. But beyond this, the further strengthening of Cyprus' relations with the socialist countries, and in general the world democratic and anti-imperialist powers, as well as with the nonalined states, can help neutralize the imperialist designs on Cyprus and promote our people's anti-imperialist struggle for a just and peaceful Cyprus solution.

The AKEL Central Committee and Central Control Committee plenary session has noted the increasing political activities in our country and the growing demand for elections. Our party reiterates it is time to hold elections for village and municipal authorities and for a new parliament. The electoral system to be applied must insure just representation of all the parties in parliament. In our opinion, the best system is that of simple proportion.

Bearing in mind the present stage of our struggle and putting above party interests the Cypriot people's interests, and with the belief that the people's patriotic unity is needed more than ever for the promotion of a Cyprus solution, AKEL appeals to all the parties: In view of parliamentary or other elections, an all-party conference must be held to bring about understanding and universal national unity and cooperation based on a minimum agreed program.

Our party firmly believes that the interests of the Cypriot people and of our national cause require that the elections should not be an element of division and conflict but a landmark for further universal and patriotic unity of the people's patriotic forces so as to jointly face any difficulties and to pursue a realistic, peaceful, and just Cyprus solution free from any dangerous demagogy.

[Signed] The AKEL Central Committee. Nicosia, October 20.

Appendix D

CALENDAR OF CYPRIOT-COMMUNIST BLOC ACTIVITIES IN 1968
(Compiled by the American Embassy in Nicosia.)

Jan. (n.d.)　　The Cypriot firm Photos Photiades, Ltd., signed a trade agreement with Communist China to import furniture equipment and preserved foodstuffs in return for the export of chromium in the value of approximately £100,000 each way.

Jan. 11　　The Cyprus Council of Ministers approved in principle the making of an airline agreement between Cyprus and Czechoslovakia.

Jan. 13　　Yugoslavia offered undergraduate scholarships to sons and daughters of Greek Cypriots—except civil servants.

Jan. 22　　Yugoslav fruit importers' delegation arrived on the island as guests of the Ministry of Commerce to negotiate the purchase of local fruit.

Jan. 26　　Czechoslovakian archeologist arrived for a two-week visit arranged through the Department of Antiquities.

Feb. 2　　The Central Council of the Czechoslovak Trade Unions issued a memorandum supporting Cyprus' struggle against imperialism. In a letter addressed to PEO it refers to the Turkish threats for invasion, describing them as a NATO plot.

Feb. 3　　A Peace Movement delegation from East Germany visited Cyprus as guest of the Cypriot Peace Movement. It was met at the airport by officials of AKEL, the East German-Cypriot Friendship Society, and the Cypriot Peace Movement. Members of the delegation spoke at a meeting on February 5 about strengthening relations between the two countries.

Feb. 5　　Mr. Rodas, Cypriot Controller of the Vine Products Scheme, returned from Moscow. It is reported that he signed an agreement with the Soviet authorities for the export of 5,000 tons of Cyprus raisins valued at £300,000.

Feb. 8	Cypriot stage actors Evis Gabrielides and Jenny Gaitano-poulou left on a short visit to East Germany as guests of its Theatrical Center.
Feb. 9	By decision of the Cyprus Council of Ministers published in the gazette, the government recognizes the diplomas in Civil Engineering granted by the Lumumba Friendship University of Moscow.
Feb. 10	It was officially announced that a limited number of scholarships were to be awarded to Cypriots for six months of training in textile engineering. The training is to be given in Poland under the auspices of the U.N. Industrial Development Organization.
Feb. 12	The Cyprus Electricity Authority signed a three-year contract with the NAFTA Petroleum Company of Cyprus to import 400,000 tons of Soviet oil valued at £2,500,000. Repayment is to be made by the export of Cyprus spirits to the Soviet Union.
Feb. 15	The local communist organizations DEOK, PEO, EDON, POAS, POGO, and EKA decided to send representatives to the World Youth Festival in Sofia, Bulgaria, between July 28 and August 6, 1968. It was announced that the Cypriot delegation would consist of about 100 members.
Feb. 23	The Soviet Embassy celebrated the fiftieth anniversary of the Soviet army. The Press Attache informed the press about the significance of the day and the role played by the Red Army in world progress, peace, and freedom. In addition, the Military Attache gave a cocktail party attended by Ministers, Members of the House, and other dignitaries. Also, the Cyprus-Soviet Association scheduled a festive gathering for February 28. The Soviet Military Attache addressed the gathering and stated that the Soviet Union will continue to grant every kind of aid to the brotherly Vietnamese people in their just struggle against imperialist aggressors.
Feb. 26	Mr. Dinos Constantinou, member of the Politbureau of the AKEL Central Committee, left for Budapest to participate together with AKEL Secretary General Ezekias Papaioannou in the conference of communist and workers' parties.
Feb. 29	Mr. Pantelis Varnavas, Secretary-Organizer of PEO, attended the conference of Soviet syndicates held in Moscow.

March 3	Cyprus participated again in the Leipzig Spring Fair, March 3 to 12.
March 3	Dr. Paul Vandel, President of the East German Society for Friendship with Foreign Peoples, arrived in Cyprus March 2 as guest of the local Friendship Society with East Germany. During his short visit Dr. Vandel was received by President Makarios and gave a lecture at the Cyprus Scientists' Association on "Present Education in East Germany."
March 6	The Soviet delegation of the Afro-Asian Peoples' Solidarity Organization, headed by Philosophy Professor Bakhitov, arrived in Nicosia. Bakhitov stated that the delegation came to Cyprus to exchange views with the representatives of the Cypriot Solidarity Committee on current problems and to broaden and strengthen the ties of Soviet and Cypriot friendship.
March 13	The Cyprus-Czechoslovak Friendship Society offered a full-time university scholarship in Czechoslovakia.
March 14	Soviet author Boris Bolevoe arrived in Nicosia on March 13 and participated in a World Peace Council delegation which arrived on the island to demonstrate support in the Cyprus problem.
March 15	Cypriot firms signed trade agreements with the Foreign Trade Service of East Germany to export citrus fruits. The agreement was signed during the Leipzig Fair.
March 16	Dr. Mathees Papapetrou, President of the Cypriot-East German Friendship Society, returned from Berlin where he attended the International Preliminary Committee meeting for the Congress to be held in Helsinki in June on "The German Problem and European Security."
March 17	The Secretary-General of the World Peace Council, Mr. Romesh Chandra from India, and Italian Senator Bentaralia arrived on the island together with leaders of the AAPSO movement to demonstrate support in the Cyprus issue.
March 18	A Cyprus-Polish trade protocol was signed in Nicosia on March 17. The protocol is to be in force for one year and the value of goods exchanged on each side is to amount to £460,000.
March 21	A five-man Soviet trade delegation, led by the chief of

225

the Administration for Trade with Western Countries, Manshule, arrived in Nicosia by air on March 20 for a one-week visit to discuss the renewal for five years of the Bilateral Trade Agreement between Cyprus and the U.S.S.R.

March 28   Cyprus and the Soviet Union signed a five-year trade and payments agreement on March 27. The agreement calls for an exchange of goods valued at more than £12 million.

March 28   A delegation from the Cyprus Potato Export Council headed by A. Azinas, Commissioner for Cooperative Development, announced that it would leave in a week for East Germany to negotiate the sale of potatoes (spring crop).

March 29   A Cyprus-Bulgaria trade protocol was signed in Nicosia. It is to be in force for one year with the value of goods to be exchanged on each side to be £650,000.

March 29   A Hungarian trade union delegation arrived in Nicosia on March 28 and attended the meeting of the local Shoe Industries' Labor Union.

April 2   The Commissioner for Cooperative Development, Andreas Asinas, left for the German Democratic Republic. He will try to sell 500 tons of Cyprus tobacco or exchange it for East German industrial goods.

April 2   The Czechoslovak Airlines inaugurated a weekly Nicosia-to-Prague service.

April 3   The Potato Export Council sent a three-man delegation to the German Democratic Republic to negotiate the sale of the island's potato spring crop.

April 4   Soviet author Sergey Smyrnoff, Secretary of the Moscow Authors' Association and President of the Committee for Solidarity with the Greek People, arrived in Cyprus on April 3. He was accompanied by Mr. V. Koplikoff, Deputy Director of the Office of European Relations of the Soviet Friendship Societies. The Soviet delegation remained on Cyprus about fifteen days.

April 10   The East German football team "Forverts" came to Cyprus at the invitation of Nicosia communist team "Omonia." The East German team played "Omonia" and the Limassol team AEL in Nicosia.

April 11	The Vice-President of the Chamber of Foreign Trade of the German Democratic Republic, Mr. Kurt Wolf, visited the Chairman of the Cyprus Chamber of Commerce and Industry, Representative Michael Savvides, and discussed the trade relations between Cyprus and the GDR.
April 13	Two East German legal experts, Messrs. Peck and Urlman, gave a press conference in Nicosia on the new constitution of the German Democratic Republic. Earlier they met Cypriot Attorney-General Criton Tornaritis.
April 15	The President of the Soviet Solidarity Committee with Greek Democrats, Mr. Sergey Smyrnoff, met with the President of the corresponding Cypriot committee, Mr. Vias Markides. The two presidents decided to maintain closer cooperation on future activities.
April 24	The Deputy General Secretary of AKEL, Andreas Fantis, left for Budapest to attend preliminary meetings of the committee for the preparation of the international communist and labor party congress, to be held in Moscow in November and December of 1968.
April 24	The Cypriot Students' Association (OEFEK) announced that it will accept applications for one scholarship to the Soviet Union and one to Bulgaria. The scholarships were granted to OEFEK by the International Students' Federation.
April 26	A trade protocol renewing the Trade and Payments Agreement between Cyprus and the German Democratic Republic was signed in Nicosia. Goods to the value of approximately £900,000 would be exchanged on each side. This represented an increase of 20 per cent as compared with the previous year.
May 2	The Soviet Under-Secretary for Postal Services, Mr. Holof, stopped at Nicosia airport in transit to Moscow from Damascus.
May 7	The German Democratic Republic opened a two-day canned meat exhibition at its Trade Mission offices in Nicosia.
May 8	Soviet visitors: *Pravda's* chief editor for the Department on European Countries, Bragin, and Moscow Radio's Mustafayev arrived in Nicosia as representatives of the Soviet Journalists' Union for a ten-day stay in Cyprus at the invitation of the Cyprus Editors' Union.

227

May 9	AKEL's General Secretary Papaioannou sent a congratulatory telegram to the Central Committee of the Czechoslovak Communist Party on the occasion of the country's liberation anniversary.
May 10	Czechoslovak activities: Czechoslovak Ambassador to Cyprus Rejmon arrived from Athens on May 9 to attend the reception given by the Czechoslovak Embassy in Nicosia on May 10, which marks the twenty-fourth anniversary of Czechoslovakia's liberation.
May 12	A delegation of three Cypriot farmers, representing the communist farmers' union (EKA) and the right-wing PEK, visited the German Democratic Republic from May 1 to 9. They attended the Congress of Agricultural Organizations in Magdebourg, GDR. EKA General Secretary Michaelides spoke at the Congress thanking the people and government of GDR for their support in the Cypriot struggle. The Chairman of the Congress, in turn, assured the Cypriot delegation of continuing support for President Makarios, the Cyprus government, and the Cypriot people in the struggle for independence and territorial integrity.
May 13	President Archbishop Makarios gave a formal luncheon at the Presidential Palace in honor of departing Soviet Ambassador Yermoshin.
May 15	President Archbishop Makarios received the Soviet press delegation. House President Clerides had received the delegation on May 14.
May 16	A Soviet journalists' delegation visited the *Halkin Sesi* and *Bozkurt* offices.
May 17	It was officially announced that the Cyprus church will be represented at the fiftieth anniversary celebrations of the Moscow Patriarchate. The Cypriot church delegates, Bishop Yennadios and Archmandrite Sariyiannis, are to depart for Moscow on May 22.
May 21	A three-member AKEL delegation including the party's Deputy General Secretary A. Fantis, left for Rumania at the invitation of the Rumanian Communist Party for inter-party talks.
May 24	The World Peace Council held a meeting in Nicosia from June 6 to 7. The leader of the Soviet delegation, playwright A. Korneychouk, arrived by ship in Famagusta on May 23 accompanied by his wife. Korneychouk is

Vice-President of the Soviet Peace Council and a member of the Governing Board of the World Peace Council.

June 2   World Peace Council Secretary-General Romesh Chandra arrived in Nicosia to attend the WPC Presidium meetings, June 5 to 8.

June 4   The Cypriot communist yough organization, EDON, announced that Cyprus would participate in this year's World Youth Festival in Sofia from July 28 to August 6, with a delegation comprising of 120 persons.

June 5   A three-day session of the World Peace Council opened in Nicosia. It was attended by about 50 members from various countries, including the United States, the U.S.S.R., France, Canada, and India. The congress was opened by the chairman of the Cyprus committee of WPC, Representative Potamitis. Dr. Lyssarides greeted the delegates and thanked them for selecting Cyprus for the congress. The Presidium continued its session behind closed doors and debated various questions, including Vietnam, the Middle East, and Cyprus.

June 7   The World Peace Council Presidium confirmed full support for the Cypriot people's struggle for an independent, self-contained, sovereign, unitary, unfettered, and demilitarized Cyprus, where the rights of the Turkish Cypriot minority will be defined and ensured. The Cyprus government and the people of the island would have the WPC's support in applying a policy of neutrality against pressures and conspiracies which seek to entangle Cyprus directly or indirectly in NATO or other imperialist military parts.

June 7   Rumania offers a post-graduate scholarship in Petrol Refining and Petrochemical Industrial Engineering.

June 8   President Archbishop Makarios received in audience June 7 the members of the World Peace Council Presidium. His Beatitude stated, inter alia, that "your efforts are much appreciated. The people of Cyprus, who are peace-loving, are watching your meetings with great interest. Cyprus is passing through a difficult stage. Your efforts for peace also help the peaceful settlement of the Cyprus problem."

June 14   The director of the Vine Products Scheme, Mr. Rodas, left for Moscow in connection with the renewal of the trade agreement to export raisins and wines to the U.S.S.R.

June 18	Cypriot representatives Lyssarides and Ioannides supported the territorial integrity and sovereignty of the German Democratic Republic at a meeting held in Helsinki on June 8 and 9 on the subject "Recognition of GDR and European Security."
June 20	The Cypriot Church delegation, comprised of Bishop Yennadios of Paphos and Archmandrite Saryiannis, who represented the Church at the celebrations for the fiftieth anniversary of the Moscow Patriarchate, returned home June 19.
June 22	A direct Nicosia-Prague air service was inaugurated with the arrival in Cyprus of 30 Czechoslovak personalities aboard a Czechoslovak airliner. The visitors, who will stay in Cyprus for five days, were led by Czechoslovakian Under-Secretary for Transport Jan Dufek. They included Vice-President of the National Assembly Valo, First Deputy Finance Minister Ler, Deputy Heavy Industry Minister Belovsky, the Director of the Premier's Office, the Lord Mayor of Prague Ludvik Cerny, and other officials.
June 26	The Cypriot Minister of Agriculture, Mr. Tombazos, left by air for East Germany to visit the Leipzig Agricultural Fair
June 27	Cypriot personalities left for a five-day visit to Czechoslovakia as guests of Czechoslovak airlines. They included Director-General of the Ministry of Interior Anastassiou, Director of Civil Aviation Ienopoulos, Director of Tourism Montis, House Member Anastassiades, President of the Cyprus Development Corporation Colocassides, and AKEL General Secretary Papaioannou.
June 29	Twelve Cypriot farmers left aboard the Soviet steamship *Felix Tserniski* for a seventeen-day visit to the Soviet Union. The farmers were accompanied by Union of Cypriot Farmers (EKA) Larnaca District Secretary Kakoullis.
June 30	Two hundred Cypriots were studying at various educational institutions in the Soviet Union, it was announced by Soviet Ambassador Tolubeyev on June 28. The Ambassador was talking at the Cyprus-Soviet Friendship Society on the occasion of a graduation ceremony for students of Russian. Toulembeyef said that knowledge of Russian is an important factor in obtaining scholarships to the U.S.S.R. and encouraged prospective candidates to learn the language by joining the language

classrooms organized by the Cyprus-Soviet Friendship Society.

June 30   At the World Youth Festival in Sofia, Cypriot representatives sat on the Presidium in three meetings: (a) the meeting concerning the Middle East problem; (b) the conference on the subject "The Role of Youth Organizations in Social Problems of Their Countries," on which subject the Cypriot delegation prepared a report to the International Preparatory Committee; and (c) the special meeting for the religiously minded, at which Cyprus represented the Greek Orthodox religion. The Cypriot delegation is to depart by sea on July 22 and arrive in Cyprus on August 11, 1968.

July 4   The Mayor of Famagusta, Mr. A. Pouyouros, and Municipal Councilor Prodromos Papavassiliou left for East Germany on July 3 as guests of Rostok city's Mayor, Mr. Flek.

July 4   The Mayor of Karavas, Mr. John Harmandas, left July 3 for East Germany as guest of the GDR government.

July 4   The Minister of Agriculture, Mr. G. Tombazos, spent a week in East Germany, June 26-July 2. During his stay Tombazos visited the Leipzig Trade Fair and other towns as guest of the President of the GDR Agricultural Council, Mr. G. Evalt.

July 13   The Czechoslovak government will offer a limited number of scholarships to Cypriots for study at the Prague International Banking School from November 15, 1968, to May 15, 1969.

July 13   The General Secretary of the Farmers' Union in East Germany, Mr. Sperling, arrived on the island July 12 for a month's stay as a guest of EKA (the communist farmers' union).

July 20   East Germany's Under-Secretary for Health, Dr. Gehring, arrived on the island July 19 for talks with the Cypriot Minister of Health on the renewal of a technical cooperation agreement between the two countries.

July 20   A 96-man Cypriot delegation boarded the liner *Feliks Dzerzhinsky* for Bulgaria, to take part in the Ninth World Youth and Students' Festival. Five more Cypriots left for Sofia by air. Fifteen to twenty Cypriot students studying at various European universities were also

231

expected in the Bulgarian capital. In all, about 120 Cypriot youths will take part in the Festival. They include dancers, singers, musicians, athletes, writers, men of letters and the arts, and youth leaders. The Cypriot delegation will take part in the Festival's cultural and athletic programs, as well as in seminars on various youth problems. Cyprus will also take part in a children's painting competition and a poster competition.

July 24   The Ministers of Health of East Germany and Cyprus signed a renewal of the Medical Cooperation agreement for five years. The renewed agreement provides for technical cooperation, medical treatment of Cypriots in East Germany, supply of educational material for the Nursing School at the Nicosia General Hospital, and the granting of scholarships.

Aug. 8   A five-man delegation of the Cypriot-Soviet Friendship Society headed by its President Andreas Pouyouros, Mayor of Famagusta, left August 7 for a two-week visit in the Soviet Union as guests of the sister association in the U.S.S.R. The delegation will have contacts on cultural relations between the two countries.

Aug. 8   Eighteen Cypriot tourists left for the U.S.S.R. on August 7 under a Cypriot-Soviet Friendship Association sponsored trip. They will stay for 15 days and visit Moscow, Kiev, Leningrad, and Riga.

Aug. 11   Thirteen Cypriot children accompanied by two escorts left by sea for the U.S.S.R. to spend a month's holiday in the children's home at Artek.

Aug. 11   Twenty-five young Cypriots, members of the Cypriot communist youth organization EDON, left by sea for a 15-day visit to the Soviet Union.

Aug. 21   A new contract for the supply of more than 13,000 tons of Cyprus spirits during 1968–70 was signed in Limassol on August 20 by the Vine Products Council and the relevant Soviet commercial organization. The value of the spirits amounted to 2 million pounds.

Aug. 25   The Cypriot communist party, AKEL, issued a resolution on August 24 supporting Soviet intervention in Czechoslovakia.

Aug. 29   The Soviet Minister for External Trade, Nikolas Patolitchev, paid a short visit to Cyprus in transit to Moscow

232

from Syria. He was met at Nicosia Airport by Minister of Commerce Nicos Dimitriou and the Soviet Ambassador to Cyprus.

Sept. 10   A group of 13 Cypriot children returned from the Soviet Union, where they spent their summer vacation at Artek.

Sept. 18   Seven Cypriots were granted education scholarships by East Germany and left for their studies.

Sept. 19   A group of 27 Cypriots granted university scholarships by Czechoslovakia departed.

Sept. 22   A five-man farmers' delegation from the communist farmers' union (EKA) departed Wednesday, September 18, for a fifteen-day visit to East Germany.

Sept. 26   Giannis Katsourides, a member of the AKEL Secretariat, departed for Budapest to take part in the work of the preparatory committee for the next international conference of communist and workers' parties, scheduled to take place in Moscow in November.

Sept. 29   Minister of Education Dr. C. Spyridakis and Under-Secretary to the President P. Stavrou departed for Belgrade for the opening of the "Treasures of Cyprus" art exhibition.

Oct. 1   Three delegates of the Soviet Communist Youth League (Komsomol) arrived on the island for a week's visit as guests of the local communist youth organization, EDON.

Oct. 3   It was officially announced that the governments of Cyprus and Yugoslavia have agreed on a mutual abolition of passport visas for a stay of up to three months or for persons in transit.

Oct. 3   Education Minister Spyridakis returned from Belgrade, where he opened the exhibition "Treasures of Cyprus." He stated upon return that he found that Yugoslavia was still interested in the Cyprus issue and that it supports a solution safeguarding the island's independence and integrity. There is a general desire, he added, for closer relations in the cultural field.

Oct. 5   A Soviet women's delegation forwarded five cases of pharmaceuticals for presentation to the Nicosia General Hospital through the local communist women's association, POGO.

Oct. 5	The East German Under-Secretary for Agriculture, Dr. Noi, arrived on the island to negotiate an agricultural cooperation agreement with Cyprus.
Oct. 8	A five-year Cypriot-East German Agricultural Cooperation Agreement was signed at the Cypriot Ministry of Agriculture. The agreement provided for mutual assistance and information on questions concerning the protection of animals and plants.
Oct. 23	Cyprus was represented at the International Congress on Town Planning and Architecture held in Moscow. G. Phaedonos of the Cyprus Town Planning Department was the Cypriot representative.
Oct. 23	Following an invitation by the Bulgarian Communist Party Central Committee, an AKEL delegation consisting of E. Papaioannou, General Secretary, Dinos Constantinou, Politbureau member, and Achilleas Achilleos, Central Committee member, left for Sofia. The delegation discussed with representatives of the Bulgarian Communist Party political questions of common interest.
Oct. 28	Five hundred tons of spirits for the Soviet Union were loaded on the Soviet ship *Diraspol*.
Nov. 5	A four-man Soviet delegation of the Cypriot-Soviet Friendship Society arrived by air for a seven-day visit to Cyprus. During its stay it will have meetings and contacts with Cypriot officials and other personalities, attend celebrations in honor of the Russian revolution's anniversary, and visit museums and other sights on the island. The delegation will be composed of Trade Minister Dimitriy Pavlov, Moscow Theological Academy Director Bishop Filaretos, Professor Andrey Beletskiy, and Aleksey Toporikov. On November 6 the delegation will be received by President Makarios. A group of 15 Soviet tourists arrived on the same plane. It included leading artists and scientists. The artists of the group will appear on November 6 at the Nicosia Municipal Theater as part of the celebrations program in honor of the Russian revolution.
Nov. 6	Negotiations between the Cyprus government and INA enterprise of Zagreb on oil prospecting and exploration in Cyprus are to end soon. A team of INA engineers and technicians will arrive early in December to explore the most suitable sites and make preparations for the test drilling to begin. Under a draft contract, the drilling will

start early in 1969 so that the economic reserves and other conditions for oil exploration can be established as soon as possible.

Nov. 10   Three Cypriots were granted university scholarships by East Germany. They are Andreas Petrides from Paphos, Miss Chrystalla Seah from Athienou, and Pangratios Kadis from Strovolos.

Nov. 27   Mr. A. N. Tutushkin, president of the Soviet import organization Soyuzplodoimport arrived on November 26 at the invitation of the Cyprus Vine Products Commission. Mr. Tutushkin visited the Minister of Commerce and Industry and discussed the possibility of increasing Cyprus' agricultural exports to the U.S.S.R.

Nov. 29   Trade negotiations on a new trade agreement between the Cyprus Republic and East Germany began at the Commerce and Industry Ministry yesterday.

Nov. 30   The Cypriot Ministry of Health announced that, in accordance with the Health Agreement between Cyprus and East Germany, a German health delegation arrived on the island, which, in cooperation with officials of the Cyprus Ministry of Health, made the necessary arrangements for the organization of a medical exhibition relating to the health conduct of people.

Dec. 4   The Cyprus Vine Products Commission and the Soyuzplodoimport company signed a contract on December 3 for the purchase by the Soviet Union of Cyprus' entire 4,000-ton raisin crop of 1968, valued at £250,000. Soyuzplodoimport was represented by its president, Tutushkin, who is on a visit to Cyprus. In August 1968 the two organizations signed another contract for the purchase by the Soviet Union of 13,500 tons of spirits valued at £2,000,000. The whole quantity of spirits is to be supplied by the end of 1970.

Dec. 5   The East German Minister of Foreign Economic Relations, Mr. Soalle, arrived on the island December 4 to negotiate a new long-term trade-and-payments agreement with Cyprus. The East German Minister was met at the airport by Cypriot Minister of Commerce Dimitriou.

Dec. 7   Cyprus and East Germany signed on December 6 a new five-year Trade and Payments Agreement. The two countries have also signed a protocol which provides for the 1969 trading activities between them, valued at £1,100,000 each way.

Dec. 10   A Soviet five-man trade delegation from the Soviet Ministry for External Trade arrived in Cyprus yesterday for trade talks.

Dec. 11   The East German Trade Delegation signed an agreement to purchase 400 tons of Cyprus tobacco.

Dec. 12   The East German President of the Cypriot-East German Friendship Society arrived on the island to sign the 1969 protocol for cooperation between the two brother societies.

Dec. 21   PEO General Secretary Andreas Ziartides returned to December 20 from East Germany, where he attended the 18th Congress of the WFTU General Council, held in Berlin between December 16 and 20.

Appendix E

BIOGRAPHIES OF ACTIVE AKEL MEMBERS
(Most are current or past members of the Central Committee, but are not listed in any particular order of importance.)

Ezekias Papaioannou, General Secretary

Born in Kellaki, 1908. Papaioannou has been a communist since his early youth. In 1930, he went to England where he was an active member of the British Communist Party. He served in Spain with the International Brigade in 1936 and later ran a communist bookshop in London. In 1945, though still abroad, he was elected to the Central Committee of AKEL, and when he returned to Cyprus the following year, he went at once into the front rank of AKEL leadership. In 1947, he became Organizing Secretary of the party, and after having acted in the post for a year he became General Secretary in 1949. In this job he was a full-time paid party official and was also employed on the staff of the communist newspaper *Neos Democratis.* He was detained in 1955 after the proscription of the party, but escaped to England. Papaioannou has several times represented AKEL at conferences abroad, including Iron Curtain countries. His wife is also an active communist and he is one of the five AKEL Members of Parliament. He has been granted honorary membership in the Communist Party of the Soviet Union.

Andreas Fantis, Deputy General Secretary

Born in Kaimakli, 1918. As a schoolboy Fantis was expelled for his communist activities; he was a member of KKK, the Communist Party of Cyprus, proscribed in 1933. On the founding of AKEL in 1941, he became a member of the Central Committee and has served on it ever since. In 1946 he became a member of the Politburo of AKEL. In May 1957 Fantis succeeded to the post of General Secretary. He has made many trips abroad to communist-sponsored meetings; he has represented AKEL at the annual congress in London of the Cypriot branch of the British communist party.

Andreas Ziartides, General Secretary of PEO

Born in Agios Omologitis, 1919. Ziartides is the driving force of AKEL and the Pan-Cyprian Federation of Labor (PEO). A member of AKEL since it started, he was elected to its Central Committee in 1943 and has served there ever since, holding various offices. In 1943 he also became General Secretary of the PSE, and in 1947 took over PEO. He has attended many communist-organized conferences behind the Iron Curtain. A detention order was issued while he was attending a WFTU Congress in Vienna, but he stayed on in Austria as a paid official at the

237

main office of the communist-controlled WFTU. When this was closed by the Austrian authorities, he went to England, where he remained in close touch with the BCP until he returned to Cyprus in 1957. Ziartides has five convictions for crimes of a political nature, including one for 18 months for conspiracy to overthrow the government by force in 1946. He is now a member of Parliament.

Pavlos Georghiou, Member of the General Secretariat

Born in Kaimakli, 1918. Georghiou was a former member of the Central Committee and the Politburo of KKK. He joined AKEL in 1941 and sat on the Nicosia District Committee, on which he served in various offices. He was elected to the Central Committee in 1943, and in 1949 he became a full-time paid official as Central Organizing Secretary, a post he held when the party was proscribed in 1955. He has been a member of the Vigilance Bureau. Georghiou escaped from detention in December 1955.

Giannis Katsourides, Member of the General Secretariat

Born in Nicosia, 1913. Katsourides was a member of the KKK underground from 1938 on. He joined AKEL soon after its foundation, and in 1944 he was alleged to have been the Secretary of the Nicosia District Committee. In 1948 he was in the Vigilance Bureau of AKEL, was responsible for the Central and the Nicosia District, and became a paid official in 1949. By 1953 he was in charge of the Vigilance Bureau, and about the same time, he became a member of the Central Committee. In 1955 Katsourides evaded arrest, and the detention order against him was never served. He also has been head of the Finance Office and the Organizational Secretary.

Costas Partassides

Born in Episcipi, 1918. Partassides is the ex-mayor of Limassol and a communist of long standing. He has been a member of AKEL since it was founded and was elected to the Central Committee in 1943. He has held various offices in the Committee and has done much public speaking on behalf of the party, but heart trouble has curbed his activities. As a member of the Pan-Cyprian Peace Committee, he represented it at the Warsaw Peace Congress in 1950. Partassides has also taken a hand in the organization of AON (the precursor to EDON).

Michaelakis Georghiou Olymbios

Born in Limassol, 1924. Olymbios has been a member of AKEL since 1941. In 1950 he was a member of the Nicosia District Committee, and in the following year he was working as a full-time paid employee of the Central Committee responsible for the Central Finance Bureau. In 1953 he was appointed General Secretary of AON, a post he held until its proscription. As a member of the council of the World Federation of Democratic Youth (WFDY), an international communist front organization, he attended the international youth festivals at Bucharest in 1953, and at Warsaw in 1955, as well as the WFDY council meeting in

Peking in August 1954. He has been a contributor to various communist newspapers, and is a member of the Pan-Cyprian Peace Committee. His wife is a leading member of a Cypriot communist organization for women and with him helped organize EDON.

Christos Petas, General Secretary of Nicosia-Kyrenia District

Born in Neon Chorion, 1922. Petas joined AKEL in 1941 and was elected to the Nicosia District Committee in 1943. He was a member of the Nicosia District Secretariat in 1944 and was elected to the Central Committee in 1947. He was a full-time paid party official and has been working for the communist newspaper *Neos Democratis*. He has also been connected with the Union of Cyprus Farmers (EAK), of whose Secretariat he was a member in 1949; a year later, he was on EAK's Central Committee. He was a member of the National Liberation Coalition (EAS), a communist-sponsored organization, and was its Organizing Secretary in 1954. Petas has three convictions for political offenses and was detained between 1955 and 1957. He is a carpenter by trade and has written a number of articles for communist publications.

Georgios Christodoulides

Born in Chlorakas, 1919. Christodoulides has been a member of AKEL since 1942. He was elected to the Central Control Committee of the Second Pan-Cyprian Congress of AKEL in 1943 and has assisted the party actively in many fields. In 1955, besides his work as a member of the District Secretariat, he sat on the Executive Committee of PEE, and on the Preparatory Committee he was engaged in organizing the AON festival. He was detained from 1955 to 1957.

Giangos Potamitis, Deputy, Lawyer

Born in Limassol, 1903. He was a lawyer in Cyprus, 1926–27, in the Sudan, 1927–37, and returned to Cyprus in 1938. Since 1955 he has been president of the Pan-Cyprian Federation of Labor and a member of the World Peace Council. He has been an AKEL member of the House of Representatives for the district of Limassol since 1960. He is the Advocate for LOEL, Ltd. He participated in the international conference for peace, disarmament, and international cooperation, in Berlin in 1954, Helsinki in 1955, Colombo in 1957, Stockholm 1958–59, New Delhi 1961, Moscow 1962; in the conference of the International Association of Democratic Jurisconsults, Leipzig 1954, Budapest 1964, in the "peace through justice" conference of the American Bar Association in Athens in 1963, and others. He was a member of the Committee of the Greek Community of Khartoum-Sudan, 1936–37; member of the board of governors of the Cyprus Bar Association; member of the International Association of Democratic Jurisconsults. He was awarded the Frederic Joliet-Curie gold medal for peace.

Lambros Gomatas

Born in Marathovouno, 1923. Gomatas is a full-time paid Secretary of the Paphos District of PEO and a member of its General Council. In

1955 he was a member of AKEL Area Committee for Ktima and of the AKEL Club at Paphos. Before their proscription, he was lecturer and Inspector of the EAK and the AON Clubs, and was reported to be a member of the "Red Hand," which is said to have been an extremist group of fanatics within AKEL, but little information on this group is available.

Haralambos (Hambis) Antonis Michaelides, General Secretary of EKA

Born in Zylophagou, 1921. Michaelides has been an active communist since 1947, when he was a member of the Larnaca District Committee of AKEL, subsequently becoming its Acting Secretary in 1949, and then becoming its Secretary in 1950. In 1949 he was elected to the Central Committee of EAK and became its General Secretary in 1950, a post he held until EAK was proscribed; he was detained in December 1955. In 1954 he was elected to the Central Committee of AKEL and continued in office until he was detained. In 1953 he visited the U.S.S.R. and Poland, and attended two communist-inspired conferences. In 1955 he led a Cypriot delegation on a visit to Rumania. He has been head of the Agrarian Office and is now a member of Parliament.

Minos Kyprianou Perdios, Member of the Central Control Commission

Born in Limassol, 1906. According to Perdios, he joined the KKK in 1931, having previously been in touch with party members. After the proscription of KKK, he was a member of that party while it continued to function illegally, and visited the United Kingdom to consult the Communist Party of Great Britain on its behalf. In 1939 he became a member of the Central Committee of KKK, and was a member of the founding of the Central Committee of AKEL in 1941, continuing in office until 1947. He subsequently became editor of the AKEL organ *Democratis*, in which capacity he was jailed for three months in 1949 for publishing a seditious article. In the same year he was elected a reserve member of the Central Committee of AKEL and became a full member again in 1951, holding this position at the time of AKEL's proscription and his detention in 1955. He has been head of the Educational Office.

Giannis Sophocles

Born in Paphos, 1923. He has been a member of AKEL for many years and has taken a special interest in farming and trade union matters. He was elected to the Central Committee of AKEL in 1947 and became Secretary of EAK and a member of the General Council of PEO. He continued to serve on the Central Committee until the proscription of AKEL, at which time he was also District Secretary. He was detained from 1955–57. He has written for AKEL publications in London.

Gregoris Spyrou

Born in Lakatamia, 1924. Spyrou joined the AKEL in 1951 after a career as a clerk. In 1947 he was a full-time paid official in the AKEL central office, and by 1950 was Organizing Secretary of the Nicosia

District Committee, responsible for the women's section in Nicosia. In 1952 Spyrou was elected to the Central Committee and was still a member and a paid official when he was detained in December 1955. He was made responsible for the Nicosia-Kyrenia District Rural Bureau in 1958 and is still responsible for village cadres.

Dinos Constantinou
Born in Famagusta, 1925. He graduated from the Famagusta Commercial Lyceum and in 1949 went to Czechoslovakia, where he studied economics at the University of Prague. A member of AKEL since 1949, he became Party Secretary for Famagusta in 1958. A year later he was elected to the Central Committee of AKEL and moved to Nicosia, where he took charge of the Party Cultural and Finance Office. In 1962 he became a permanent member of the Central Committee and in 1970 was named a permanent member of the Politburo.

Georgios Savvides
Born in a Cypriot village, 1920, and raised in Kyrenia. He graduated from the Pancyprian Gymnasium in 1937 and studied at the Athens School of Philosophy; later he studied biology at the University of Prague, specializing in genetics. Savvides was one of the founding members of EDON. He is a member of the Council of the Cyprus Peace Movement and the Committee on the Afro-Asian Solidarity Organization. Since 1941 he has been a member of AKEL and since 1959 a member of the Central Committee. At the last Party Congress he was elected Chairman of the Central Control Committee.

Nicos Mavronicolas, Lawyer
Mavronicolas is a lawyer in Paphos and has displayed little significant party activity. A native-born resident of Paphos, during the 1970 election he was chosen to represent the district over the incumbent Chyrsis Dimetriades, who among other things was not a resident and thus less likely to win in an open election.

Christos Koutellaris
Born in a Cypriot village, 1919. He became an AKEL member in 1944, was president of AKEL's collective farm near Kyrenia in 1954, and has since been a salaried member of the communist farm movement. He is a member of the party's Central Committee, responsible for agrarian matters. Koutellaris is also Assistant General Secretary of EKA, the Union of Cypriot Farmers.

Appendix F

RESOLUTION TO SOVIET UNION

(*Haravghi,* March 7, 1970. Translation from the Foreign Broadcast Information Service *Daily Report: Middle East & Africa,* March 10, 1970.)

[Resolution of the 12th AKEL Congress to the Soviet Union]

[Text] The 12th AKEL congress unanimously passed yesterday, amid moving manifestations, the following resolution to the Soviet Union:

The 12th AKEL congress reaffirms once more the deep respect and unlimited gratitude of the working people of Cyprus for the firm and unselfish assistance which the USSR has offered and is still offering to the Cypriot people's anti-imperialist liberation struggle. The Cypriot people do not forget that during Cyprus' most critical moments the Soviet Union offered its unlimited support and decisively helped avert the dangers which threatened our country's independence and integrity.

During extremely difficult moments for our country, when the imperialist enemies of Cyprus were trying to internationally isolate the Cyprus Republic and annihilate it, the Soviet delegate at the Security Council defended and fraternally supported our just cause. When Cyprus was threatened by foreign invasion in 1964 and 1967, with its strong and explicit warnings the USSR Government interrupted and thwarted NATO's plans for the partition and enslavement of Cyprus.

The Soviet Union has supplied the Cyprus Republic with valuable economic aid and armament for its defense. This, together with its firm, moral, diplomatic, and political support, has been a serious factor in Cyprus' struggle. Even recently when imperialist pressures and conspiratorial activities were intensified to convert Cyprus into a nuclear and missile base in the place of their bases lost in Libya, and while terrorist organizations instigated by foreigners were internally undermining the Cyprus Republic, the Soviet Union through the TASS statement of 18 February 1970 protected once more Cyprus' independence and peace, and gave a serious warning to the organizers of the criminal designs for a coup and a plot against the Cyprus Republic and its government.

The TASS statement is proof of the strong Soviet solidarity and support for the Cypriot people and the Government of the Cyprus Republic.

The imperialist enemies of Cyprus and their organs were disturbed by this explicit expression of decisive solidarity for the Cyprus Republic and tried to indulge in demagogy by creating confusion. Their efforts led to a fiasco because the Cypriot people know from experience who are their faithful friends and relentless enemies.

The development of political, economic, and cultural relations between the Cyprus Republic and the USSR is a decisive factor for the independent development and progress of Cyprus, a protective shield of security for the Cypriot people, and a factor promoting peace in the Mediterranean and the Middle East for the sake of all peoples of the area.

The 12th AKEL congress expressed once more the deep gratitude of the party and the patriotic Cypriot people for Lenin's glorious party, for the USSR Government, and the great Soviet people for their solidarity with the Cypriot people and the Cyprus Republic and their unselfish, unlimited, and decisive support and aid to our struggle for a completely independent, territorially integral, sovereign, and prosperous Cyprus.

RESOLUTION TO MAKARIOS
(Haravghi, March 8, 1970.)

[Resolution of the 12th AKEL congress to President Makarios]

[Text] After hearing and discussing the report submitted on behalf of the Central Committee of our party by Secretary General E. Papaioannou, the 12th AKEL congress authorized the Presidium to submit to Your Beatitude the following:

1. AKEL has unreservedly supported your decision for a change in the Cyprus policy toward a feasible Cyprus solution within the present Cyprus and international conditions. Your patriotic decision, approved by the patriotic majority of the people, is an important service to Cyprus and its cause.

2. AKEL firmly maintains that the Cyprus problem is a political problem which can and must be solved through the only correct way— the inter-Cypriot talks. We do not overlook the existing difficulties, but we believe that if the method of talks presents difficulties, then the method of violence, the revival of the Greek-Turkish dialog, or the five-party conference will lead straight to destruction and partition. The talks must be continued and must be successful, and our party will support every initiative and every bold decision leading to the success of the talks, to the acceptable feasible solution.

3. AKEL has condemned lawlessness and terrorism whose main target is the patriotic policy declared by Your Beatitude. Our party agrees with you that terrorist activity causes irreparable damage to the Cyprus cause. We have given the government, both inside and outside Parliament, our unlimited support on measures for suppressing and eradicating lawlessness. We wish to assure you that you will have our unlimited support in implementing the approved measures. Without the decisive suppression of lawlessness and terrorism, and the collection of the illegally held arms, it would be impossible to hold free and uninfluenced elections or to effectively promote a Cyprus solution.

4. AKEL has consistently applied and followed in recent critical years the policy of unity of the people's forces. This shall be our policy in the future as well. Now that we are on the eve of elections, and in the future, we shall continue working for the unity of all the people's forces in the struggle for a territorially integral, unified, sovereign, independent, and demilitarized Cyprus.

RESOLUTION ON ASSASSINATION ATTEMPT
(Moscow in Greek to Cyprus 1800 GMT 8 Mar 70 M.)

[Text] Delegates taking part in the 12th congress of the Restorative Party of the Working People in Nicosia met today in their final meeting full of indignation at the machinations of the agents of imperialism. The delegates urgently passed the following resolution:

On the final day of its work, the 12th AKEL congress learned with indignation that the fascist agents of imperialism had raised their criminal hand against the president of the Republic of Cyprus, Archbishop Makarios. The congress stigmatizes this criminal, treacherous act, which is undoubtedly part of the imperialist plans for establishment in Cyprus of a fascist state of affairs and partition of the country in furtherance of NATO's aggressive plans, which our party has condemned. The 12th AKEL congress demands that the criminals be arrested immediately and punished, and that decisive measures be adopted to eradicate the provocative, fascist activities in our country.

Closing the work of the congress today, the reelected AKEL secretary general, Ezekias Papaioannou, called on all party members to struggle actively to carry out the decisions of the 12th congress. There is no doubt that the assassination attempt on President Makarios was the work of the agents of imperialism, Papaioannou declared. On behalf of AKEL, Papaioannou summoned the Cypriot people to unity, vigilance, and mobilization of all their forces to foil the imperialist machinations against the country.

OTHER RESOLUTIONS
(*Haravghi*, March 8, 1970.)

[Excerpts] The 12th AKEL congress unanimously passed a resolution expressing the party's determination to work for developing relations of friendship and cooperation with the Turkish Cypriots and for removing mistrust and hatred.

Turkish Cypriot Ahmed Sadi had earlier stressed: "With the implementation of the imperialist policy of 'divide and rule,' so much blood has been shed and such a gap has been created between the two communities that it difficult . . . to have it closed within a short time. With the continuation of the talks, however, we can arrive at a satisfactory result.

244

The delegates gave Sadi an extremely warm and enthusiastic welcome. Interpreting the feelings of solidarity of the Cypriot working people for the struggle of our neighbor Arab peoples, the congress passed a resolution strongly condemning the gangster-like Israeli aggression, supporting a Middle East solution on the basis of the Security Council resolution of November 1967, and stressing that the enemy of the Cypriots and the Arabs is international imperialism, particularly American imperialism.

LIST OF DELEGATES
(*Haravghi,* March 6, 1970.)

[Text] The 12th congress of the Restorative Party of the Working People (AKEL) is attended by delegations of the communist and workers parties from the following 16 countries:

Soviet Union: K. N. Grishin, deputy chairman of the party Control Committee; N. K. K. Kirichenko, first secretary of Crimea obkom; (K. Shemigov) of the International Relations Department.

German Democratic Republic: Paul Froehlich, Politburo member; Edith Baumann, Central Committee member; Hans (Jungbluch), head of the Department on Relations with Capitalist Countries.

Czechoslovakia: Jan Pelnar, Central Committee member; Vaclav Frybert, of the Department of International Relations.

Hungary: Janos Brutyo, chairman of the Central Control Committee; Istvan Dobi [as published] of the Department of International Relations.

Romania: Mihai Dalea, member of the Romanian Communist Party Central Committee and chairman of the Central Party Collegium; Ghizela Vass, Central Committee member and section chief of the party Central Committee.

Bulgaria: Krustyu Trichkov, alternate member of the Politburo; Stavri Markov, of the Department of International Relations.

Yugoslavia: Macac Keleman, member of the Central Committee Presidium; Aco Janoski, of the International Department.

Britain: Reuben Falber, assistant secretary general.

France: Réné Andrieu, Central Committee member and chief editor of *L'Humanité.*

Italy: Umberto Cardia, Central Committee member and deputy.

Federal Republic of Germany: Georg Polikiet, Central Committee member.

Israel: Tewfik Toubi, Politburo member and Central Committee secretary; Pnina Feinhaus, chairman of the Central Control Committee.

Jordan: Fuad Qassis, Politburo member.

Iraq: Bakir Ibrahim, Politburo member.

Lebanon: Mahmud Wawi, Central Committee member.

Syria: Ahmad Bakkari, Politburo member.

Khamis Saliba of the periodical "Problems of Peace and Socialism."

Khambis Mikhail is also attending the congress on behalf of the progressive Cypriots in England, and Ahmed Sadi on behalf of the progressive Turks.

RESOLUTION ON MID-EAST
(Haravghi, March 11, 1970.)

[Text] The 12th Congress of the Restorative Party of the Working People (AKEL), interpreting the solidarity of the progressive forces of Cyprus toward the Arab peoples, has unanimously passed the following resolution:

"The 12th AKEL congress addresses a warm salute and cordial greetings to the peoples of the Arab states fighting against imperialism and the reactionary warlike circles of Israel for the defense of their national independence and integrity.

"It denounces the aggressive war declared by the Israeli Zionists in 1967, with the encouragement and reinforcement of the American imperialists, against the UAR, Syria, and Jordan. It denounces with abhorrence the aggressive criminal actions being continued by the same circles against the Arab people and land.

"It considers the occupation of Arab territories by the state of Israel a gangsterite action contrary to the principles and aims of the United Nations, and the main cause for the deterioration of the situation in this region.

246

"It maintains that the settlement of this problem must be sought through the application of the Security Council resolution dated 22 November 1967, providing for the withdrawal of Israeli troops from all occupied territories as the primary prerequisite for the settlement of other related issues.

"It considers the struggle of the Cypriot people for the completion of their independence, the territorial integrity of Cyprus, and the abolition of foreign military bases, as directly related to the struggle of the Arab peoples. The common enemy of the Cypriots and Arabs is international imperialism, and particularly American imperialism, which, in order to secure the huge profits it gains from the exploitation of Middle East oil, tries to turn Cyprus into a NATO military base for the protection of these interests.

"Without failing to appreciate the warlike intentions of the imperialists and Zionists of Israel, the Cypriot people express the conviction that a peaceful settlement of the problem will be found, corresponding to the just cause of the Arabs and the vital interests of all peoples in the region. A guarantee of this is the unity and determination of the national liberation, anti-imperialist Arab forces; their reinforcement by the new democratic, anti-imperialist regimes of Sudan and Libya; and the invaluable, extensive aid provided them by the force of the Soviet Union and the other progressive forces of the world."

AKEL CONGRESS SENDS GREETINGS TO TURKISH CYPRIOTS
(*Haravghi,* March 18, 1970.)

[Text] Dear Turkish compatriots: The 12th AKEL Congress addresses warm greetings to you and on this occasion again assures you that the party of the people of Cyprus will firmly support, just as it has done for the past 35 years, the need for friendship and cooperation between the Greek and Turkish working people of Cyprus.

It is a joint responsibility of Greeks and Turks in Cyprus peacefully in Cyprus [as published], and this is how they must live in the future so that our country may progress and prosper. The Greeks and Turks of Cyprus are linked by common interests and problems. The present unrest is artificial; it is the creation of the imperialists, the common enemy of the Greeks and Turks of Cyprus, who want to keep Cyprus as a base in the Eastern Mediterranean for the promotion of their interests.

AKEL has always maintained that whatever the differences between the Greeks and Turks of Cyprus, they can be settled peacefully through talks in Cyprus.

Foreign intervention in the Cypriot people's internal affairs in recent years has caused many hardships to both Greeks and Turks and has prevented the unimpeded development of Cyprus. We have seen a new situation during the past 2 years—the inter-Cypriot talks, which aim at a Cyprus solution within the framework of a unitary, democratic, and demilitarized Cyprus based on UN principles and with the Turkish Cypriots' rights fully safeguarded and consolidated.

Dear compatriots, it is the joint responsibility of Greeks and Turks in Cyprus to make every effort to safeguard peaceful coexistence and insure the success of the talks.

We assure you again that AKEL will consistently struggle, as it always has, to apply the policy of mutual understanding, respect, and friendship and cooperation between Greeks and the Turks for the progress of Cyprus.

Long live the friendship and cooperation of the Greeks and Turks of Cyprus.

Notes

Complete author's names, titles, and publication data are given in the Bibliography, pp. 263–67.

Chapter 1

[1] Lee, *Great Britain and the Cyprus Convention Policy of 1878,* pp. 164–65.

[2] Monroe, *The Mediterranean in Politics,* p. 49.

[3] *Haravghi* (Dawn), November 27, 1969.

[4] Hill, *History of Cyprus,* Vol. IV, p. 593n.

[5] Yiavopoulos is alive and now living in Argentina, but there is no record of his having been active with that country's small Trotskyite Workers' Party, the Partido Obrero–Trotzkista. Besides his name being dropped from the November 27, 1966, commemorative issue of *Haravghi,* Vatiliotis too was excluded along with Vassiliou. For some unexplained reason, Skeleas led the list of personalities, which may or may not indicate the special position he holds in the communists' view of their history in Cyprus. The issue also carried photographs and brief sketches of some of the other founding members of KKK, who are apparently still held in high regard by the present AKEL leadership. These were, in order from left to right as they appeared on the page:

Costas Skeleas. Born in Limassol in 1896, he formed one of the first communist groups. Participated in the First Congress of the party, at which time he was elected General Secretary. Up to the time of his exile in 1931 he worked as a stonemason.

Christos Christodoulides. Born in Limassol in 1902, he was the half-brother of Skeleas. A high school graduate, he was involved in literary work in the first communist groups and participated in the First Congress of the party. For some time he worked at the Public Bank as a teller.

Katina I. Nikolaou. Born in Limassol in 1904. In 1924 she became involved with the early communist groups. In 1926 she participated in the party's First Congress. For 15 years (1924–39) she was a teacher, and in the last 20 years has played an active leading role in the women's democratic movement.

Marcos Marcoulis. Born in Limassol and studied medicine. A participant in the first Marxist youth groups; also attended the First Party

Congress of the KKK. Since then he has been in the forefront of the popular movement. (He is shown in military garb.)

Christos Savvides. Born in Limassol in 1901. Assisted in the organization of the first communist groups and took part in the First Party Congress of the KKK. In 1941 he participated in the founding of AKEL and was elected a member of its Central Committee. He remained an active member of the party until his death in 1963.

Charalambos Solomonides. Born in Limassol in 1896. One of the founding members of KKK in 1922. In 1925 he published the official organ of the KKK, *Neos Anthropos*. Following AKEL's formation he continued to play an active role. He died on August 31, 1965.

Kyp. Koukoulis. Born in Myrtou in 1902. Joined the builders' union of Limassol at the age of 22. In 1926 he represented communist youth at the First Party Congress. In 1931 he was elected a member of the party's Political Bureau. He later withdrew from active participation in the party but has never renounced his ideology.

Christos Artemiou. Born in Limassol; mingled with first Marxist groups at a very early age; participated in the First Party Congress.

[6] *Neos Anthropos,* Dec. 24, 1926, quoted in *Communism in Cyprus,* p. 4.

[7] Degras (ed.), *The Communist International Documents, 1919–1943,* p. 150.

[8] *Neos Anthropos,* Jan. 8, 1927, quoted in *Communism in Cyprus,* p. 4.

[9] Thomas, *The Spanish Civil War,* p. 377. Some 160 Greeks were also members of the International Brigades serving in the Dimitrov Battalion. *Ibid.*

[10] Interview with Stavros Pandzaris (a former KKK member), Nicosia, 1969.

[11] Interview with Servas, Nicosia, 1969.

[12] Statement of former Colonial Governor Sir Charles Woolley, quoted in *Cyprus: The Dispute and the Settlement,* p. 5.

[13] Interview with Pandzaris, 1969.

[14] Quoted in *Communism in Cyprus,* p. 10.

[15] Quoted in *Communism in Cyprus,* p. 8.

[16] It may be interesting to note that the Zionists had a plan for colonizing Cyprus which dated back to before the turn of the century, when Theodor Herzl founded the movement. Herzl tried to sell the idea

to the British as a stroke which would eliminate at once the problems with both the Greeks and the Turks. Were the Zionists to move into Cyprus, he argued, "the Moslems will move away, the Greeks will gladly sell their land at a good price and emigrate to Athens or Crete." Purcell, *Cyprus*, pp. 210–12.

[17] For a complete recount of this strike, see Lavender, *The Story of the Cyprus Mines Corporation*, pp. 294–99.

[18] *Democratis*, January 1949. Self-criticism was instituted in the AKEL during 1944 and has been used ever since.

[19] *International Press Correspondence*, December 17, 1931.

[20] *Hansard* (Commons), Vol. 414, col. 218, quoted in *Cyprus: The Dispute and the Settlement*, p. 7.

[21] Fifis Ioannou in: Communist Party of Great Britain, *We Speak for Freedom*, p. 51.

[22] *Ibid.*, p. 94. Coincidentally, similar conditions exist in Greece today and a current debate about the support AKEL has given to the *enosis* case would probably provoke an equal amount of acrimony among communists.

[23] Kousoulas, *Revolution and Defeat*, p. 221.

[24] *Communism in Cyprus*, p. 9. The claimed figure of 20,000 EAS members seems high, since AKEL was estimated to have only 2,000 card-carrying members at that time. See *The Economist*, May 14, 1948.

[25] *Cyprus: The Dispute and the Settlement*, p. 10.

[26] *Cyprus Mail*, April 21, 1956.

[27] *Neos Komos* (Athens), November 1951.

[28] *The Road to Freedom*, Program of the Eighth AKEL Party Congress, March 1954. Later Papaioannou explained in an article that union of Cyprus with Greece could only come about if it were demilitarized and refused any NATO ties. See also "For the Independence and Progress of Cyprus," *World Marxist Review*, December 1966, p. 11.

[29] Quoted in *Communism in Cyprus*, p. 13. See also *Neos Democratis*, August 10, 1954 for the appeal by AKEL to Makarios to talk about "the best way of handling" such help.

[30] *Survey of International Affairs, 1954* (London: Oxford University Press, 1957), p. 181.

[31] See Communist Party of Great Britain, *Allies for Freedom*, pp. 74–77.

[32] *Ibid.*, p. 75.

[33] *Neos Anthropos*, August 10, 1954.

[34] See *The Road to Freedom*.

[35] "Democritus," *The Leadership of AKEL*, p. 17. AKEL was called upon to help in the struggle as early as January 1955 by EMAK, EOKA's predecessor formed in Greece.

[36] *Neos Democratis*, April 30, 1955.

[37] For an account of Grivas' work in "X," see Barker, *Grivas: Portrait of a Terrorist*.

[38] *Neos Democratis*, May 1, 1955.

[39] *Ibid.*, September 4, 1955.

[40] *Ibid.*, September 9, 1955.

[41] AKEL's aversion to the use of hostilities in the *enosis* struggle was expressed in *Neos Democratis* as early as December 18, 1954, when some isolated sabotage first occurred against the British. See "Democritus," *The Leadership of AKEL*, p. 25.

[42] See Xydis, *Cyprus: Conflict and Conciliation, 1954–1958*.

[43] *The Cyprus Gazette*, December 14, 1955. This British move was described by Grivas as an effort to give AKEL "martyrs" and thus strengthen it in the long run. See: Foley, ed., *The Memoirs of General Grivas*, p. 17.

[44] *Haravghi*, November 27, 1966. There was no mention of the number of AKEL members who might have been killed, or by whom (e.g., EOKA assassins).

[45] "Democritus," *The Leadership of AKEL*, pp. 38–42.

[46] The American journalist was George Weller, and the piece was carried by the *Chicago Daily News*, April 4, 1955.

[47] Foley, ed., *The Memoirs of General Grivas*, p. 104.

[48] *Ibid.*, p. 35.

[49] *Ibid.*, p. 135.

[50] Foley, *Island in Revolt*, p. 177.

[51] Alastos, *Cyprus Guerrilla*, p. 194.

[52] The full text may be found in Great Britain, *Cyprus,* Cmnd. 1093 (London: H.M.S.O., July 1960).

[53] For an account of the behind-the-scenes maneuvers at the London meeting, see Alastos, *Cyprus Guerrilla*, pp. 181–201.

[54] *New York Times,* February 24, 1959.

[55] Alastos, *Cyprus Guerrilla*, p. 202.

[56] *Haravghi,* October 10, 1959.

Chapter 2

[1] *Haravghi,* June 24, 1960.

[2] Article 73, paragraph 12 of the Constitution of the Republic of Cyprus.

[3] *Neos Democratis,* May 1, 1955.

[4] For a treatment of AKEL's current view of the Cypriot Turks, see the article by Georgios Pefkos in the weekly journal of the Communist Party of Great Britain, *Comment,* April 1968, p. 237. Sadi also attended the Twelfth Congress in March 1970 as the representative of the "progressive Turks." *Haravghi,* March 6, 1970.

[5] *Elevtheria,* June 1, 1953. Under the British, the elected municipal councils had practically no authority over local affairs, which in practice came within the domain of the colonial District Commissioners. As such, the stake in these elections was not great enough to arouse the nationalists to great efforts and the voter turnout was usually low.

[6] *Haravghi,* August 2, 1960.

[7] Karayiannis, *The Cyprus Problem,* p. 65.

[8] The constitutionally stated duties of the Party Congress are as follows: (a) Hears and approves the reports of the outgoing Central Committee and Control Commission. (b) Elects the members of the new Central Committee and Control Commission. (c) Reviews and amends the Constitution and Program of the party. (d) Determines the party's tactics on current policy problems. See *The Constitution of*

253

AKEL, Approved by the Tenth Party Congress, March 1962 (Kaimakli: Printko, Ltd., 1962) for a detailed picture of the organization and duties of the various units of the party. The fifth regular plenum of the party's Central Committee and Central Control Committee announced that the AKEL Twelfth Congress would be held in March 1970, four years to the month after the Eleventh Congress. (*Haravghi,* February 26, 1969.) This action amounted to an *ultra vires* amendment to the AKEL Constitution, which had originally provided for three-year intervals between congresses.

[9] *Haravghi,* June 19, 1960.

[10] *Ibid.,* June 10, 1964. When the Central School was founded it was lauded as the first step toward the establishment of a "Marxist Institute" in Cyprus. *Neos Democratis,* February 1962.

[11] Christos Petas in *Neos Democratis,* October 7, 1961.

[12] *Haravghi,* April 18, 1962.

[13] *Neos Democratis,* February 1962.

[14] *Neolaia,* June 11, 1960. Compulsory conscription into the National Guard was effected in 1964 and this has also made it difficult for AKEL to recruit among young men in Cyprus.

[15] Petas, *loc. cit.* An *aktive* is less an organizational meeting than a gathering used to obtain the views of cadres (composed of the most reliable members).

[16] *Neos Democratis,* February 1962, article by Christos Lasettas.

[17] *Haravghi,* August 6, 1961.

[18] *Ibid.,* November 16, 1968.

[19] *Ibid.,* October 10, 1969.

[20] Personal interview with Giangos Potamitis, the advocate for LOEL, September 1966. According to Potamitis, LOEL was started after a communist-inspired strike in 1946 at the leading distillery caused the firing of 40 workers. With help from AKEL, the company was launched by workers and is supported by the "workers and the peasants who buy their products." LOEL is a big importer from and exporter to communist countries.

[21] *Haravghi,* August 16, 1961.

[22] *Activities Report of PEO* (Nicosia: March 1961), p. 134. PEO even managed to raise 23,000 pounds sterling at a "Pan-Cyprian Dance" in 1960 by selling 48,682 men's tickets and 17,989 women's tickets. *Ibid.*, p. 132.

[23] *Directory of Trade Annual, 1961–1965* (Washington: International Bank for Reconstruction and Development, 1966), paragraph 105.

[24] *Haravghi*, September 11, 1962.

[25] *Neos Democratis*, December 1962.

[26] *Haravghi*, September 11, 1962.

[27] See, for example, W. Granger Blair, "Communism in Cyprus," *New York Times*, August 30, 1960. See also Philip Windsor, *NATO and the Cyprus Crisis*, Adelphi Paper no. 14, p. 8.

[28] See the editorial "The Formation of Parties," *Haravghi*, February 8, 1969. The emergence of political parties in Cyprus is treated at length in Chapter 4.

Chapter 3

[1] *Cyprus: A Handbook of the Island's Past and Present*, p. 239.

[2] *Haravghi*, October 9, 1968. For a British view of the strategic significance of Cyprus, see Verrier, "Cyprus: Britain's Security Role."

[3] For a picture of this period in considerable depth, see Adams, *U.S. Army Area Handbook for Cyprus*, pp. 209–36.

[4] A complete study of the Cypriot constitution and the problems that it generated may be found in Adams, "The First Republic of Cyprus," pp. 475–90.

[5] For a detailed coverage, see Adams and Cottrell, "The Cyprus Conflict." The Greeks adhere to the *rebus sic stantibus* principle of international law while the Turks stress the equally valid *pacta sunt servanda* concept.

[6] For a treatment of the U.N. role in Cyprus, see Adams and Cottrell, "American Foreign Policy and the U.N. Peacekeeping Force in Cyprus."

[7] *Cyprus Mail*, February 19, 1969. To speculate on the date of the next elections in Cyprus is risky. It is safe to say that unless there is some sort of an agreement with the Turks in the present intercommunal talks, Makarios will not risk the "unity" of the Greek Cypriot

community by allowing competition between political parties. At this writing the elections were reportedly set for July 1970.

[8] *The Program of AKEL, 1962* (Kaimakli: Printko, Ltd., 1962), p. 8. Kaimakli is the leftist "workers' suburb" of Nicosia.

[9] From Nihart, ed., *World in Arms: A Politico-Military Almanac.*

[10] The following excerpt provides a succinct comparative rundown of the Cypriot economy: "In 1960, per capita income in Cyprus was £184.8, in 1966 (for Christians) it was £260.5. . . . Only Israel, with its enormous volume of aid from world Jewry, has a higher per capita income in the Middle East, and even so it has more labor problems than Cyprus. Since 1965 there has been full employment (that is, an unemployment rate of under 2 per cent), though one must allow for the fact that this does not apply to the Turkish enclaves, and the fact that military service has been introduced." From Purcell, *Cyprus,* p. 55.

[11] For a more complete look at the main religions in Cyprus, see French, *The Eastern Orthodox Church;* Seligman, *The Turkish People of Cyprus;* and Attwater, *The Christian Churches of the East.*

[12] Psomiades, "Soviet Russia and the Orthodox Church in the Middle East," pp. 371–81. This is also cited in Psomiades, *The Eastern Question,* p. 87.

[13] Stephen Barber, in a review of Adams and Cottrell, *Cyprus Between East and West,* in *Orbis,* Fall 1968, p. 9.

[14] This account was given in a personal interview with Costas Kononas in Nicosia, October 1967. Kononas is editor of the right-wing paper *Patris* and former General Secretary of the KKK.

[15] "Democritus," *The Leadership of AKEL,* p. 5.

[16] This quotation was in the account of a speech Papaioannou delivered some five months after the Tenth Party Congress, as carried by *Pravda* on July 28, 1962. The translation differs somewhat in wording, though not in meaning, from the official English translation of the Tenth Party Congress program. See *The Program of AKEL* (Kaimakli: Printko, Ltd., 1962), p. 5.

Chapter 4

[1] *Haravghi,* September 11, 1962.

[2] *Ibid.,* March 12, 1969, and see *ibid.,* January 16, 1962.

[3]OHEN is the Orthodox Christian Youth Union and OEKA (not EOKA) is the Organization for the Control of the Communist Menace. The utility of these groups, however, is limited. See *Agon,* March 19, 1969, for a review of how the police have the situation in hand in Cyprus.

[4]Giannis Katsourides in *Neos Democratis,* December 1962. This article discusses the 1962 "organization plan" adopted at the Tenth Party Congress.

[5]*Haravghi,* October 11, 1961; the Turkish Vice-President could constitutionally veto proposed legislation in certain key areas.

[6]*Ibid.,* November 23, 1961.

[7]*Cyprus Mail,* January 1, 1969. For the next elections, a proportional representation system is undoubtedly what the communists would like to see.

[8]*Haravghi,* February 12, 1960. EDMA, the first nationalist party after independence, also pushed a socialist economic policy but with little success.

[9]*Ibid.,* February 26, 1969.

[10]*Ibid.,* September 11, 1962.

[11]*Ibid.,* May 23, 1963.

[12]*Cyprus Mail,* December 10, 1962.

[13]*Haravghi,* December 13, 1962.

[14]*Ibid.,* December 18, 1965.

[15]*Ibid.,* February 26, 1969.

[16]Cyprus, Republic of, *Annual Report of the Ministry of Labor and Social Insurance for the Year 1968,* p. 108.

[17]Some of the leading PEO unions are: Pan-Cyprian Union of Construction Workers, Carpenters, and General Workers; Pan-Cyprian Union of Farm Workers; Pan-Cyprian Union of Mechanics and Electricians; Pan-Cyprian Union of Port Workers and Porters; Pan-Cyprian Union of Government and Military Workers; Union of Hotel, Restaurant, and Amusement Center Employees; and Union of General Workers.

[18]*Neos Democratis,* April 10, 1952.

[19]Voice of Cyprus radio broadcast, October 26, 1968.

[20] *Haravghi,* November 7, 1968.

[21] *Ibid.,* July 7, 1959.

[22] *Neoi Kairoi* (Nicosia), April 13, 1959.

[23] *Haravghi,* October 19, 1959.   In contrast, an AON membership of 4,500 was reported by *Neos Democratis* on March 24, 1953, at the time of the AON Fifth Pan-Cyprian Congress. The same paper reported on March 22, 1953, that 288 representatives from 85 groups attended that congress.

[24] *Tass International Service,* May 11, 1969.

[25] *Haravghi,* April 18, 1962.

[26] This information was learned in personal interviews with Servas in Nicosia, September 1966 and May 1969.

[27] *Haravghi,* June 15, 1960.

[28] *Ibid.,* June 19, 1960. Varosiotis was famous for writing Trotskyist articles.

[29] *Ibid.*

[30] This information was gained in personal interviews with Lyssarides in 1965, 1966, and 1969.

[31] *Cyprus Mail,* February 26, 1969.

[32] *Ibid.*

[33] *Ibid.*

[34] *Ibid.,* February 12, 1969.

[35] *Ibid.,* February 13, 1969.

[36] *Nicosia Domestic Service,* February 6, 1969.

[37] *Cyprus Mail,* February 13, 1969.

[38] *Haravghi,* October 15, 1959.

[39] *Ibid.,* June 22, 1960.

[40] *Ibid.,* September 11, 1962.

[41] See, for example, Papaioannou's report to AKEL's Central Committee after the Fifth Plenum in February 1969: *Haravghi*, February 23, 1969, as well as Appendix C. Also: Report of AKEL's Central Committee, to be presented to the Twelfth Party Congress, March 5–8, 1970, *Neos Democratis*, December 1969; and Appendix F.

[42] *London Daily Telegraph*, March 21, 1962.

[43] Voice of Cyprus radio broadcast, October 15, 1967.

[44] Personal interview, Nicosia, 1969.

[45] "Russia's Good Neighbor Policy on Show," *The Interpreter* (London), September 1965, pp. 5–8.

[46] *Haravghi*, November 7, 1968.

[47] *Elevtheria* (Nicosia), October 24, 1969.

Chapter 5

[1] *Haravghi*, June 15, 1960.

[2] "Democritus," *The Leadership of AKEL*, p. 25.

[3] Statement by N. S. Khrushchev in *Tass International Service*, May 4, 1958.

[4] A detailed review of Soviet policy toward Cyprus in the postwar period may be found in Adams and Cottrell, *Cyprus Between East and West*, Chapter 4.

[5] *Haravghi*, September 17, 1969.

[6] Salih, *Cyprus: An Analysis of Cypriot Political Discord*, p. 107n. The author states: "The Cypriots wanted the [British] bases to stay for economic and security reasons which had been demonstrated during the early periods of the 1963 Cypriot crises."

[7] John C. Campbell, "American Search for Partners," in Hurewitz, ed., *Soviet-American Rivalry in the Middle East*, p. 199.

[8] Interview with Ziartides, Nicosia, October 1966.

[9] *Haravghi*, December 8, 1960. Cyprus also had representation at the March 1969 meeting which prepared for the world communist party conference.

[10]*Haravghi*, March 6, 1969. Communist bloc activities with Cyprus are of the following variety: exchange of personalities; conferences and festivals; religious activities (particularly with the Russian Orthodox Church); friendship societies (such associations exist in Cyprus for all Eastern bloc countries); cultural, artistic, athletic, and other celebrations; commercial trade agreements; direct economic assistance; and participation in Cypriot trade fairs.

[11]*Pravda*, July 28, 1962.

[12]*Ibid.*, December 3, 1964.

[13]*Haravghi*, December 1, 1968.

[14]*Ibid.*, September 17, 1969.

[15]*Izvestia*, January 21, 1965.

[16]*Cyprus Mail*, January 27, 1965.

[17]*Neoi Kairoi* (Nicosia), February 8, 1965. Later, Papaioannou specifically rejected the federation principle "for a number of important considerations." *World Marxist Review Information Bulletin*, March 18, 1965.

[18]Interview with Servas, Nicosia, August 1965.

[19]*Yearbook of the United Nations, 1965* (New York: U.N. Office of Public Information, 1967), pp. 202–3.

[20]*Haravghi*, December 18, 1965.

[21]*Pravda*, January 25, 1966.

[22]*World Marxist Review*, February 1966.

[23]*Haravghi*, March 4, 1966.

[24]*Tass International Service*, March 5, 1966.

[25]*Haravghi*, September 29, 1963.

[26]Speech delivered by General Secretary Papaioannou at the Eleventh Congress of the AKEL, March 3, 1966, carried by *Tass International Service*, March 3, 1966.

[27]Voice of Truth radio broadcast, September 13, 1968.

[28]*Haravghi,* June 22, 1969. According to the *Tass International Service* on June 26, 1969, a "veteran of the AKEL," Georgios Levendis, was also in attendance at the meeting, but there was no elaboration on the role he played other than the claim that he gave a news conference in which he "denounced the splitting activity of the Mao Tse-tung group."

[29]Interview with John Gollan, London, May 1969.

[30]Drachkovitch, ed., *Yearbook on International Communist Affairs, 1966,* p. 96. Hambis Mikhail is a leader of the "progressive Cypriots in England" and attended the Twelfth AKEL Congress. *Haravghi,* Mar. 6, 1970.

[31]*Land og Folk* (Copenhagen), September 1, 1964.

[32]*World Marxist Review Information Bulletin,* August 6, 1965.

[33]Kousoulas, *Revolution and Defeat,* pp. 282–83.

[34]*Haravghi,* December 1, 1968. Three other KKE factions may also exist, the largest of which is pro-Chinese.

[35]Radio broadcast from Athens Domestic Service, January 30, 1969. When Greece withdrew from the Council of Europe in December 1969, it also abrogated the Treaty of London, concerning the Council, and the Rome Convention, concerning human rights. *Ibid.,* December 20, 1969.

[36]See Chapter 4.

[37]Interview with R. Palme Dutt, London, May 1969.

Chapter 6

[1]*Zafer* (Nicosia), September 29, 1969.

[2]*O Filelevtheros* (Nicosia), September 16, 1969.

Chapter 7

[1]*Neos Democratis,* October 1961. The communist parties of Italy and France do not have as high a percentage of workers as AKEL.

[2]*Haravghi,* June 5, 1960.

[3]*Ibid.,* November 27, 1965.

[4]Personal interview, Nicosia, November 1967.

[5] *Haravghi*, January 1, 1962.

[6] *Ibid.*, February 26, 1969.

[7] Interview with Minister of the Interior Komodromos, in Nicosia, May 1969.

Bibliography

The works cited below are mainly in the English language. As stated in the Preface, most of the Greek sources were obtained through the Foreign Broadcast Information Service *Daily Report: Middle East & Africa* or through the Joint Publications Research Service of the U.S. Department of Commerce. These two agencies are responsible for the translations which were not done specifically for this study.

Adams, T. W. *U.S. Army Area Handbook for Cyprus.* Washington: Government Printing Office, 1964.

———. "Crisis in Cyprus," *Army Magazine,* September 1964.

———. "Cyprus," *Viewpoints* (American Friends of the Middle East), March 1964.

———. "The First Republic of Cyprus: A Review of an Unworkable Constitution," *The Western Political Quarterly,* September 1966.

Adams, T. W., and Alvin J. Cottrell. *Cyprus Between East and West.* Baltimore: The Johns Hopkins Press, 1968.

———. "American Foreign Policy and the U.N. Peacekeeping Force in Cyprus," *Orbis,* Summer 1968.

———. "Communism in Cyprus," *Problems of Communism,* May-June 1966.

———. "The Cyprus Conflict," *Orbis,* Spring 1964.

Alastos, Doros. *Cyprus Guerrilla: Grivas, Makarios, and the British.* London: Heinemann, 1960.

Allen, Richard V., ed. *Yearbook on International Communist Affairs, 1968.* Stanford, Calif.: The Hoover Institution, 1970.

Attwater, Donald. *The Christian Churches of the East.* Oxford: Black-friars Publications, 1947.

Barker, Dudley. *Grivas: Portrait of a Terrorist.* New York: Harcourt, Brace, 1960.

Blair, W. Granger. "Communism in Cyprus," *New York Times,* August 30, 1964.

263

Brown, Neville. "Cyprus: Bi-Nationalism Under Stress," *The New Middle East* (London), February 1970.

Christodoulou, Demetrios. *The Evolution of the Rural Land Use Pattern in Cyprus*. London: Geographical Publications, Ltd., 1959.

Communism in Cyprus. Nicosia: Government Printing Office, n.d. Published in the mid-1950's by the British as a possible rationalization for proscribing the AKEL in 1955.

Communist Party of Great Britain. *Allies for Freedom: The Report of the Second Conference of Countries Within the Sphere of British Imperialism*. London, 1954.

——. *We Speak for Freedom: Conference of the Communist Parties of the British Empire*. London, 1947.

Cyprus: The Dispute and the Settlement. Prepared by the Information Department, Royal Institute of International Affairs. London, New York: Distributed by Oxford University Press, 1959. (Chatham House Memoranda)

Cyprus: A Handbook of the Island's Past and Present. Nicosia: Greek Communal Chamber, 1964.

Cyprus, Republic of. *Annual Report of the Ministry of Labour and Social Insurance for the Year 1968*. Nicosia, 1969.

Degras, Jane, ed. *The Communist International, 1919–1943*. 3 vols. London, New York: Oxford University Press, 1956–65.

"Democritus" (George Cacoyannis). *The Leadership of AKEL and the Armed Struggle–A Marxist Critique*. English ed. Cyprus: Privately published, June 1959.

Drachkovitch, Milorad, ed. *Yearbook on International Communist Affairs, 1966*. Stanford, Calif.: The Hoover Institution, 1967.

Durrell, Lawrence. *Bitter Lemons*. New York: Dutton, 1957.

Eden, Anthony. *Full Circle*. London: Cassell, 1960.

EOKA. *The Communist Leadership Against the Cypriot Struggle*. (In Greek.) Nicosia, 1958. A criticism of AKEL's failure to join in the anti-British rebellion.

Foley, Charles. *Island in Revolt*. London: Longmans, 1962.

——, ed. *The Memoirs of General Grivas*. New York: Praeger, 1965.

Foot, Sir Hugh (Lord Caradon). *A Start in Freedom.* New York: Harper and Row, 1964.

French, Reginald Michael. *The Eastern Orthodox Church.* London: Hutchinson House, 1951.

Hill, Sir George. *The History of Cyprus.* 4 vols. Cambridge: Cambridge University Press, 1952. This is considered the authoritative reference on Cypriot history.

Home, Gordon C. *Cyprus Then and Now.* London: J. M. Dent, 1960.

Hurewitz, J. C., ed. *Soviet-American Rivalry in the Middle East.* New York: Praeger, 1969.

Ivanov, M. "Cyprus: A New Republic," *International Affairs* (Moscow), September 1960.

Karayiannis, George. *The Cyprus Problem, December 1963–August 1964.* Nicosia: Pan Publishing House, 1967.

Kilic, Altemur. *Turkey and the World.* Washington: Public Affairs Press, 1959.

Kousoulas, Demetri George. *Revolution and Defeat.* London: Oxford University Press, 1965.

Kyriakides, Stanley. *Cyprus: Constitutionalism and Crisis Government.* Philadelphia: University of Pennsylvania Press, 1968.

Lanitis, Nicolas C. *Rural Indebtedness and Agricultural Cooperation in Cyprus.* Limassol, 1944. The first book on agriculture in the island written from a theoretical viewpoint.

———. *Trade Unionism and the Provision for Social Service.* Nicosia, May 1940. An investigation of the trade union movement in Cyprus at a time when the KKK was moribund and the movement that would found AKEL was beginning to stir.

Lavender, David S. *The Story of the Cyprus Mines Corporation.* San Marino, Calif.: The Huntington Library, 1962. A company-sponsored version of the operations and benefits to Cyprus from this American enterprise. Gives a good account of the company's fight with the communist labor unions.

Lee, Dwight E. *Great Britain and the Cyprus Convention Policy of 1878.* Cambridge, Mass.: Harvard University Press, 1934.

Luke, Sir Harry. *Cyprus: A Portrait and an Appreciation.* London: Harrap and Company, 1957.

Maier, Franz Georg. *Cyprus: From Earliest Time to Present Day*. London: Eleck Books, Ltd., 1968.

Mayes, Stanley. *Cyprus and Makarios*. London: Putnam, 1960. This is an uncomplimentary story of the role the Archbishop played in the EOKA struggle and should be read in contrast to the book by Doros Alastos on the same period.

Meyer, Albert, and Simos Vassiliou. *The Economy of Cyprus*. Cambridge, Mass.: Harvard University Press, 1962.

Middle East Record 1960. London: Weidenfeld and Nicolson, 1962.

Middle East Record 1961. London: Weidenfeld and Nicolson, 1967.

Monroe, Elizabeth. *The Mediterranean in Politics*. London: Oxford, 1938.

Nihart, Brooke, ed. *World in Arms: A Politico-Military Almanac*. McLean, Va.: T. N. Dupuy Associates, 1970.

Papaioannou, Ezekias. "For the Independence and Progress of Cyprus," *World Marxist Review*, December 1966.

Pefkos, George. "A Report on the Cyprus Problem," *Comment* (Communist Party of Great Britain), April 1968.

Petas, Christos. "Backgrounds of Party Members," *Neos Democratis*, October 7, 1961.

Psomaides, Harry. *The Eastern Question: The Last Phase*. Thessalonika: Institute for Balkan Studies, 1968.

———. "Soviet Russia and the Orthodox Church in the Middle East," *The Middle East Journal*, Autumn 1957.

Purcell, H. D. *Cyprus*. London: Benn, 1969. A comprehensive, scholarly, and irreverent history and analysis of the Cypriot scene.

Road to Freedom, The. Program of the Eighth AKEL Party Congress, March 1954.

Salih, Halil Ibrahim. *Cyprus: An Analysis of Cypriot Political Discord*. Brooklyn: Theo. Gaus' Sons, Inc., 1968. A balanced treatment of the political problem by a Turkish-American scholar, despite a decidedly pro-Turkish twist at the end.

Seligman, Adrian. *The Turkish People of Cyprus*. London: Press Attaché's Office, Turkish Embassy, 1956.

Stampolis, Anthony. *The Social and Economic Development of Cyprus.* Nicosia: Ministry of Labour and Social Insurance, 1963. A study sponsored by the U.S. Educational Foundation; gives a good rundown of the Ministry's attempts to institute reforms which the nationalists believe to be effective against communism.

Stephens, Robert. *Cyprus: A Place of Arms.* New York: Praeger, 1966. A good journalistic treatment of the contemporary problem.

Tevetoglu, Fehti. *Cyprus and Communism (Kibris ve Kommunism).* Ankara: Ajans-Turk Matbaasi, 1966. The story of AKEL as seen by the Chairman of the Foreign Relations Committee of the Turkish Senate. It is printed in Turkish and has not been translated into English except for this study.

Thomas, Hugh. *The Spanish Civil War.* New York: Harper Colophon Books, 1963.

"The Uninterrupted Struggle of the People of Cyprus for a United, Completely Independent, Non-aligned and Prosperous Cyprus," Report of the AKEL Central Committee, *Neos Democratis,* December 1969.

United States. Department of Labor. Bureau of Labor Statistics. *Labor in Cyprus.* Washington: Government Printing Office, April 1963.

———. Department of State. Bureau of Intelligence and Research. *World Strength of the Communist Party Organizations, 21st Annual Report.* Washington: Government Printing Office, 1969.

Weir, W. W. *Education in Cyprus.* Larnaca: American Academy, 1952.

Windsor, Philip. *NATO and the Cyprus Crisis.* Adelphi Paper no. 14. London: The Institute for Strategic Studies, November 1964.

Woodhouse, C. M. *Apple of Discord: A Survey of Recent Greek Politics in Their International Setting.* London: Hutchinson and Co., Ltd., 1948. A book by the World War II head of the British Military Mission in Greece; one of the best accounts of the communists' role in the Greek Civil War.

Verrier, Anthony. "Cyprus: Britain's Security Role," *The World Today,* March 1964.

Xydis, Stephen G. *Cyprus: Conflict and Conciliation, 1954–1958.* Columbus: Ohio State University Press, 1967.

Index

Index of Persons

Venizelos, Eleutherios, 18

Wawi, Mahmud, 246
Weller, George, 252
Winster, Lord, 36
Wolf, Kurt, 227
Woolley, Sir Charles, 250

Xenophontos, Michael, 205
Xenos, Glafkos, 83

Yennadios, Bishop, 228, 230
Yermoshin, 228
Yerodiakonou, Kyriakos, 23
Yiavopoulos, Nicolas Othon, 13,
    14, 249

Zachariades, Nicos, 38, 46, 49n,
    174, 217
Zavallis, Achilleas, 207
Zenon, Lefkios, 22n, 23
Ziartides, Andreas, 27, 28, 48—
    53 *passim,* 65, 67n, 68, 78,
    126, 128, 134, 162, 173, 199,
    205, 207, 216, 236, 237, 238,
    259
Ziartidou, Kioula, 138

Index of Subjects

African communist parties: 178
Agriculture, role in economy: 99—100
Aktives, establishment of: 71—72
Annexation by Britain: 11
Army of Cyprus: 97. *See also* Military forces; National Guard
Asian communist parties: 178
Australian communist party: 177

Bases, foreign military: 4, 6—7, 38, 47—48, 54, 56, 58n, 87, 98—99, 101, 126, 159, 184, 196
Book stores, communist-operated: 83
"Brezhnev Doctrine": 171
British communist party, 172—77 *passim*
British Empire. *See* Great Britain

Cabinet
  communist representation in: 61
  proportional representation in: 89
Capital, from Cypriots abroad: 101
Canadian communist party: 177
Censorship, by government: 82
Central Treaty Organization (CENTO): 119
Ceylon communist party: 177
Children. *See* Youth
Civil service
  Enosis, effect on bureaucracy: 93
  EOKA members integrated into: 93
  proportional representation in: 55, 89
Coalition government, aspirations of elements in: 90—93
Comintern
  control of party discipline: 4, 6, 19, 32, 36, 49—50, 50n, dissolution of: 26
  recognition of AKEL by: 14, 156
Commercial interests, support of communists by: 74—76, 182. *See also* Industry
Communication, conduct by communists: 79—84, 154—55
Communications facilities, U.S.: 4
Communism, popular attitude toward: 2, 6, 8, 12—13, 15—17, 30—31, 47, 60, 142, 152, 202
Communist International. *See* Comintern
Communist parties, Cypriot. *See* Communist Party of Cyprus (KKK); Progressive Party of the Working People (AKEL)

277

Greek Cypriot, nature of: 108, 112, 204
independent governmental body for: 89
number in AKEL: 2, 133
percentage of population: 85
ruling groups: 109
social structure and patterns of life: 108–10
support of EOKA: 52n
Gross national product: 102
Guerrilla warfare, by EOKA: 48

Imports, exclusivity in distribution: 95
Income
per capita: 99
sources of: 99–101
Independence
as acceptable course for future: 123
British encouragement of: 10
communist support of: 35–39, 43, 57, 58n, 120, 126, 130, 156, 185, 192
divisiveness resulting from: 56, 88–90, 122
EOKA's demand for: 50
ethnarchy's demand for: 41
political problems resulting from: 54–57, 89, 121–23
popular reaction to: 56, 58, 122
proclaimed: 4, 57
purposes of: 88
secret societies, role in: 94
Soviet position on: 58n, 161, 170
Indian communist party: 177
Industry, communist attitude toward: 100, 198. *See also* Commercial interests
Invasions
defensive mechanisms against: 94–95
historic attitude toward: 15–18
variety of invaders: 86
Islam, attitude toward communism: 116
Israeli communists: 173
Italian Communist Party: 2n, 173

Journalists' Association: 83

Labor class, communist influence among: 6, 8
Labor organizations
assassinations of officials: 52–53, 62
commercial interests, support from: 75
communist influence in: 21, 27–29, 34, 50, 60, 70, 134–36, 179, 182, 193
communist members in: 73
competition against communists: 188–90

Politburo, composition: 67n
Soviet Union, dependence on and discipline by: 133, 156–58, 161–66, 170, 179, 183–85, 193, 200, 203
surveillance of by government agencies: 202
tactics, political: 180, 191–92
world communism, position in: 164–66
world communist issues, attitudes toward: 170–71
Propaganda, communist
activities in: 48, 50–51, 67, 126
foreign bases as element in: 87–88, 184–85
by radio and television: 83
by Soviet communist party: 4
Publications, communist. *See* Press, communist

Radio broadcasting, clandestine: 83, 151
Religion, practices and influence of: 113–16
Research Institute: 203
Right-wing parties: 147
Riots. *See* Violence
Rural areas, communist interest in: 63

Security forces
police and military forces: 96–99
provisions relating to: 54–55
Self-determination. *See* Independence; Nationalism
Self-government. *See* Independence; Nationalism
Sino-Soviet dispute, communist position on: 6, 79, 170, 184
Socialists
doctrine of: 144–48
exploitation by: 11–12
Society
central values in: 109
class distinctions in: 103–12
Greek community structure: 108–9
life, insular characteristics of: 93–96
strata of classes: 103–8
structure and patterns of life: 108–12
Turkish community structure: 110–12
Sovereignty, limitations on: 119, 171
Soviet bloc
Cypriot students in: 70, 137
financial support from: 76–77
trade with: 76
Soviet Union
AKEL, relations with: 6, 7, 19, 32, 132–33, 156, 158–59, 162–70, 183–85
Church, political use of: 114–15
Cyprus in foreign policy of: 153–54, 158–62, 192
federation, position on: 7, 133, 140, 166–67, 170, 174

282

United States
    Cyprus, relations with: 120–21
    role in U.N. on Cyprus question, 48
Urban areas
    growth of: 103, 107
    social status in: 109

Violence. *See also* Guerrilla warfare
    anti-Soviet demonstrations: 153
    actions charged to EOKA: 45, 48
    communist aversion toward: 48, 50, 52, 182
    communist role in: 124–26
    communist threats of: 47–48
    over *Enosis*: 33
    by labor organizations: 18, 20, 29–30, 35–36, 124–25
    outbreak of 1931: 18, 124
    outbreak of 1963: 89, 122, 124
    by Turkish community: 53
Voting. *See* Elections

Women's groups, communist influence among: 138–39, 179
Working class. *See* Labor class
World War II, communist behavior during: 21–22, 25, 26–29, 152, 157

Youth
    communist interest in: 15, 60, 62, 69–70
    groups, communist influence among: 139–40, 179

Zionism, communist attitude toward: 28–29
Zurich Agreement of 1959: 4, 54, 58, 119